Counseling Programs for
Employees in the Workplace

COUNSELING PROGRAMS FOR EMPLOYEES IN THE WORKPLACE

JUDITH A. LEWIS
Governors State University

MICHAEL D. LEWIS
Governors State University

Brooks/Cole Publishing Company
Monterey, California

Brooks/Cole Publishing Company
A Division of Wadsworth, Inc.
© 1986 by Wadsworth, Inc., Belmont, California 94002. All rights reserved.
No part of this book may be reproduced,
stored in a retrieval system, or transcribed, in any form or by any means—
electronic, mechanical, photocopying, recording, or otherwise—
without the prior written permission of the
publisher, Brooks/Cole Publishing Company,
Monterey, California 93940, a division of Wadsworth, Inc.

Printed in the United States of America
10 9 8 7 6 5 4 3 2 1

Library of Congress Cataloging in Publication Data

Lewis, Judith A., [date]
    Counseling programs for employees in the workplace.

    Includes index.
    1. Employee counseling.   I. Lewis, Michael D.,
[date]   . II. Title.
HF5549.5.C8L49 1985   658.3′85   85-7868
ISBN 0-534-05256-8

Sponsoring Editor: *Claire Verduin*
Marketing Representative: *Thomas L. Braden*
Editorial Assistant: *Linda Wright*
Production Editor: *Phyllis Larimore*
Manuscript Editor: *Lawrence Kenny*
Permissions Editor: *Nadine Kirtz*
Interior and Cover Design: *Katherine Minerva*
Art Coordinator: *Michele Judge*
Typesetting: *Vail-Ballou Press, Inc., Binghamton, New York*
Printing and Binding: *R. R. Donnelley & Sons Co., Crawfordsville, Indiana*

TO KEITH LEWIS

Preface

The demand for counseling services in corporate settings has grown rapidly in recent years. Most major organizations are now planning or implementing counseling programs based in the workplace and designed to deal with employees' personal or career concerns. And in the near future, it's likely that most adults will begin to take these programs for granted, whether they are employed by public or by private organizations.

Who manages and staffs such employee assistance programs (EAPs) and career development systems? Typically, an employee counselor or consultant is either a helping professional who has moved from the public to the private sector or a person whose background in business has been enhanced by some clinical training. As worksite-based programs become more professional, they will be staffed primarily by people who possess both clinical and managerial skills and whose training has focused specifically on the role of counseling programs in the organizational context. A person who is considering employee counseling as a career will need to be aware of the conceptual framework upon which such programs are based, as well as the types of activities and skills that are involved.

This book provides such an overview. Sections are devoted to EAPs, which help employees deal with personal or health problems that might affect their productivity, and to career counseling programs, which promote effective decision making in the context of organizational human resource planning. The appendices describe a number of existing programs and thereby demonstrate the variety and scope of services currently being implemented. Our emphasis throughout the book is on the practical methods an individual needs to know if he or she is to carry out such important tasks as policy formulation, training, assessment, counseling, and consultation. The reader will learn how to design and carry out programs that can meet the real needs of organizations and their employees.

A number of people were instrumental in helping us develop these materials. Special thanks need to go to the people responsible for the model programs reviewed as part of the text. Also, at early stages, Bree Hayes, Thelma Whitehead, Byron Romey, Les Netland, Art Zaragoza, and many others provided valuable information about employee assistance programs. Keith Lewis provided valuable assistance in proofreading and indexing. Steven Shatkin, Joanne Cooper, Jim Williams, and Steve Rollin provided valuable insights in their reviews of an earlier draft. And finally, the editorial and production staff members at Brooks/Cole continue to be models of excellence in their own right.

Judith A. Lewis
Michael D. Lewis

Contents

PART FIVE   THE SCOPE OF EMPLOYEE COUNSELING PROGRAMS   217

List of Exhibits

*Counseling Programs for
Employees in the Workplace*

Part One

INTRODUCTION

Chapter One

E MPLOYEE COUNSELING PROGRAMS: AN OVERVIEW

Many counselors are currently venturing into previously unknown territory. They are moving from human service agencies to corporate headquarters; from public schools to factories, banks, and hospitals; from serving children and youth to working with adult employees of a variety of organizations. These counselors are meeting a new and growing demand for the services of professionals who can adapt their skills and make the transition to counseling employees where they work.

Counseling programs geared specifically for employees in or near their work settings have grown steadily in recent years, primarily because employers have come to recognize the importance of developing and preserving valuable human resources. Managers have begun to listen to the ideas of people like Peters and Waterman, whose best-selling book on corporate excellence exhorts,

> Treat people as adults. Treat them as partners; treat them with dignity; treat them with respect. Treat them—not capital spending and automation—as the primary source of productivity gains . . . In other words, if you want productivity and the financial reward that goes with it, you must treat your workers as your most important asset (1982, p. 238).

Now that these ideas have entered the mainstream of thought among the ranks of executives, we find a new readiness in the business world to absorb the concepts and talents that the counseling profession has to offer. Just a few years ago, a mere handful of professionals provided for the counseling needs of business and industry. Now, new programs begin operation and existing services expand every day. The thousands of programs now operating represent "a hundredfold increase in a quarter of a century" (Tuthill, 1982, p. 64). The growth of employee counseling services in the public sector is just as dramatic; people who work for governmental units or educational institutions are also being served for the first time. In both the profit-making and the nonprofit sectors, policy makers have learned that services to employees play a dual role: they increase productivity while concurrently enhancing employees' well-being.

What are the kinds of services that counselors might be able to provide in worksite-based programs? Many professionals have been able to use their human relations skills to move into such areas as training, consultation, organizational development, personnel, and sales. The focus of this book, however, is on programs that can be defined by a clear *counseling component*. Counselors now can make a transition to the private sector by changing work settings without changing careers. Increasingly, organizations provide employees with services that any professional would be likely to interpret as falling within the purview of what we traditionally call *counseling*. In the context of these programs, one individual can help another to learn about self and environment, set goals, examine alternatives, change behaviors, and manage problem situations. Although worksite-based counselors become involved in such activities as training, consultation, and organizational development, they also spend at least part of their time counseling employees directly.

Our purpose in this text is to prepare counselors for providing such services by building an understanding of the nature, scope, and functions of today's employee counseling programs. In subsequent chapters, we will describe a variety of approaches to employee counseling programs. The appendices that follow will demonstrate the range of current programming by providing concrete examples of widely varying programs that are now in operation in the United States.

In general, counseling services for employees can be divided into two major categories. *Employee assistance programs* are focused on employees' mental and physical health and deal with personal problems that might, even indirectly, affect job performance. *Career development programs* use assessment, counseling, planning, and training to help individuals make and act on career decisions within the context of the organization's human resource plans. Each of the two approaches is built on the theory that individual and organizational needs can be compatible.

EMPLOYEE ASSISTANCE PROGRAMS

The central purpose of an employee assistance program is to provide timely, professional aid for people whose personal problems might otherwise lead to work impairment, absenteeism, accidents, conflicts in the work setting, or even job termination. Employee assistance programs (EAPs) have become prevalent because problems in living—stress, alcoholism, drug dependency, family conflicts, interpersonal difficulties, financial pressures, and other issues—affect almost everyone and can, in turn, impact on work performance and productivity. When an organization's managers choose to allocate resources for an EAP, they know that they are simultaneously providing a valued employee benefit and building a more stable, efficient work force.

These programs normally offer services to all employees of the organization as well as to their immediate family members. The counseling may be provided either by professionals who are, themselves, employed by the sponsoring company or by counselors working under consulting contracts. Whether programs are based on internal or external models, virtually all contemporary EAP's share a number of common features in terms of the kinds of counseling services offered.

1. *Counseling Is Short-Term.*

The EAP model does not lend itself to the provision of long-term therapy. In fact, many EAP service providers actually limit their work to assessing their clients' difficulties and making referrals to appropriate community treatment resources.

Of course, it is preferable to offer problem-solving help along with assessment and referral. Many of the organization's employees will feel that they can benefit from some immediate assistance in decision making, life planning, or stress reduction but that they have no need or desire for more intensive treatment. In these situations, counselors should be prepared to offer short-term counseling to help their clients examine their own lives and make action plans for resolving troublesome issues. These plans may include further counseling, but they are just as likely to involve such self-help activities as developing new leisure activities, building new skills, enhancing support networks, or making other life changes. Counselors in EAP settings need to develop approaches that allow them to be useful even when they see each client for only a few brief sessions. The key to effective employee counseling is intervening in a way that helps clients to increase the degree of independent control they can maintain over their lives.

2. *Counseling Is Offered both to Employees Referred by Others and to Individuals Who Refer Themselves.*

An important element in an employee assistance program is the provision of training sessions for managers, supervisors, and union representatives. Through such training sessions, key members of the organization learn to use the EAP effectively. When supervisors have been trained to confront employees whose work performance has slipped and to make appropriate referrals to the EAP counselor, the program can perform one of its primary functions: preventing the need for serious disciplinary action against the employee. If a program is well integrated into the organization, many referrals come from supervisors, from union representatives, and from co-workers concerned about an individual's physical or psychological health.

Although participation in the program is always voluntary, referral from a supervisor undoubtedly forces some employees to recognize the seriousness of problems they might otherwise have ignored.

The employee assistance program can help with problems at a much earlier stage of development through encouragement of employee self-referral. Employee orientation is just as important as supervisory training. If employees and their families learn that the EAP is accessible, professional, and appropriate for mild, as well as serious, problems they tend to use the services before work performance has been affected.

3. Counseling Is Confidential.

An EAP's effectiveness depends on the degree of trust engendered among employees. The question of confidentiality is especially important in workplace programs because clients are rightfully concerned about their employment records. They do not want to share personal problems with counselors unless they are sure that their careers can in no way be affected. For this reason, employee assistance programs are based on policies, signed by both managers and service providers, that clarify the program's role in the organization. Such policies emphasize the intent to maintain complete confidentiality and include statements to the effect that participation in the EAP will not affect promotions, working conditions, or continued employment. Thus, when a counselor sees an individual who has been referred by a supervisor, he or she maintains contact with the supervisor in order to evaluate the effectiveness of the intervention but does not share any information about the client's communications without specific, written permission. When a counselor sees an individual on a self-referral basis, no information, not even the name of the client, is released to the organization. Although general information about the number and types of employees seen is shared with management as an evaluation mechanism, all information protects the anonymity of each client seen.

4. Counseling Is Convenient and Accessible for Clients.

Employee assistance programs have obvious benefits for organizations, since they enhance the quality of the work force. EAPs are just as important, however, from the vantage point of helping professionals concerned about mental health-related issues. Pointing out that the world of work may be the "last frontier for the delivery of mental health and substance abuse services," Roman (1981) states,

> The work world represents a "mother lode" for both movements . . . The extent to which work is invested with meaning in the lives of most Americans is an open question, but the work organization's preeminence as a physical community for most American men and an increasing proportion of American women is an undeniable fact. With the decline of traditional "communities" of residence and growing instability of family life, the workplace may represent the most stable single environment in the lives of many people (p. 12).

That the work setting provides, at the very least, an appropriate setting for interventions is stressed even more strongly by House (1981).

> Work and work organizations are potentially powerful and efficient mechanisms of planned social intervention and change. That is, for any given input of time, money, and manpower researchers can potentially produce a greater impact on more normal or premorbid adults through the workplace than through any other single formal organization or institution (p. 8).

Thus, one of the most compelling characteristics of the EAP is that it provides a setting through which counselors can reach a sizable number of adults. These adults can be reached early, while they are still employed, before the onset of major mental or physical problems.

If counselors are to make use of the positive aspects of this delivery system, they need to recognize and act on the importance of making counseling convenient, comfortable, and accessible. This task can be accomplished by making appointments that conform to clients' work schedules, day or evening, and by choosing offices that allow for privacy and convenience. If external services are provided, away from the organization's physical plant, they should be in offices situated near the employees' home or work settings. If the program is an internal effort, within the employing organization, care should be taken to maintain offices that are informal and set apart from managerial settings. To gain the full benefit of an EAP, employees should feel comfortable seeking counseling services, regardless of the nature of their problems.

Today, most employee assistance programs are "broad brush," meaning that they deal with a variety of issues and problems. Employees with widely varying concerns are encouraged to use the system, and supervisors are urged to refer employees, not because they have diagnosed specific problems, but because they recognize unexplained changes in job performance. This broad, general approach is, in fact, fairly new in the EAP field. Although contemporary programs deal with many more issues, the movement has its roots in "industrial alcoholism programs" that have been in existence for decades.

Industrial Alcoholism Programs

It is not surprising that alcoholism has been seen as a high priority problem by a large number of American companies. The Department of Health and Human Services estimates that the problem costs the country roughly $50 billion per year ("Battling employee alcoholism," 1982), and a high percentage of that cost is absorbed by companies through absenteeism, turnover, loss of productivity, industrial accidents, and the costs of medical care for secondary ailments.

> North American Rockwell Corporation, with 100,000 employees, has placed the cost of alcoholism to its operations at $250 million a year, or $50,220 per alco-

holic employee each year. Gulf Oil Canada, Ltd., with 11,000 employees, has estimated the annual cost to be $400,000. The United California Bank of Los Angeles, with 10,000 employees, estimates the cost at $1 million a year. The Illinois Bell Telephone Company places the cost of alcoholism in wage replacements alone at $418,500 a year. The U.S. Postal Service estimates an annual cost of $168 million, and the U.S. General Accounting Office places the cost of alcoholism among federal civilian employees at $550 million a year (Follmann, 1978, p. 224).

Alcoholism is costly to any organization. Especially at the later stages in its development, it affects dramatically the job performance of workers who previously might have been highly competent. Direct, measurable expenses result from accidents, absenteeism, illness, and the need to replace employees whose alcoholism cost them their jobs. Less measurable but equally real costs come from the alcoholic's increasing problems with judgment and decision making.

Although the problem of alcoholism has been apparent for some time, industrial responses did not come about until managers were convinced that the problem could be resolved. Treatment and recovery can be as dramatic as the problem itself, but few members of the American public realized this before the advent of Alcoholics Anonymous and the introduction of the notion that alcoholism could be thought of as a treatable disease.

The 1940s saw the establishment of a number of alcoholism programs in major corporations. These industrial programs were based on the idea that alcoholics in the work force could be identified by supervisors and referred for treatment. Supervisory training focused on the symptoms of alcoholism, with supervisors being taught to make preliminary diagnoses and to refer affected workers to the program.

Although these early programs represented significant strides and certainly saved a number of lives, supervisors tended to be very cautious about making referrals, often waiting until the alcoholic's symptoms could no longer be overlooked.

> Finally, because of the stigma associated with the disease, supervisors wanted to be certain beyond all doubt that alcoholism really was the problem. Fearing the embarrassment of misidentification, the supervisors waited until the employee evidenced several obvious chronic stage symptoms. Usually supervisors conferred with their own superiors, with the personnel department or the occupational nurse. Confidentiality was compromised and the end result was often an ultimatum to the employee to stop drinking or be terminated, a proposal comparable to telling a tubercular to stop coughing or be terminated (Wrich, 1980, p. 13).

In the 1950s and 1960s, a subtle change took place in the nature of industrial programming. Because supervisory searches for alcoholics tended to identify workers in such late stages, new methods of case finding had to be pioneered. Instead of teaching supervisors to look for physical symptoms, trainers began to focus on changes in job performance. "Supervisors were asked simply to perform the jobs for which they were being paid— to monitor individual job performance and conduct corrective interviews where indicated" (Dunkin, 1982, p. 8). Employees could then be given a choice between seeking treatment or accepting the next stage in the disciplinary process. Supervisors did not attempt to label or diagnose their employees' problems, although the fact that treatment providers tended to be clearly identified as alcoholism specialists signified an implied diagnosis.

A high degree of success was consistently documented for clients who were reached. Companies with alcoholism programs reported both high recovery rates for treated employees and impressive financial savings for the organizations. Success rates improved so steadily that practitioners began to joke that they would "average about 105 percent in the near future" (Weiss, 1980, p. 30).

General Motors, in 1973, tracked the job performance of 71 alcoholic employees and found an 85.5% reduction in lost workerhours and a 72% decrease in sickness and accident benefits paid ("More help for troubled employees," 1979).

Employees of Kennecott Copper Corporation who used the company's EAP showed a 52% improvement in attendance, a 74.6% drop in worker's compensation costs, and a 55.4% decrease in health care costs (Witte and Cannon, 1979).

Scovill Manufacturing Company, with 27,000 employees, saved $186,550 annually, after the costs of treatment and rehabilitation had been deducted (Follmann, 1978).

The Bell Telephone Company found that an EAP brought about a 72% recovery rate among identified alcoholics. Sickness disability cases dropped from 662 in the five years before the program started to 356 in the following five years, resulting in a $459,000 savings. Job accidents decreased 80% (Follmann, 1978).

Allis–Chalmers Corporation saved an estimated $80,000 per year by implementing an alcoholism program (Follmann, 1978).

The Pontiac Division of General Motors saved $9,878 on disability insurance benefits and 10,850 hours lost from work each year on 25 alcoholic employees (Follmann, 1978).

All of these figures point up the success of industrial alcoholism programs at a time when few other identification or treatment modalities were able to show significant gains. Yet, the statistics gathered tended to show only the results achieved by identified alcoholics. Few programmers could say what percentage of the total target population had actually been reached. Supervisors had begun to feel more comfortable making referrals, since their confrontations were based on job performance rather than on medical symptomatology. But in terms of penetration rate (reaching the right numbers of troubled employees), many problems still existed under this model.

One major drawback of the industrial alcoholism programs was that the emphasis on supervisory referral tended to concentrate most efforts on the lower echelons of the work force, whose output was likely to be monitored by first-line managers. In reality, executives and professionals are just as likely to be affected by alcoholism. Moreover, the company's investment in them tends to be sizable. As long as the program stressed alcoholism and spent major efforts in training first-line supervisors, executives tended to avoid personal involvement.

Identifying the program with alcoholism treatment also continued to delay referrals at all levels. As long as the program was labeled in terms of alcoholism, a supervisory referral carried an implied, if unspoken, diagnosis. Supervisors remained cautious and labor representatives wary.

Finally, basing programs on alcoholism alone ignored the fact that any number of other problems—physical, psychological, social, and behavioral—can also affect job performance. Providers of services began to realize that, if a program to assist alcoholics is effective, other problems might also be amenable to the same kind of solution. In fact, a broad, general program, not associated specifically with chemical dependency, might provide a more encouraging environment for serving alcoholics whose denial of their problems made them avoid participation in specialized services.

The creation in the 1970s of the National Institute on Alcohol Abuse and Alcoholism and the institute's interest in industrial programming helped to bring new consultants, new research, and new ideas into the field. As programs proliferated, contemporary concepts for employee assistance came to the fore.

Contemporary Concepts

The employee assistance concept, like the alcoholism programs that spawned it, recognizes the importance of the work situation to people troubled with alcoholism or other issues. Many individuals who would never consider reaching out for counseling or treatment on their own do accept help when their jobs are on the line. In both traditional alcoholism programs and contemporary, broad-brush approaches, "the essence . . . is that they create a system of intervention that uses job performance to create a crisis that motivates the problem employee to seek help" (Sherman, 1983, p. 48). The contemporary employee assistance program, however, deals just as effectively with individuals whose job performance has not yet been affected by their problems and who desire help for the sake of their own well-being. Table 1.1 provides a summary of the major differences between traditional alcoholism programs and broad-brush EAPs.

As the table indicates, the major differences between traditional and contemporary programs lie in the breadth and timing of the services offered.

Table 1.1. *Traditional versus contemporary programs*

Traditional Programs	Contemporary Programs
Emphasis on alcoholism as the basis of the problem	Broad-brush approach; any issue appropriate for service
Emphasis on supervisory referrals	Combination of supervisory referral, self-referral, and referral by others
Problems identified at late stages in development	Services offered at earlier stage in problem development
Services offered by medical or alcoholism specialists	Services offered by generalist counselors with expertise in chemical dependency and other areas
Focus on troubled employees with job performance problems	Focus both on employees with work problems and on employees/family members with no performance problems
Confidentiality for referred employees	Confidentiality for referred employees; anonymity for self-referred employees or family members

While traditional programs focused on one major health issue, contemporary approaches use similar methods to deal with a variety of employee problems. While traditional programs provided intervention only when job performance had been affected, contemporary EAPs use self-referral systems and avoid stigmatization in the hope that employees will seek help earlier.

Preventive Programming

The next step for employee assistance programs is likely to be toward still earlier interventions designed with prevention in mind. Even now, the most sophisticated of the contemporary EAPs emphasize educational workshops to enhance employees' awareness of concepts related to mental and physical health. As part of the employee assistance "package," counselors offer seminars on such diverse topics as stress reduction, burnout, alcoholism and addiction, parenting, communication skills, marriage enrichment, financial management, and career and retirement planning. Clearly, these interventions are meant to prevent the problems that tend to bring individual employees to the counselor's office.

Currently, educational/preventive interventions tend to fall into three categories. EAP practitioners (1) provide general information that might be useful for any adult population, (2) conduct focused workshops to prevent the problems that are most prevalent among employees of the specific organization, and (3) coordinate support groups or special interventions for groups of employees who might be at risk because of some special event or characteristic. Thus, an EAP counselor, noting a large number of self-referrals dealing with marriage issues, might provide marriage enrichment workshops for the general employee population and more intensive, small-group interventions (still voluntary) for people coping with recent divorces. The counselor might provide stress management training for the company at large, but coordinate special meetings for an employee group temporarily under special work pressure.

Increasing numbers of programs are also seeking a closer integration with corporate initiatives oriented toward wellness/health promotion or toward enhancing the quality of work life. EAPs have a readily apparent commonality of purpose with wellness programs, which are designed to encourage employees' efforts toward developing health-oriented lifestyles. While only large corporations have the resources needed to provide fully equipped fitness centers, smaller organizations can also devise methods for supporting employee efforts. As Ardell and Tager (1982) point out, the dimensions of wellness include nutritional awareness, physical fitness, environmental sensitivity, stress awareness and management, and, above all, self-responsibility. Their five-dimensional program is illustrated in Figure 1.1.

The concepts of wellness and health promotion involve teaching individuals the skills and knowledge needed for maintaining good nutrition,

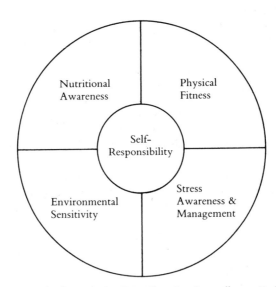

Figure 1.1. Dimensions of wellness. Note. From Planning for wellness (2nd ed.) (p. 7) by B. D. Ardell and M. J. Tager, 1982, Dubuque, IA: Kendall/Hunt. Copyright 1982 by Kendall/Hunt. Reprinted by permission.

fitness, stress management, and healthy environments. These individuals can then use their knowledge as a basis for taking responsiblity for their own physical and mental health. In corporate settings, wellness programs tend to include a combination of educational programs, informal support groups, health screenings and appraisals, fitness activities, and training in medical self-management. EAP counselors are beginning to realize that these concepts make a great deal of sense as preventive interventions that complement direct, individual services.

Effective counselors also recognize that helping troubled clients involves both strengthening their abilities to withstand stress and, at the same time, attempting to lessen the stressfulness of the environment. Counselors dealing with the employees of a specific organization have a significant advantage in this area, since they can assess and attempt to alter negative conditions in the work environment.

> Although individual coping techniques may be quicker and easier, improvements in the work place may have a more pervasive and long-lasting impact . . . Teaching people how to cope with a stressful job is certainly helpful, but it may not be as effective as making the job less stressful to begin with (Maslach, 1982, pp. 118–119).

EAP counselors, in their roles as consultants, can help in the identification and possible lessening of stressful working conditions. Environmental characteristics to examine include physical stressors, such as noise level or crowding, as well as such job situations as lack of control, ambiguity and insecurity, faulty reward systems, overly repetitive work, poor communication patterns, and too little opportunity for growth and involvement. Viewing the organizational environment from a more positive perspective, employee assistance professionals can play major roles in the development of quality of work life improvements. Ozley and Ball (1982) present the following definition of "quality of work life," as adapted from the work of the American Center for the Quality of Working Life:

> Quality of work life improvements are defined as any activity which takes place at every level of an organization which seeks greater organizational effectiveness through the enhancement of human dignity and growth . . . a process through which the stakeholders in the organization—management, union(s) and employees—learn how to work together better . . . to determine for themselves what actions, changes and improvements are desirable and workable in order to achieve the twin and simultaneous goals of an improved quality of life at work for all members of the organization and greater effectiveness for both the company and the union(s) (p. 27).

These ideals are obviously compatible with those of counselors, whether the work being performed is in the context of an EAP or a career development program.

CAREER DEVELOPMENT PROGRAMS

Seeking commonality between the needs of the individual employee and those of the organization as a whole is a major focus of career development programs.

> In individual career planning the focus is heavily concentrated on a wide range of matters related to life and career planning—the individual is central to these concerns. In organizational career management, planning, systems development, and coordination of the various personnel-related efforts receive major attention. Yet in both instances, a common ground exists where individuals (can) facilitate institutional plans and institutions (can) support individual development and growth (Burack and Mathys, 1980, p. 36).

In a systematic career development effort, "the organization determines its own needs, individual employees are given the opportunity to plot their own careers, and then those two data points are matched up or aligned" (Leibowitz and Schlossberg, 1981, p. 72).

The components of the system thus include both activities oriented toward the organization's goals and programs designed to meet employees' objectives. Organizationally focused activities include human resource allocation, recruitment, selection, performance appraisal, succession planning, job design, and personnel systems—all processes that help companies make the most of their employees' efforts. Career planning is the process that helps the individual employee to obtain information and make decisions about the future course of his or her work life. Career development is the outcome of these two sets of components, the reality of what actually happens in the employee's career. This conceptualization can be understood most clearly through an examination of the model designed by Gutteridge and Otte (1983, p. 23) and shown in Figure 1.2.

As Figure 1.2 indicates, individual career planning and institutional career management come together to bring about an outcome that, ideally, fulfills both employee and organizational goals.

Organizational Initiatives

Employers initiate career programs because they expect clear performance results. In general, these programs are expected to provide some combination of the following outcomes (Moravec, 1982, p. 29):

- More effective development of available talent to aid when promoting from within.
- Self-appraisal opportunities for employees considering new or nontraditional career paths.

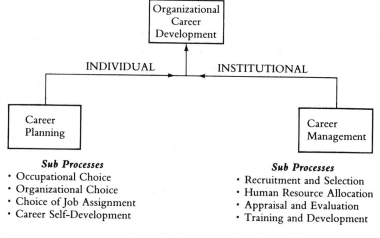

Sub Processes
- Occupational Choice
- Organizational Choice
- Choice of Job Assignment
- Career Self-Development

Sub Processes
- Recruitment and Selection
- Human Resource Allocation
- Appraisal and Evaluation
- Training and Development

A. Career: The sequence of a person's work-related activities and behaviors and associated attitudes, values and aspirations over the span of one's life.

B. Organizational Career Development: The outcomes emanating from the interaction of individual career planning and institutional career management processes.

C. Career Planning: A deliberate process for becoming aware of self, opportunities, constraints, choices and consequences; for identifying career-related goals; and for programming work, education and related developmental experiences to provide the direction, timing and sequence of steps to attain a specific career goal.

D. Career Management: An ongoing process of preparing, implementing and monitoring career plans undertaken by the individual alone or in concert with the organization's career systems.

Figure 1.2. A working model of organizational career development. Note. From "Organizational career development: What's going on out there?" by T. G. Gutteridge and F. L. Otte, 1983, Training and Development Journal, 37 (2), pp. 22–26. Copyright 1983 by American Society for Training and Development. Reprinted by permission.

- More efficient deployment of human resources within and between divisions and/or geographic locations.
- A demonstration of a tangible commitment to EEO, affirmative action, and the corporate image.
- Satisfaction of employees' personal development needs.
- Improvement of performance through on-the-job training experience provided by horizontal and vertical career moves.
- Increased employee loyalty and motivation, leading to decreased turnover.
- A method of determining training and development needs.

Like employee assistance programs, career planning services help to build a stable, high-performance work force. Career programs are also similar to EAPs in that they are relatively new. Although managers have always been interested in fitting the right person to the right job, they did not always see the importance of utilizing counselors to help in the individual's life planning. The growth of purposeful career development programs awaited a number of contemporary trends, including changes in the values and makeup of the work force, the increasing complexity of technology, advances in management theory, and new information about adult development. In addition, many companies have initiated programs in response to their own immediate crises or challenges.

Work force changes.   Human resource development functions have expanded in recent years, in part because of distinct changes in the values and needs of employees. At one time, employees tended to remain attached to one or two companies throughout their careers, with loyalty to the organization and acceptance of the employer's authority being the norm (Immundo and Eisert, 1982). Especially in white-collar and technologically sophisticated organizations, however, these values have changed. American workers have become more concerned about their own growth and development and more willing to change employers for the sake of new challenges or advancement. Employees are not *dis*loyal or *un*committed, but they may have multiple loyalties and commitments—to their professions, their families, their avocations, and their personal well-being.

Just as employers have had to learn to deal with changing values, they have also had to cope with changes in the nature of the work force. Women, minorities, young people, and dual-career couples have focused attention on the facts that employees have widely varying needs and that the work organization must be willing to provide options appropriate for a diverse population of workers.

It is expensive to replace employees who leave to seek greener pastures. New workers need to be recruited, selected, oriented, and trained, and of course the employees who are lured away tend to be those with highly developed skills and competencies. Employers have learned that they can retain such valued employees by allowing individual needs to be recognized and met. They know that people tend to remain with a company if they have the opportunity to choose and act on their own goals and priorities within the organization. Good career development programs teach employees how to work toward their own objectives while continuing to do productive work for the company.

Technological advances.   Rapid changes in technology have also posed special problems for many organizations. Technological growth has brought a need for skilled technicians and professionals, and some companies have found themselves in the unenviable position of having a number of unfilled technical positions along with a plethora of untrained personnel.

Long-range human resource planning can help such companies make better predictions about their future needs. Then career planning services can be used to help current employees set their own goals and select viable training options based on accurate information. A comprehensive career development system lets employees make practical, informed decisions and allows managers to choose the cost-effective alternative of promoting from within when new positions arise.

Advances in management theory.   Career development programs have also become prevalent because of managers' increased understanding of the nature of motivation and leadership in work settings.

Today, effective managers understand that motivating employees toward high performance is a complex process that can be examined from a number of perspectives. For example, many managers have come to accept the possible implications of Maslow's (1954) hierarchy of needs. This hierarchy includes, from the most fundamental to the highest, physiological needs, needs for safety and security, needs for belonging, esteem and status needs, and self-actualization needs. Once the fundamental needs have been met, workers might be motivated by having the chance to work toward the realization of higher needs, up to and possibly including self-actualization.

Similarly, Herzberg (1975) points out that, while maintenance factors such as salary and job security can be associated with job dissatisfaction, the real motivators are factors like the opportunity for growth and accomplishment and the chance to demonstrate competence. Vroom's (1967) expectancy theory postulates that people are most highly motivated if they expect that their efforts will be rewarded and if the rewards offered happen to be important to them.

Each employee is motivated by a different set of needs and values. Career planning programs provide a chance for individuals to clarify their goals and identify the paths they can take within the organization to reach their personal objectives and earn valued rewards. These programs are motivating both because they let employees work toward enhancing their own job satisfaction and because they allow supervisors to be sensitive to employees' needs when setting performance objectives. Career development programs would have been anachronistic when money and security were seen as the only motivators and coercion the only prod. Career planning does fit today's more realistic understanding of the motivation process.

Career development programs also complement contemporary approaches to managerial style. Organizational theorists have long been aware of the distinction between what McGregor (1960) terms "Theory X" and

"Theory Y." Theory X managers assume that people dislike work, hope to avoid responsibility, and need coercion and control to make them work toward the company's objectives. Theory Y managers, in contrast, assume that workers desire the opportunity to achieve and are willing and able to exercise self-direction if they are committed to organizational goals. The Theory X manager is concerned with production, rather than with workers' needs for involvement, while the Theory Y manager tends to emphasize the human aspects of the work organization.

A number of theorists, including Blake and Mouton (1978), now note that a manager does not have to choose between concern for people and concern for production. The most effective managers are those who realize that employee commitment and productivity go hand in hand. Attending to employees' career goals and priorities enhances their desire to perform well in their current positions and increases their commitment to the organization.

Adult development.   No longer can we expect that a career plan selected in youth will last a lifetime. We know now that development and change occur throughout the life span and that individuals can expect to change course several times during the adult years. Just as individual personalities, values, and attitudes change, so do environmental factors. Some adults may desire to alter their career directions, even to the point of making drastic changes in midlife. As Brewer, Hanson, Van Horn, and Moseley (1975) point out, "Increased life expectancy and realization of the discrepancy between original aspirations and mid-life achievements are causing many individuals . . . to make major changes to seemingly unrelated fields" (p. 228). Just as often, adults find themselves forced to make changes due to shrinking job markets or other economic factors. Career-related programs in organizational settings reflect the reality that change will happen in any event and that careful planning simply influences its direction.

Responses to crises or challenges.   In many instances, organizations have created career development systems in response to immediate and unique needs. At the Lawrence Livermore National Laboratory, for instance, a highly respected program was begun in the early 1970s in response to "a strongly felt need, or hurt" (Hanson, 1981, p. 80). A reduction in funds brought about the need to terminate the positions of employees who had acceptable performance records, including scientists and engineers who had been with the organization in specialized capacities and who could see few employment options for themselves. This reduction in force created a challenge for the organization.

> There was "hurt" for both employees and management. Management wanted to do something to prevent a recurrence of the problem. Employees who had watched terminated friends deal with their problems wanted to save themselves from a similar experience . . . Management wanted employees to take more

responsibility for their own careers—to be less dependent on the organization (the managers) to "take care of them." This objective became a central theme of the program (Hanson, 1981, p. 81).

In other organizations, the immediate challenge to address career development needs might relate to different issues. Frequently, equal employment opportunity and affirmative action are at the heart of the earliest efforts. Career planning programs designed to encourage the development of women, minorities, and handicapped workers often prove so effective that services are subsequently broadened to include other employee groups. In every instance, an organization creates a career development program because that program serves some organizational goal, whether long-term or immediate.

Services to Employees

Employees also have specific goals that can be met through career development programs. Participation in the career planning components allows them to find their own answers to such universal concerns as (Burack and Mathys, 1980, pp. 301–302):

1. What are my skills and what are the possibilities for developing them or gaining new ones?
2. What do I really want for myself insofar as work is concerned?
3. What's possible for me, given my (current) abilities and skills?
4. What's really required for certain jobs?
5. What training will be required if I choose to pursue a certain career objective?

The search for these answers involves both obtaining accurate, up-to-date information about career possibilities in the organization and learning about oneself through participation in activities oriented toward self-exploration and planning.

Employees can determine what career paths are realistic for them only if the organization provides information about current and future job openings, promotion criteria, opportunities for job enrichment, and career ladders. With this information made available as part of the career development system, employees can perform their part in the process by assessing their own abilities, skills, and goals. Exploration can be facilitated by counselors through the use of career workshops, self-assessment tools, training, individual counseling, and management of transitions.

Career workshops.   Most comprehensive career development systems use some form of workshop or seminar to engage employees in planning. Workshops vary in length from hours to days but tend to cover similar ground. Usually, group interaction is used to help participants examine themselves realistically in the organizational context. Common elements include some form of individual self-assessment, appraisal of policies and available career paths in the organization, analysis of the fit between career aspirations and organizational requirements, career action planning, and implementation tactics (Gutteridge and Otte, 1983). Obtaining knowledge about oneself and the organizational environment is only the first step. Participants help one another to emerge from these experiences with specific, concrete plans for working toward the long-range goals they have identified. In many cases, they are ready to take such immediate steps as embarking on new training programs or seeking more challenging positions. If workshops or seminars are effective, employees should also come out of them with new-found planning and decision-making skills. As Walz (1982, p. 12) points out, "a mountain of data does not an effective career plan make," and seminars should introduce systematic decision-making models that can be used throughout the life span.

Self-assessment tools. Similar analyses can also be completed by individuals using workbooks or other planning tools designed for self-administration. Although this approach lacks the depth that can come from human interaction, it makes career planning possible for people who cannot attend structured workshops or who want to proceed at their own pace.

Some companies use manuals or workbooks that lead individual employees through the same steps that they would take if they were participating in workshops. These self-guided instruments include exercises designed to assess personal interests and goals and to provide practice in skills related to planning and decision making. Tests and inventories that assess interests or aptitudes are also in wide use, but they are most beneficial if employees learn to use the resulting data as part of a more comprehensive decision-making process.

Training. Both in-house training opportunities and tuition reimbursement programs can fall under the auspices of a career development system. Training can be directed toward technical competency or interpersonal proficiency, current tasks or future plans, formal academics or on-the-job experience. What is most important is that participants see training as one aspect of planned career development rather than as an end in itself.

If education and training are recognized as methods of achieving career-related or organizational objectives, it becomes apparent that they can take many forms. Kaye (1983) categorizes resources for career development as (1) training and education related to specific topics; (2) experience-based training, including special projects, job rotation, and other chances for new experiences; and (3) support-guided development that allows for the sharing of experiences among individuals and groups. This orientation stresses that individuals have many options for development beyond the traditional emphasis on formal learning situations.

Individual counseling.   Meeting the needs of individuals also requires provision for individual counseling. When such counseling is provided by the employee's supervisor, it can most accurately be called *career coaching*. In the context of a performance appraisal, a properly trained supervisor can move from evaluation toward an emphasis on development, helping the employee to devise appropriate plans for doing the current job more effectively and for moving toward future goals. In a *career pathing* program, "employees and supervisors plan a career progression that takes into account present experience and skills and identifies what kind of additional self-development and training experiences individuals will need to prepare themselves adequately for future career goals" (Walz, 1982, p. 15). Regular reviews of the career path and the employee's progress form a major component of the career pathing concept, and supervisors can play an important role because they combine knowledge of the employee's current contribution with awareness of the organization's needs.

Increasingly, career development programs also include the provision of individual counseling by professional helpers. The focus of professional counseling tends to be on helping the employee with the processes of self-assessment, organizational awareness, and long- and short-term planning. The goals, and even the procedures, used in individual career counseling have much in common with those used in seminars or workshops. Work with individuals forms a valuable adjunct to the group approach, allowing human resource professionals to provide additional assistance to those who need it and providing a mechanism that employees can use to seek help with specific, career-related issues. In many situations, even a well-planned career path can be blocked until an employee finds objective, confidential assistance in dealing with unexpected problems or developing new coping strategies.

Managing transitions.   Counselors are also proving valuable in the effort to help individuals deal with major career transitions, including retirement, relocation, and job change. Retirement planning sessions, whether offered through individual or group methods, have become almost routine aspects of many organizations' career development programs. The recognition that retirement has major social and psychological, as well as economic, impact on individuals and families has brought with it an emphasis on careful planning well in advance of the event itself.

Similar considerations have brought attention to the need to provide counseling for families facing temporary relocations or permanent transfers to new geographical areas. These changes call on all of the family's coping resources, and corporations are beginning to find that more and more relocation requests are meeting resistance (Sherwood and DeSimone, 1983). Especially when relocations are international in scope, counselors are needed both to assess a family's potential adjustment and to help in predeparture planning, on-site adjustment, and repatriation (Fontaine, 1983).

Finally, outplacement counseling is coming into wide use to help employees manage the ultimate transitional crisis: job loss. As Knowdell (1983) points out, organizations take on the costs of supporting individuals through this transition because of managerial concern for the company's public image, the need to retain the goodwill of remaining employees, the hope of minimizing grievances and lawsuits, the desire to cut down on unemployment insurance premiums, and the financial savings brought about through timely severance. Through outplacement services, a terminated employee is helped to deal with the emotional trauma of sudden unemployment while assessing individual career options and learning practical strategies for job search. The methods counselors use are similar to those needed for dealing with other aspects of career planning. The change in focus involves the need to deal with immediate concerns and to encourage the individual's rapid return to appropriate employment. Professional counselors, trained to aid individuals in self-exploration and decision making, can help their clients make successful adjustments in difficult situations.

PROFESSIONAL COMPETENCIES

Most trained counselors have the basic helping skills needed for the delivery of worksite-based services. Counselors may find it necessary to adapt their skills to the special nature of employee counseling programs. Each counselor should focus attention on developing skills associated with all of the following major competency areas: (1) program development and management, (2) short-term counseling/assessment, (3) resource utilization/networking, (4) organizational consultation, (5) education and training, and (6) public relations and marketing. In the context of employee counseling programs, effective counselors need solid competencies in each of these areas, with consulting, program management, and marketing being as important to program success as the provision of direct services.

Program Development and Management

Counselors in all settings need skills in program development and management in order to ensure that services remain focused on their programmatic goals. "The survival of human service programs depends on how well they are managed . . . [and] human service professionals have no choice but to accept increased responsibility for management and supervision in their own settings" (Lewis and Lewis, 1983, p. v).

In employee counseling programs, an orientation toward effective management is even more important. Few counselors in the foreseeable future will be able to move into established programs and take their places as direct service specialists. Most employee counseling programs are new, and a majority of the counselors currently being hired are required to develop innovative efforts in organizations that have not had EAPs or career development programs in the past. These programs are also small, with individual counselors being called upon to develop and implement a variety of services under minimal supervision. Especially in corporate settings, employee counseling providers must prove themselves as effective managers who can plan and carry out efficient delivery systems.

Counseling and Assessment

In employee counseling systems, individual services are heavily oriented toward assessment of clients' strengths and special needs. EAP counselors are required to assess a variety of medical and psychological concerns with enough accuracy and insight to make appropriate referrals. Of special importance for these counselors is the ability to recognize and evaluate chemical dependency problems and to choose treatment resources that can meet clients' needs. Career development counselors, too, concentrate much of their effort on helping individuals to measure and evaluate their interests, aptitudes, and career objectives. Both EAP and career-oriented counselors know that their most important role is to assess situations effectively enough to allow clients to meet identified needs through their own or external resources.

Counseling, as well as assessment, is utilized in work settings. The counselor's approach must, however, be oriented toward practical problem solving. Employee counselors know that clients requiring long-term therapy will be served most effectively outside the work setting. The role of the employee assistance or career counselor is to help clients develop plans that can be implemented independently. Having this kind of impact on the basis of just a few sessions requires a counselor with a special kind of skill.

Resource Utilization/Networking

An employee counselor is a human link, connecting clients with a variety of community and organizational resources. Knowledge of local agencies and helath care systems is especially important for EAP counselors, who must be able to increase their clients' options and choose resources objectively from as large a number of alternatives as possible. Employee counselors of all types must also be aware of resources within the organization, including services provided by management, labor unions, and medical and personnel departments. The company's "benefit package" determines a great deal about what resources are available to employees, and counselors must be familiar with employee benefits in general and the company's package in particular.

Organizational Consultation

Even if counselors did nothing but assist individual employees, they would need to know their organizations well. Filipowicz (1979) points out that an organization-based counselor has a decided advantage over "the practitioner in the community agency who is isolated from the dimension of the employee's work environment, and lacks familiarity with his milieu, management, and groups with whom the employee must interact" (p. 20). An employee assistance counselor needs to know how environmental stressors within the work setting affect clients as well as how individual problems impact on the work organization in return. Counselors dealing with career issues are in even greater need of expertise in assessing the work environment. Their goal is to help individuals develop career plans that meet the needs of both the employee and the organization, and they can accomplish this task only if they have intimate knowledge of corporate human resource policies and plans.

Counselors in work organizations also need competency in assessing and affecting organizational characteristics. All counselors need close involvement with human resource policies. Many professionals also play major roles as internal organizational development consultants. Burke and Schmidt (1979, p. 201) identify organizational development in terms of a "strategy . . . to change the organization's culture from one of dealing with problems 'as we have always done' to a culture that (1) takes full advantage of the human resources the organization has available, and (2) allows for a process to develop which will insure that the organization can plan and implement needed change at all levels." The development of such processes is highly relevant to the well-being of individual employees and to the work of the counselor. Professionals in EAPs or career development programs can move naturally into major roles as internal organizational development consultants if they have the broad expertise needed.

Education and Training

Although counselors spend some time in direct, one-to-one counseling with individual employees, they often concentrate even more on working with groups. In employee assistance programs, workshops and educational programs dealing with such issues as stress management, financial planning, family issues, or substance abuse help to prevent the occurrence of mental and physical health problems, while training programs for supervisors and employee representatives form the backbone of the EAP itself. Career development programs also depend on group efforts, with counselors presenting career planning workshops for general employee populations as well as group efforts designed for people facing major transitions. The content of training sessions varies widely, but all counselors need the ability to design and carry out meaningful educational experiences for large and small groups.

Marketing and Public Relations

At some future date, employee counseling programs will have a long record of success, and managers of all organizations will assume that such programs are needed. Currently, however, the concepts involved in employee assistance and career development programs are new to most people, and professionals need to be proactive in convincing decision makers to budget for them. Counselors must sell their programs, first to get them initiated and then to make sure that they are trusted and used by managers, unions, and employees. Developing and maintaining employee programs requires public relations skills, since programs can be successfully implemented only if they are visible, trusted, and respected.

SUMMARY

Employee counseling programs are designed to play the double role of enhancing employees' well-being and increasing their productivity. Employee assistance programs are focused on mental and physical health issues and provide aid for people whose personal problems might otherwise lead to problems in job performance. Although based on industrial alcoholism programs, most EAPs are now "broad brush," providing short-term counseling and referral for any employee desiring help. Career development programs are also aimed toward assisting individuals in the context of the work organization. Through individual counseling, workshops, assessment tools, training, and transitional management, counselors assist employees to make career plans that fulfill individual and organizational goals.

Both employee assistance and career development programs require that counselors have strong competencies in program development and management; short-term, assessment-oriented counseling; resource utilization; organizational consultation; education and training; and public relations and marketing. With these skills, large numbers of counselors can be absorbed into this new and rapidly growing field.

REFERENCES

Ardell, D. B., and Tager, M. J. (1982). *Planning for wellness* (2nd ed.). Dubuque, IA: Kendall/Hunt.

Battling employee alcoholism (1982). *Dun's Business Month, 120* (6), 48–53.

Blake, R. R., and Mouton, J. S. (1978). *The new managerial grid.* Houston: Gulf.

Brewer, J., Hanson, M., Van Horn, R., and Moseley, K. (1975). A new dimension in employee development: A system for career planning and guidance. *Personnel Journal, 54* (4), 228–231.

Burack, E. H., and Mathys, N. J. (1980). *Career management in organizations: A practical human resource planning approach.* Lake Forest, IL: Brace-Park Press.

Burke, W. W., and Schmidt, W. H. (1979). Primary target for change: The manager or the organization. In C. R. Bell and L. Nadler (Eds.), *The client-consultant handbook* (pp. 192–209). Houston: Gulf.

Dunkin, W. S. (1982). *The EAP manual.* Washington, DC: National Council on Alcoholism.

Filipowicz, C. A. (1979). The troubled employee: Whose responsibility? *Personnel Administrator, 24* (6), 17–22, 33.

Follmann, J. F. (1978). *Helping the troubled employee.* New York: AMACOM (American Management Association).

Fontaine, C. M. (1983). International relocation: A comprehensive psychosocial approach. *EAP Digest, 3* (3), 27–31.

Gutteridge, T. G., and Otte, F. L. (1983). Organizational career development: What's going on out there? *Training and Development Journal, 37* (2), 22–26.

Hanson, M. C. (1981). Implementing a career development program. *Training and Development Journal, 35* (7), 80–90.

Herzberg, F. (1975). One more time: How do you motivate employees? In Harvard Business Review Editors (Eds.), *Harvard Business Review—On management.* New York: Harper & Row.

House, J. S. (1981). *Work stress and social support.* Reading, MA: Addison-Wesley.

Immundo, L. V., and Eisert, M. P. (1982). *Managing your human resources: A partnership approach.* New York: AMACOM (American Management Association).

Kaye, B. (1983). Career development puts training in its place. *Personnel Journal, 62* (2), 132–137.

Knowdell, R. L. (1983). Outplacement counseling in business and industry. In R. L. Knowdell, C. McDaniels, A. Hesser, and G. R. Walz (Eds.), *Outplacement counseling* (pp. 1–58). Ann Arbor: ERIC/CAPS (Educational Resource Information Center/Counseling and Personnel Services).

Leibowitz, Z. B., and Schlossberg, N. K. (1981). Training managers for their role in a career development system. *Training and Development Journal, 35* (7), 72–79.

Lewis, J., and Lewis, M. (1983). *Management of human service programs.* Monterey, CA: Brooks/Cole.

Maslach, C. (1982). *Burnout: The cost of caring.* Englewood Cliffs, NJ: Prentice-Hall.

Maslow, A. (1954). *Motivation and personality.* New York: Harper & Row.

McGregor, D. M. (1960). *The human side of enterprise.* New York: McGraw-Hill.

Moravec, M. (1982). A cost-effective career planning program requires a strategy. *Personnel Administrator, 27* (1), 28–32.

More help for troubled employees. (1979, March 12). *Business Week,* 97–102.

Ozley, L. J., and Ball, J. S. (1982). Quality of work life: Initiating successful programs in labor management organizations. *Personnel Administrator, 27* (5), 27–33.

Peters, T. J., and Waterman, R. H., Jr. (1982). *In search of excellence: Lessons from America's best-run companies.* New York: Harper & Row.

Roman, P. M. (1981). *Prevention and health promotion programming for work organizations: Employee assistance program experience.* DeKalb, IL: PRN Monograph, Prevention Resources Project, Northern Illinois University.

Sherman, P. A. (1983). The alcoholic executive. In J. S. J. Manuso (Ed.), *Occupational clinical psychology.* New York: Praeger.

Sherwood, M. B., and DeSimone, J. A. (1983). Relocation counseling: Current status and potential. In J. S. J. Manuso (Ed.), *Occupational clinical psychology* (pp. 202–214). New York: Praeger.

Tuthill, M. (1982). Joining the war on drug abuse. *Nation's Business, 70* (6), 64–66.

Vroom, V. H. (1967). *Work and motivation.* New York: Wiley.

Walz, G. R. (1982). The career development diamond: Touching all the bases. In G. R. Walz (Ed.), *Career development in organizations.* Ann Arbor: ERIC/CAPS (Educational Resource Information Center/Counseling and Personnel Services).

Weiss, R. M. (1980). *Dealing with alcoholism in the workplace.* New York: National Industrial Conference Board.

Witte, R., and Cannon, M. (1979). EAP's: Getting top management's support. *Personnel Administrator, 24* (6) 23–26, 44.

Wrich, J. T. (1980). *The employee assistance program: Updated for the 1980's.* Minneapolis: Hazelden.

Part Two

EMPLOYEE ASSISTANCE PROGRAMS

Chapter Two

COMPONENTS OF THE EMPLOYEE ASSISTANCE PROGRAM

Employee assistance programs vary in terms of the services they provide because each is designed to meet the unique needs of a specific work organization and employee group. In general, however, effective EAPs share a number of features. Each program, regardless of where it is placed in the organization, should include some provision for each of the following components:

- Clearly stated policies and procedures to guide the program and its implementation.
- Training programs for supervisors and employee representatives.
- Employee orientation and information mechanisms.
- A system for offering confidential counseling, assessment, and referral.
- Educational and preventive efforts.

The combination of these components enables the EAP to have an impact on the organization and its employees. Nothing short of a complete system can be truly adequate, regardless of whether services are provided through an internal program or by consultants working on a contractual basis.

INTERNAL VERSUS EXTERNAL PROGRAMS

Perhaps the single most important distinction among employee assistance programs is that some are offered internally, within the company, and some externally, through consultants who are not, themselves, employed by the organization they serve.

The Internal Model

Early employee assistance programs were based on the internal model. Organizations with EAPs provided services through counselors or resource persons who were, themselves, company employees.

This approach remains prevalent among major organizations. Depending on the size of the firm, one or more specialists staff an EAP office within the company. These employee assistance specialists manage and deliver the program, providing consultation, training, and education as well as direct services to individuals. In most instances, individual services are limited to short-term problem solving, assessment, and referral. Counselors keep close track of available community resources so that when an employee is assessed as needing treatment of any kind, an appropriate referral can be made. Referrals take into account both individual needs and the constraints of the company's health benefit package. Ideally, employee assistance specialists are closely involved with managers, supervisors, and employees, so their clients include both individuals who refer themselves and employees whose job performance has aroused supervisory concern.

This close involvement constitutes the strength of the internal model and makes it worthy of consideration by an organization large enough to support such an effort. An EAP is only successful insofar as it is used, and an internal consultant can do a great deal to keep the program visible to potential clients. The service provider's presence at the worksite can encourage drop-ins from employees or supervisors who might be undecided about making the commitment to seek help.

The internal EAP counselor might also be trusted because of his or her knowledge of the company and its characteristics. A counselor who knows the system can be both a helpful advocate for a client with work-related problems and a useful consultant for managers.

The possibilities of having an impact on the organizational environment are also enhanced for internal practitioners. The credibility that comes with being part of the organization can help practitioners address problems that may become apparent through their work. If a number of individual employees develop problems that can be attributed to a stressor in the work environment, an alert EAP counselor can reach managers or union stewards who might have the power to bring about needed changes. If nothing else, an internal EAP coordinator can certainly influence the company's resource policies and health care benefits.

Although the internal model possesses some benefits, it is not appropriate for all work settings. A major characteristic of the internal program is that it is practical only for organizations employing a large number of people at a worksite. It has been suggested that a company can justify one internal mental health professional for every 2,500 employees ("More help for troubled employees," 1979). If this rule of thumb were followed, most organizations would be perceived as too small to warrant hiring a full-time EAP provider. Planners may disagree about the most appropriate ratio of employees to counselors, but they know that it is cost-effective to employ full-time counselors only if there are enough employees in the location to keep them busy. Some organizations have attempted to make employee assistance the part-time obligation of a member of the personnel department, but this option is inappropriate. The EAP is based on the notion that counseling is confidential and that employment records will not be affected by participation. A personnel specialist attempting both to provide EAP services and to make management decisions would find himself or herself plagued by role conflicts.

Thus, small or medium-sized companies usually find it in their best interests to contract with external consultants for EAP service delivery. In fact, however, many large organizations also find the external model preferable, either because of its cost-effectiveness or because of the increased ease in guaranteeing the confidentiality of services.

The External Model

An external employee assistance program includes every component found in the internal system, including training, prevention, and consultation, as well as direct service delivery. For instance, the brochure of one consulting firm (PACE, n.d.), states that

> The PACE professionals can provide a full range of employee assistance services to meet the needs of the individual company, including:
>
> *Consultation* on the development of EAP policy and procedures.
> *Training* for managers, supervisors, and union leaders.
> *Dissemination* of information to all employees.
> *Assessment, referral,* and short-term *counseling* services for employees and their families.
> *Recommendations* to management for improving productivity and preventing employee problems.
> *Reports* summarizing service use and highlighting the prevalence of preventable problems.
> *Presentation* of educational mental health programs available to employees at no extra cost.

Thus, external programs can be as comprehensive as internal systems. The one unique characteristic of the external model is that services are provided by consultants who are not employees of the company. These consultants are paid on a contractual basis and usually meet with clients in offices located away from worksites. (Some consultants deliver services on-site at a company while maintaining their identities as outsiders. Although this model has not been common in the past, it can be expected to become more prevalent as a third approach, possibly combining some of the benefits of the internal and external alternatives.)

When an external employee assistance program is initiated, consultants assist in the development of policy and procedure statements to be signed by managers and employee representatives. The consultants then take responsibility for training supervisors, orienting employees, and providing ongoing information. At the heart of such programs, of course, is the provision of counseling, assessment, and referral services for employees.

Most external programs are based on telephone appointment systems. When an employee wishes to see a counselor, he or she calls a telephone number that has been made available to all members of the organization. An appointment is made to suit the employee's convenience, usually during nonworking hours at an office close to home or work. The counselor makes an assessment of the client's situation. If short-term problem solving assistance is all that is needed, the counselor provides this service. If more help—medical, psychological, legal, financial, or social—is necessary, a referral is made to an appropriate professional or agency. There should be no cost to the employee for EAP counseling. Referrals to other agencies should take into account the employee's insurance coverage and ability to pay. If employees or family members refer themselves to the employee assistance program, no information—not even their names—is shared with the employing organization. If employees are referred to the EAP by their supervisors, the counselor may maintain contact with the supervisor. Even then, however, no information about the content of the counseling sessions is provided unless the client requests that data be shared.

The fact that counseling services are located outside of the workplace makes them appealing to many employees. Internal programs do very well in attracting both supervisory referrals and self-referrals of rank and file workers. Often, however, executives, managers, and people in technical/professional fields are found to be out of reach of these programs. Although every good employee assistance program, whether internal or external, stresses confidentiality and keeps assessment data out of personnel records, ambitious executives and professionals often fear that their careers will be compromised if they admit to the existence of personal problems. Use of the program by highly placed executives is also affected by the tendency of managers to avoid asking for help from people who occupy even slightly lower places in the organization's hierarchy.

The placement of assessment counselors outside of the organization can sometimes encourage reluctant managers and professionals to seek help for themselves or their families. Counselors in external programs have the objectivity and professional identity that come from being outside of the organization. Yet, unlike helpers in general community agencies, they are associated with the employing company closely enough to know the work setting and its stressors. These characteristics can encourage self-referrals from the employees in whom the company has invested the most.

Another strength of external programs lies in the variety of professional skills offered by service providers. An external consulting firm may use a number of assessment counselors, each with a distinct specialization or area of expertise. These counselors can address a wider variety of problems and issues than a single internal consultant can. As Leeman (1974) points out, "since the counselor's supervision comes from the outside organization, the company obtains professional expertise otherwise unavailable to it" (p. 24).

Finally, external consultants can bring a certain objectivity to an examination of organizational issues that an employee of the firm might not have.

> A position outside the company's organizational structure protects the counselor from conflicts of interest between her own job security and her professional standards. She can help employees reach decisions in their own best interest—sometimes even decisions to seek employment elsewhere. At the same time, she is confident that in the long run this approach is also in the company's interest (Leeman, 1974, p. 22).

The Best of Both Worlds

No generalization can be made about the comparative effectiveness of internal or external models. The best approach is always the one that most closely meets the needs, values, and resources of a specific organization. Each EAP provider needs to make sure that his or her program builds on the strengths inherent in the model being implemented and avoids its pitfalls.

Practitioners in internal programs should make full use of the fact that their credibility allows them to have an impact on the organizational climate. If EAPs are closely integrated with other human resource functions, policies relating to such efforts as staffing, performance appraisal, job design, industrial safety, and labor relations can show sensitivity to employee concerns and take into account the need to prevent stress-related problems. As Hollmann (1981) points out, "It makes little sense to rehabilitate troubled employees and let them return to the same environment which caused or contributed to their problem" (p. 40).

Internal EAP consultants are in a good position to integrate their services into the organizational environment. They should also try to duplicate some of the strengths of external programs by continually emphasizing confidentiality and privacy. Scrupulous care should be taken to avoid any possibility of betraying confidences. Self-referrals can be generated, but only if counselors use every available communication process to reiterate the broad goals of the EAP and to emphasize that services are meant for everyone. Sessions that focus on such nonthreatening concepts as wellness, with attention paid to educational activities, might attract the participation of executives and professionals.

An external consultant tends to have little difficulty convincing employees of the privacy and professionalism of services but faces an uphill battle when attempting to integrate the EAP with the organization's human re-source processes. Managers tend to ask for assistance only in dealing with troubled employees or in solving pressing problems, so a consultant must be aggressive if he or she is to maintain visibility within the organization. Close contact must be kept with union and management representatives who are unlikely to initiate ongoing communication, and employees need constant reminders that the EAP is there to serve them. The primary challenge faced by the external consultant is to remember that an employee assistance program is meant to serve the entire organization, as well as the individuals within it.

NATIONAL STANDARDS FOR EMPLOYEE ASSISTANCE PROGRAMS

Because employee assistance programs have a great impact on work organizations and employees, EAP consultants should expect to be accountable for the services they provide. Increasingly, EAPs are recognized as comprehensive systems that must be consistent with high standards of excellence. Internal and external programs are expected to meet identical standards.

The early 1980s saw the implementation, for the first time, of suggested standards for employee assistance programs. Such organizations as the Association for Labor-Management Administrators and Consultants on Alcoholism (ALMACA), the National Council on Alcoholism (NCA), the National Institute on Alcohol Abuse and Alcoholism (NIAAA), and the Occupational Program Consultants Association (OPCA) joined forces with representatives of labor and management to develop a set of standards appropriate for industrial alcoholism and broad-brush employee assistance programs. Although these standards are voluntary, they are accepted by most practitioners in the field as appropriate guidelines for action. Each EAP counselor should use these standards as a basis for program development and implementation. The standards, which were developed by a broadly based task force, are reprinted in full as Exhibit 2.1.

EXHIBIT 2.1. *National Standards for EAPs*

1. Policy and Procedures
   1.1 Policy statement:
      An organization shall adopt a written policy statement on alcoholism and other problems covered by the EAP. This will be signed by the chief executive and union head where appropriate, and will

reflect management and labor attitudes and agreements as to the program's objectives. The policy should state that alcoholism is a disease responsive to treatment and rehabilitation and should specify the responsibilities of management, union representatives, and employees as they relate to the program. The EAP need not in any way alter management's responsibility or authority or union prerogatives. Participation in the EAP will not affect future employment or career advancement, nor will participation protect the employee from disciplinary action for continued substandard job performance or rule infractions.

1.2 Confidentiality:

Written rules will be established specifying how records are to be maintained, for what length of time, who will have access to them, which information will be released to whom, and under what conditions, and what use, if any, can be made of records for purposes of research, evaluation, and reports. Client records maintained by an EAP should never become part of an employee's personnel file. Adherence to Federal regulations on the confidentiality of alcohol and drug abuse records (42 CFR Part 2) is required of programs even indirectly receiving Federal funds.

1.3 Procedures for individuals referred by management and/or union representatives:

Each EAP will prepare written procedures for action initiated by management and/or union representatives. This will provide for assessment by EAP staff, evaluation by professionals, referral for treatment, feedback to the referral source, and follow-up. For alcoholism cases there should be a follow-up at least monthly for a minimum of one year.

1.4 Procedures for voluntary use of the program by employees/family members:

Procedures for individuals who refer themselves will provide for assessment by EAP staff, evaluation by professionals, referrals for treatment, and follow-up. The program will initiate no contact with management concerning individuals who refer themselves, consistent with confidentiality regulations.

2. Administrative Functions

2.1 Organizational position of the EAP:

Operation of or responsibility for the EAP should be positioned at an organizational level high enough to insure the involvement of senior management and/or union leadership in sustaining the program.

2.2 Physical location of the EAP:

The physical location of the EAP should facilitate easy access while insuring confidentiality.

2.3 Record-keeping system:

Each EAP will have a record-keeping system carefully designed to protect the identity of the client, while facilitating case management and follow-up and providing ready access to statistical information.

2.4 Relation of the EAP to medical and disability benefit plans:

There should be a review of medical and disability benefits to insure that plans adequately cover appropriate diagnosis and treatment for alcohol, drug, and mental health problems. Where feasible, coverage should include out-patient and day treatment care. The EAP staff should be familiar with provisions of the medical and disability benefit plans so they can advise clients clearly as to the extent, nature, and cost of the recommended treatment and reimbursement available.

2.5 Malpractice/liability insurance:

The organization should conduct a legal review of all aspects of the program. The purpose is to insure that there should be adequate protection for all EAP staff and the organization against possible malpractice/liability claims.

2.6 Qualifications of EAP staff:

The EAP staff should combine two primary qualifications:

1. Appropriate managerial and administrative experience.
2. Skills in identifying problems, interviewing, motivating, referring clients, and, where appropriate, in counseling or related fields. Experience and expertise in dealing with alcohol-related problems are essential.

3. Education and Training

3.1 Communicating EAP services to employees and their families:

It is important that employees and their families are informed about the organization's EAP and the services it offers, and are continually updated by various educational techniques on its existence and availability. Information about the EAP should be made available to all new employees and their families.

3.2 Employee education:

An organization should have a major commitment to on-going education about alcohol use and alcoholism. Additional efforts should be made to educate employees about other recognized problem areas.

3.3 Orientation of management and union representatives:

Management and union representatives should be thoroughly informed about their key role in utilizing the EAP services. Orientation for management and union representatives should be updated regularly.

4. Resources

4.1 Resource file on providers of assistance:

Each EAP should maintain correct information about alcoholism

treatment services and other resources. These include Alcoholics Anonymous, Al-Anon, Alateen, and other self-help groups, appropriate health care, community services, and other professionals.
5. Evaluation
   5.1 Program review and evaluation:
   There should be a periodic review of the program to provide an objective evaluation of operation and performance.
   5.2 Staff performance evaluation:
   There should be an annual evaluation review of EAP staff performance.

■

These standards, based on the collective experience of a number of researchers and practitioners, affirm the organizational focus of the employee assistance concept. Primary emphasis is placed on the importance of disseminating accurate information to all members of the company, including managers, union representatives, employees, and family members. EAP practitioners can devise procedures that fit the exigencies of the organization. They must, however, use every possible mechanism to ensure that all concerned know how to use the system and are aware of its possibilities and limitations.

The fact that the EAP is a system is underscored by the attention paid in the standards to policy and administrative functions. Novices in the field might believe that they can concentrate solely on the provision of services to troubled individuals. In fact, however, an effective employee assistance program has an impact on the organization as a whole and is, in turn, affected by other organizational policies. When a company initiates an employee assistance program, its members are making a commitment to adopting an altered view of the value of troubled employees and accepting the notion that treatment and rehabilitation are appropriate methods of addressing mental and physical health problems. For many firms, this step represents a major reorientation, one which cannot be made without the authentic involvement of labor and management. An EAP that is considered the sole domain of the professional service provider is doomed to failure, and the standards help to prevent this error.

Just as the EAP counselor interacts closely with the firm itself, he or she must also develop ties with a number of external resources. The standards provide a sorely needed reminder to counselors to maintain current files on professional and self-help resources in the community and to become thoroughly familiar with employee benefit plans. With this familiarity comes the equally important responsibility of providing input to encourage adequate insurance coverage for alcohol, drug, and mental health-related treatment.

Perhaps the most important contribution of the standards is their encouragement of confidentiality and ethical behavior. Although the standards allow for procedural variation, they provide clear guidelines concerning individual privacy. A counselor attempting to work in accordance with the standards would have no choice but to maintain confidentiality for all clients and anonymity for self-referring employees. If the organization's policy statement includes voluntary acceptance of the standards, managers are unlikely to press for exceptions to the rules of confidentiality or professional ethics.

POLICY STATEMENTS

In keeping with the suggested standards for employee assistance programs, each EAP should have a clear policy statement on which to base its operations. In fact, designing the statement of policy should be the first step taken when a program is being considered. Although an EAP consultant can play a major part in presenting ideas for consideration and in drafting the actual document, the policy must reflect the thinking of the people who will be affected by the program's success. The longevity of the program may well be a function of the time and care taken to obtain extensive input from managers, first-line supervisors, employee representatives, and service providers. The resulting document should combine consistency with national standards and attention to the special needs of the unique organization. An examination of several existing policy statements—all in actual use in employee assistance programs—can point up a few of the commonalities and distinctions among programs. The "Personal Assistance Program" used by Kemper Insurance Company is shown below as Exhibit 2.2. The program, which has been in existence for a number of years, is managed and implemented as an internal EAP open to all employees.

EXHIBIT 2.2. EAP *Policy Statement: Kemper Insurance Company*

In accordance with our general personnel policies, which are based on the underlying concept of regard for the employee as an individual, as well as a worker:

1. We believe that alcoholism, drug addiction and emotional disturbance are illnesses and should be treated as such.
2. We believe that the majority of employees who develop alcoholism, other drug addiction or emotional illness can be helped to recover and the company should offer appropriate assistance.
3. We believe the decision to seek diagnosis and accept treatment for any

suspected illness is the responsibility of the employee. However, continued refusal of an employee to seek treatment when it appears that substandard performance may be caused by illness is not tolerated. We believe that alcoholism, other drug addiction or emotional illness should not be made an exception to this commonly accepted principle.

4. We believe that it is in the best interest of employees and the company that when alcoholism, other drug addiction or emotional illness is present, it should be diagnosed and treated at the earliest possible date.

5. We believe that the company's concern for individual alcohol drinking, drug taking and behavioral habits begins only when they result in unsatisfactory job performance, poor attendance or behavior detrimental to the good reputation of the company.

6. We believe that confidential handling of the diagnosis and treatment of alcoholism, other drug addiction or emotional illness is essential.

The objective of this policy is to retain employees who develop any of these illnesses by helping them to arrest its further advance before the condition renders them unemployable.

■

The Kemper policy statement reflects the prevalence of supervisory referrals to that company's EAP. Focus is placed on the effect of alcoholism, drug addiction, and other problems on job performance and on the importance of basing referrals on detrimental, job-related behaviors. Another policy statement, currently used in a school system EAP, differs in emphasis and is shown in Exhibit 2.3. This policy statement reflects the philosophy of an external program, developed by PACE (Professional Assistance for Corporations and Employees) for an elementary school district in the Chicago area.

EXHIBIT 2.3. *School District Policy Statement*

The school district and the service provider recognize that alcoholism, drug addiction, and emotional difficulties are all treatable problems. In addition, we recognize that almost everyone is under some kind of stress at some time. This can show up in family problems, dependence on drugs or alcohol, trouble in interpersonal relationships, or personal distress. The decision to seek help for any of these problems is an individual matter, but it is in the best interest of school district employees and pupils if problems are diagnosed and treated at the earliest possible date.

The presence of an employee assistance program can be seen as a benefit for employees, since they can receive prompt, professional assistance for issues that concern them. In addition, the employee assistance program is beneficial for the school district and the community. Prompt recognition and treatment of problems allow the schools to retain valued employees and to keep the quality of education high.

If an individual employee choses to seek assistance through the employee assistance service, no one will be informed concerning his/her use of the service. If an employee is referred by an administrator, it will be on the basis of impaired job performance. Participation of any individual in the employee assistance program is voluntary and will not affect future employment or career advancement in any way.

It is understood that records concerning individual problems will be maintained by Professional Assistance for Corporations and Employees, Inc., only, and access will be limited to their professional personnel. Information concerning use of the EAP will not become part of the employee's personnel file. EAP evaluation reports will be statistical in nature, with information concerning individual employees remaining confidential.

This program in no way alters the roles of administrators, teachers, or the bargaining unit. The employee assistance program provides a viable alternative that is available on a voluntary basis for the benefit of the school system. The program is carried out in accordance with national standards for employee assistance programs.

■

The policy statement shown in Exhibit 2.3 reflects the realities of providing EAPs for groups of professionals. Stress is placed on self-referrals, since they can be expected to outnumber administrative referrals by a significant margin. The emphasis on the voluntary nature of the program and on careful consideration of confidentiality results from concerns expressed by the teachers who participated in developing the policy statement. The teachers also noted the importance of encouraging school district employees to use the program, not because they saw themselves as people with "illnesses," or even "problems," but because they recognized that anyone could need help in coping with temporary stress.

The broad-brush approach of the two policies shown above differs to a considerable extent from the substance abuse focus of many industrial programs. An example of an industrial EAP of long standing is provided by the General Motors program, a joint labor-management effort developed cooperatively by GM and the UAW-IUE for employees represented by the United Auto Workers. This program's policy statement, which emphasizes the disease concept of alcoholism and drug abuse, is shown as Exhibit 2.4.

EXHIBIT 2.4. General Motors Employee Alcoholism and Drug Abuse Recovery Program

1. Alcoholism and drug abuse is recognized as a highly complex disease which is treatable. For purposes of this policy, alcoholism and drug abuse is defined as a disease in which an employee's consumption of alcohol or other drugs definitely and repeatedly interferes with his job performance and/or his health.

2. Employee alcoholism or drug abuse becomes a concern when it interferes with the employee's job performance. To drink or use other drugs socially is the prerogative of the employee. The social stigma often associated with alcoholism has no basis in fact. A realistic recognition of this illness will encourage employees to take advantage of available treatment. Employees with this illness will receive the same consideration and referral for treatment that is presently extended to all employees having other illnesses.

3. Every effort should be made to identify the disease in its early stages, to work with and assist the employee, and to encourage him to obtain treatment without delay. When a represented employee is involved, it is recognized that the disease can be dealt with most effectively on a cooperative union-management basis.

4. Early identification of the alcoholic or drug abusing employee should be based entirely on evidence of poor job performance and other related factors. The immediate supervisor should refer such an employee to the plant medical director or his designated representative for further evaluation. In this regard, it is not necessary for each supervisor to know the medical symptoms of alcoholism or drug dependency. If the employee is represented by a union, an appropriate local union representative may be in a position to convince the alcoholic or drug dependent employee to seek treatment. It is the responsibility of all supervisors to carry out this policy and to follow procedures assuring that no employee will have his job security jeopardized solely by his request for diagnosis and treatment.

5. The plant medical director, or his designated representative, is available to consult with an employee about the nature of his problem and whether or not treatment is indicated, but he does not provide treatment. In each instance, medical records of employees with alcoholism or drug abuse problems will be maintained in the same confidential manner as all other medical records.

6. The decision to undertake treatment is the responsibility of the individual employee, that is, through sources qualified in the proper care and treatment of alcoholism and drug abuse. The medical department is available for referral assistance or the employee may seek help directly from any qualified treatment facility or agency. When a leave of absence is nec-

essary so that an employee may undergo medical treatment in an appropriate facility in accordance with this program, and when the employee has voluntarily submitted himself for such treatment and his seniority or length of service has not already been broken, he will be granted a sick leave of absence and he will be eligible for benefits in accordance with the GM Insurance Program.

7. The employee should be assured that if he brings his illness under control and his job performance becomes satisfactory, his job security will not be jeopardized solely by his decision to seek treatment. However, he also should be advised that he may expect no special privileges or exemptions from standard personnel administration practices. If the employee does not cooperate in obtaining treatment and his performance continues to be unsatisfactory, or if the treatment does not result in a marked improvement in his job performance within a reasonable period, management will review the employee's situation and make a determination concerning his future status as an employee—applying GM salaried policies and procedures or posted shop rules.

8. Considerate and careful follow-up is vital for effective employee rehabilitation or continuance of corrective action, whichever is appropriate.

Nothing in this statement of policy is to be interpreted as constituting any waiver of management's responsibility to maintain discipline or the right to invoke disciplinary measures in the case of misconduct which may result from or be associated with the use of alcohol or other drugs.

■

Each of the policy statements shown above reflects the special concerns of the organization being served. The General Motors policy statement, for instance, demonstrates recognition of the devastating effects of substance abuse and highlights the importance of dealing with this health issue in a way that is fair to each member of the organization. The school system policy, in contrast, focuses attention on the idea that all human beings experience stress and coping difficulties at some time in their lives. This view expresses the teachers' awareness that stress and burnout are serious issues in the school milieu and that professionals are most likely to seek help if they are encouraged to see the program as preventive rather than curative. While both the Kemper and the GM policy statements deal extensively with the role of the EAP in the disciplinary process, the school system policy tends to reflect the reality that professionals' job performance is difficult to measure and rarely subject to close supervision. Self-referral is likely to form the heart of an employee assistance program in a professional setting, and therefore the policy statement identifies the EAP as a voluntary employee benefit.

Despite differences in emphasis, the policy statements exhibit similarities that verify a fairly broad consensus in the employee assistance field. Almost all working policies include some mention of each of the following factors:

- The organization's commitment to treatment and rehabilitation of troubled employees.
- The importance of early identification of problems.
- The voluntary nature of employee participation in the program.
- The recognition that high standards of performance continue to be expected.
- The need for supervisory referrals based solely on identifiable impairment in job performance.
- The assurance of confidentiality in services and counseling records.

Whether EAPs are internal or external, focused on alcoholism or broadbrush, practitioners tend to agree on the kind of benefits they hope to provide for employees and their organizations.

SUPERVISORY TRAINING

First-line supervisors play a key role in implementing an employee assistance program, since they are called upon to identify and refer those employees who need assistance. Most EAPs are based on the assumption that supervisors should be able to recognize changes in job performance, confront the employee in terms of observable behavior, and encourage the individual to seek the help he or she needs. Ideally, the employee will be able to improve performance and avoid the next step in the disciplinary process.

EAP consultants recognize that few supervisors are able to perform these tasks effectively without special training. Harrison (1982) points out that many supervisors fail to give any critical feedback at all because (a) the task is unpleasant, (b) friendship between supervisor and supervisee might be affected, (c) the supervisor is uncertain about how to approach the problem, or (d) the supervisee's actions have not been well documented. When supervisors suspect the existence of mental or physical health problems, they tend to be even more uncomfortable with the prospect of confronting a supervisee.

Successful implementation of an employee assistance program requires that supervisors develop the knowledge, attitudes, and skills needed to blend confrontation and encouragement. The knowledge needed by supervisors includes information about the close interaction between work and personal health, the methods for recognizing and documenting changes in job performance, and the ways to make use of the EAP as a supervisory support system. Complementary attitude changes involve both increased self-awareness concerning personal anxiety in dealing with troubled supervisees and recognition that early confrontation may actually benefit employees more than "looking the other way" and letting problems persist. When supervisors become convinced of the efficacy of the EAP approach, they are ready to build their own skills in specifying behavioral expectations and communicating effectively.

The provision of training both for supervisors and for union stewards or employee representatives, who play similarly important roles in the referral system, should begin as soon as the EAP policy has been developed. Initial training sessions usually include the following components:

1. Overview of the EAP policy and related procedures.
2. An information session, often including films or video tapes, concerning job performance problems and the need to confront them.
3. An opportunity to analyze and practice personal communication skills.
4. Instruction in performance appraisal and confrontation methods, using realistic examples.
5. Role-played practice in supervisory confrontation.
6. Discussion of the special problems and concerns of the specific work environment.
7. A chance for supervisors and employee representatives to react to the employee assistance concept and to make suggestions for its implementation.

Follow-up training sessions should be offered on a regular basis, both to meet the needs of new supervisors and to update and reinforce the effects of earlier sessions. Supervisory referrals depend on the supervisors' commitment to the program and on their own feelings of competence in dealing with troubled employees. Training sessions must be practical and experiental, rather than didactic and academic, and focus on the usefulness of the information and skills for the supervisor attempting to do his or her job. The EAP is meant to make the supervisor's task easier—not more difficult—and effective training will succeed in making this point clear.

EMPLOYEE ORIENTATION AND INFORMATION

Clear communication with the company's entire work force is also important. All members of the organization, including employees and covered family members, need to know what the EAP is and how they can use it. EAP consultants should use every available communication mechanism to furnish initial information about the program's use and to maintain the visibility of the services by providing regular reminders.

The initial orientation of employees should use the organization's normal methods of disseminating information. In some organizations, mass meetings may be designed to provide an introduction to the EAP for a number of employees at one sitting. If such an orientation session can be arranged, EAP consultants can use this opportunity both to disseminate factual information about the program and to generate enthusiasm among employees. In general, orientation sessions follow some of the same steps involved in supervisory training. Some time, however brief, should be devoted to each of the following matters:

1. An overview of the policy and procedures upon which the EAP is based.
2. Statements of support for the program by executives, union representatives, and other opinion leaders.
3. Information concerning the relationship between work performance and mental and physical health.
4. Clear instructions concerning the methods to be followed for using the program.
5. Repetition of assurances concerning the voluntary and confidential nature of the services.
6. Introduction of people who will be providing services through the employee assistance program.
7. Opportunities for employee questions, discussion, and input.

The desired outcome of such an orientation session is that employees feel that the EAP is a resource that can help them to enhance their personal well-being and to maintain their effectiveness as workers.

In many organizations, large-scale orientation sessions are difficult to arrange. EAP consultants can try to arrange meetings with smaller work groups to disseminate some of the same information. Such meetings are usually brief, but offer valuable opportunities for informal discussion of employee concerns. If an organization's structure allows for a combination of large and small meetings, the consultant can incorporate the benefits of each by presenting information to a large group and following up with smaller sessions to deal with employee reactions. For instance, an employee assistance program for teachers can be introduced at a system-wide fall orientation meeting, with follow-up sessions planned for the faculty of each individual school.

Whether or not orientation meetings are held, each employee should receive written notification that an EAP has been initiated. This notification should advertise the program by including both basic information and a positive message about its potential to be helpful. The brochure or handout should incorporate material found in the program policy statement but use informal, nonthreatening language. The following example (Exhibit 2.5) is taken from an EAP delivered by PACE to a school system in Illinois. The policy statement, duplicated in a previous section of this chapter, formed the basis for the one-page handout made available to all district employees.

EXHIBIT 2.5. *School District Employee Handout*

The Employee Assistance Program:
A Service Provided for Faculty and Staff

PACE (Professional Assistance for Corporations and Employees) is now providing a new service at no cost to you. The service, an EMPLOYEE ASSISTANCE PROGRAM, is meant to provide short-term help for any kind of problem that concerns you.

The school district has contracted with PACE to provide these services because of the recognition that everyone is under some kind of stress at some time. This can show up in work or family problems, dependence on drugs or alcohol, trouble in interpersonal relationships, or personal distress. If you are trying to solve such a problem, you can now call PACE . . . If you do, a counselor will see you within a week, at a time that is convenient for you.

The counselor will try to help you resolve the immediate issue. If more than two or three sessions are needed, the counselor will recommend someone else who can work with you for a longer period of time. If additional assistance is recommended, your insurance coverage and ability to pay will be taken into account. The sessions with our own PACE counselors will be free of charge.

We are interested in helping people before any problems begin to interfere with effectiveness at work. Don't hesitate to call, even if your problems seem minor. What happens in the sessions remains confidential. No information about any individual will be shared with others.

No matter what issue might be worrying you now, call PACE . . . One of our trained professionals will try to help.

■

The information sheet is designed to encourage self-referrals by emphasizing the easy accessibility of services and focusing on the fact that help is not limited to people with serious problems. Often, a number of employees refer themselves within a few days of receiving EAP information. This phenomenon suggests that many troubled people hesitate to search for help but will accept assistance if it is offered to them.

In order to maintain the utilization of services in the long run, the counselor needs to keep the program visible. Posters in central locations, wallet-sized cards imprinted with the EAP telephone number, items in the firm's newsletter, and brief notes in pay envelopes can perform two functions: educate employees about health issues and remind individuals that they have easy access to personal help.

COUNSELING, ASSESSMENT, AND REFERRAL

When an individual seeks assistance from the employee assistance counselor, his or her current level of functioning should be assessed. The counselor should try to determine whether significant problems exist in the client's life and work. At the same time, the assessment should also identify the strengths and resources the client has for coping with stress.

Albee (1980) makes a distinction between two models for explaining problems in human behavior: the "competency model" and the "defect model." The competency model assumes that everyone has the right and the potential to maximize his or her competence to deal with stress and that distress can be handled—and even prevented—by reducing stress and building competence. The defect model, in contrast, explains disturbed behavior in terms of some flaw within the individual.

In an employee assistance program, the competency model is clearly more appropriate. From an organizational standpoint, the premise of an EAP is that employees are valued resources who might sometimes need help in order to maintain their accustomed levels of excellence in job performance. From the employees' point of view, the EAP is a benefit that allows them to enhance the quality of life for themselves and their families. The counselor's task, then, is not to find out what is "wrong" with an employee but to explore the possibilities for improving the interaction between the individual and his or her environment. The assessment process should involve a joint effort by the client and the counselor to recognize what stressors affect the individual and what mechanisms he or she uses to cope with the world. In very general terms, the purpose of this initial assessment is to find some answers to the following questions:

1. What objectives does the client hope to meet through participation in the EAP?
2. What kinds of changes or constant stressors are affecting the individual at home and at work?
3. What health factors are affecting the individual either positively or negatively?
4. How adequate are the individual's skills in such areas as problem solving, interpersonal relations, stress management, job performance, and health maintenance?
5. To what degree does the individual feel that he or she has control over his or her life?
6. What kinds of social support are available to the client from friends, family, co-workers, or others?

A broad assessment, taking into account physiological, social, and psychological factors, helps to identify the components of the client's life that he or she might wish to attack and change. As a result of this multifaceted assessment, one client might decide to work on skills in problem solving and decision making, another might choose to seek more social support by joining a self-help group, and another might change his or her work schedule in order to decrease stress. In each case, what the assessment process has done is to give direction to the individual, showing what gaps need to be filled as he or she attempts to build life mastery.

Many employees find that this assessment process meets their needs and that they can develop new plans based on what they have learned about themselves. Others decide to use the services of the EAP counselor on a short-term basis to help in skill development and life planning. Although the EAP practitioner cannot provide a lengthy therapeutic intervention, he or she can assist the client to examine alternatives and make needed changes in behavior. Pragmatic problem-solving approaches can be used to help employees manage immediate situations, with the counselor providing assistance and support as the individual moves from examining the problem to setting realistic goals to developing plans for action. In general, the clients most frequently served by counselors in the EAP setting include people working on the development of specific behaviors, individuals seeking support to deal with temporary crises, and employees hoping to improve their relationships with family members and associates.

Employees with more pressing mental or physical health problems need to be referred for help outside of the work setting. When this happens, the counselor now has sufficient familiarity with the employee's needs to present the most appropriate possible referral options. A competency-oriented model opens up many more choices than a defect model. Client and counselor need not limit their consideration to what would traditionally be called "treatment." Instead, they can examine a number of options, including self-help networks, social organizations, community action groups, and financial, legal, personal, or family counseling.

EAP counselors have to be as familiar with community resources as they are with client needs, so that referrals can be made solely to consistently effective agencies and individuals. Of course, employee assistance professionals need to maintain comprehensive files that include information about the quality and costs of services available to their clients. They also need to have the kind of subtle information about treatment philosophies and agency values that can come only from personal investigation. Ideally, each referred employee should be linked with a service provider who can meet his or her identified needs and who is also a "good fit" in terms of personality, goal orientation, and shared values.

EDUCATION AND PREVENTION

An approach to behavior change based on competency building and stress reduction also opens the door to preventing the occurrence of problems in health and behavior. EAPs have traditionally proven their effectiveness in "secondary prevention," which involves early identification and prompt treatment of problems that might otherwise become severe. Even more can be accomplished, however, in "primary prevention," which decreases the incidence of problems among a given population by concentrating efforts on people who have not shown any evidence of dysfunction.

In the context of a work organization, an employee assistance counselor can do a great deal to prevent the development of mental and physical health problems by presenting programs that build employees' coping resources.

> Such efforts, often referred to as competence training, are designed to improve the capacity of normal and at-risk populations to cope with predictable life transitions and to more effectively manage stressful situations. The premise underlying this approach is that disorders can be avoided by strengthening an individual's or group's capacity to handle environmental stress or life crises (Ketterer, Bader, and Levy, 1980, p. 271).

Educational approaches can be used to prevent the incidence of the problems most frequently seen among the employees of a given firm. A variety of methods, including workshops, seminars, film presentations, and dissemination of written materials, can be used to educate employees about such health-related issues as substance abuse, smoking, exercise, and nutrition. In addition, employees can be exposed to skill development in areas that seem to relate to individuals' ability to withstand stress and maintain good mental health. Some examples of workshops that have been popular in many EAPs include:

- Stress management
- Preventing burnout at work
- Effective parenting
- Communication skills
- Marriage enrichment
- Family support systems
- Specific approaches to stress prevention (biofeedback, self-hypnosis, relaxation training, and other mechanisms)
- Assertiveness training
- Depression
- The components of good mental health

Most employee assistance counselors try to present workshops or seminars of general interest at least four times each year. The topics covered are normally selected after consultation with managers, employee representatives, and human resource or personnel specialists. The counselor can take into account the types of problems that have been most prevalent among individual clients as well as the general concerns expressed by the organization's members. General sessions can be followed up by ongoing seminars for employees wishing to explore an issue in more depth.

An educational approach is very suitable for an EAP because the client population is made up of essentially normal adults who have been healthy enough to maintain employment. Most clients can be expected to have reasonably effective coping skills. They can learn to enhance their skills and withstand stress without the need for long-term, in-depth treatment. For these people, a newfound ability to relax, to communicate effectively with family members, or to recognize early signs of alcohol abuse can make the difference between healthy coping and stress-related crises.

At the same time, EAP professionals can help to prevent crises by addressing stressors in the one aspect of their clients' environment that they are in the best position to assess: the work setting. Kahn (1981) suggests that organizations can be made less stressful if attempts are made to take the following steps:

1. Minimize unpredictability and ambiguity . . .
2. Minimize uncontrollable events at the individual level . . .
3. Eliminate avoidance learning, that is, performance or punishment . . .
4. Minimize physical stressors . . .
5. Avoid recurring (daily) stresses . . .
6. Watch for negative affect . . . (p. 30).

The EAP specialist, in his or her role as consultant, can use such information to make the organization less stressful and more humane, thus preventing a host of physical and psychological problems.

It is also important to remember that the environment can have positive effects on individuals' development. One of the factors that affects people's ability to cope with difficulties is the availability of social networks that provide psychological and practical support. For many employees, social support systems are built and maintained in the work setting. An employee assistance program can purposefully encourage this positive characteristic by providing experiences that lead to the development of mutual support among employees.

SUMMARY

Effective employee assistance programs share a number of elements. Each EAP should include a clear statement of policy, a supervisory training program, an employee information system, a counseling, assessment, and referral service, and an educational/preventive effort.

Employee assistance programs can be divided into internal and external programs. In programs based on the internal model, services are provided by specialists who are, themselves, employed by the company. External programs are provided by consultants who are paid on a contractual basis and who usually deliver services at locations away from the worksite. Programs can be equally comprehensive whether they are based on the external or the internal model, and service providers should carefully maximize the strengths and minimize the weaknesses of the model being implemented.

A set of voluntary employee assistance program standards has been developed by a group of national organizations to provide guidelines for planning and implementing programs. These standards, which cover policies and procedures, administrative functions, education and training, resources, and evaluation, are equally appropriate for internal and external programs and their validity is widely accepted in the field.

In keeping with suggested standards, each successful EAP has a policy statement that expresses the organization's commitment to treating and rehabilitating troubled employees and emphasizes the voluntary and confidential nature of services. Supervisory training sessions ensure effective policy implementation by helping key members of the organization to play their part in referring troubled employees for assistance. Self-referrals are encouraged by the program's efforts to provide initial orientation and ongoing information for all members of the organization. Finally, the services provided, whether focused on one-to-one counseling or on prevention, help employees to develop the competencies and resources they need to withstand stress and improve the quality of their lives. The impact of the EAP is increased even more when counselors and consultants do all they can to make the work organization less stressful and more humane.

REFERENCES

Albee, G. W. (1980). A competency model must replace the defect model. In A. Bond and J. C. Rosen (Eds.), *Competence and coping during adulthood* (pp. 75–104). Hanover, NH: University Press of New England.

Harrison, E. L. (1982). Training supervisors to discipline effectively. *Training and Development Journal, 36*(11), 111–113.

Hollmann, R. W. (1981). Beyond contemporary employee assistance programs. *Personnel Administrator, 26*(9), 37–41.

Kahn, R. L. (1981). Work, stress, and individual well-being. *Monthly Labor Review, 104*(5), 28–30.

Ketterer, R. F., Bader, B. C., and Levy, M. R. (1980). Strategies for promoting mental health. In R. H. Price, R. F. Ketterer, B. C. Bader, and J. Monahan (Eds.),

Prevention in mental health: Research, policy and practice (pp. 263–283). Beverly Hills: Sage.

Leeman, C. P. (1974, March–April). *Harvard Business Review,* pp. 20–24, 152–154.

More help for troubled employees. (1979, March 12). *Business Week,* pp. 97–102.

PACE (n.d.). EAP brochure. (Available from Professional Assistance for Corporations and Employees, Inc., 3259 Broadway, Chicago, Illinois)

Chapter Three

ASSESSMENT AND REFERRAL SERVICES

Some clients come to an employee assistance counselor because they want to save their jobs. Others seek to safeguard their marriages, their friendships, or their feelings of health and well-being. No matter what specific difficulty might motivate an employee to seek help, he or she fully expects to play an active role in resolving the problem at hand. Especially in a program oriented toward adult workers, the ultimate goal of counseling is to help individuals plan their own lives in accordance with their unique values and priorities. The counselor's relationship with the client parallels the consultant's alliance with a manager.

> Consultants in the business world adopt a variety of roles—they listen, observe, collect data, report observations, teach, train, coach, provide support, challenge, advise, offer suggestions, and even become advocates for certain positions. But the responsibility for running the business remains with those who hire the consultant. Therefore, even though some of the consultant's activities can be seen as directive, the managers still make the decisions. Consulting, then, is a social-influence process, but one that does not rob managers of their responsibilities (Egan, 1982, p. 15).

Similarly, the responsibility for running his or her life belongs to the client. The counselor can identify problem areas and suggest alternative strategies for their resolution, but the process must encourage the client's active participation in every stage of assessment and treatment planning.

When clients become actively involved in assessing their current life situations, they can simultaneously learn about themselves and begin to increase the degree of control they feel they can exercise over their activities. These benefits can be realized only through an assessment process that is practical, multifaceted, and easily understood by clients.

ASSESSMENT

The basic question to be answered through the assessment process is not "What is wrong with this individual?" but "What is keeping this person from effectively managing his or her life right now?" The goal of assessment is not necessarily to place the individual in appropriate "treatment" but to devise a plan for transcending problematic situations and improving the quality of life. The best method of answering these questions and meeting these goals is through an assessment process that has the following characteristics (Lewis and Fussell, in press):

- The assessment focuses on the individual's strengths and resources as well as his or her deficits.
- The assessment is based on active involvement and understanding on the part of the client.
- The assessment process flows naturally into the planning process, so that each difficulty identified is addressed in a plan of action.
- The assessment takes into account both the stressors and the supports available in the individual's environment.

No matter what other issues might bring them to a counselor's office, most clients have in common the need to increase their sense of control over events. They need to enhance what Bandura (1982) terms "self-efficacy," or the expectation that they can be successful in taking actions that will lead to positive results. If the assessment process is taken out of their hands to be performed by an "expert," the presenting problem might be solved, but their sense of control and self-responsibility will be damaged.

> Whenever services are offered, emphasis should be placed, not on the recipient's weakness, but on his or her potential strength. An individual may seem to have many needs involving the services of the . . . counselor; perpetual dependence is never one of them (Lewis and Lewis, 1983, p. 122).

Assessment, then, is a mutual effort through which counselor and client attempt to identify life components that can be changed as the client seeks to gain mastery over his or her life, to increase self-efficacy, and to withstand stress.

The Assessment Equation

Swift (1980) cites an equation first developed by George Albee to examine the variables affecting the incidence of mental illness in general populations. This equation states that the incidence of problems is affected by the values of the following numerator and denominator:

$$\text{Incidence} = \frac{\text{stress} + \text{physical vulnerabilities}}{\text{social supports} + \text{coping skills} + \text{self-esteem}}$$

According to this equation, strategies aimed at reducing the incidence of mental health-related problems in a given population can be addressed either to decreasing the values in the numerator, especially lessening environmental stressors, or to increasing the values in the denominator by building up the coping strengths of the population's members. Thus, preventive efforts in mental health can be categorized according to whether they attack the stressors that contribute to problems or strengthen the abilities of the host to withstand stress through such mediating factors as social supports, coping skills, and self-esteem.

This equation is equally applicable to whole communities or to individuals, to the prevention of mental illness or to the assessment of any problem in living. As an assessment tool for individual clients, it serves as a way of organizing data and as a method for teaching people about the interaction between stress and coping.

When the equation is used, the initial step in the assessment process is to teach the individual client how to use it as a guide for thinking about oneself. Clients have no trouble understanding that any individual might, because of genetic or other physiological factors, be vulnerable to a specific problem or disorder. This vulnerability might never be triggered unless the individual is forced to deal with severe stress. Either a crisis-producing life event or the presence of a long-term environmental stressor can contribute to depression in one person, heart disease in another, and accident proneness in a third (President's Commission on Mental Health, 1978). Even in the presence of major stressors, people are protected from dysfunction by their abilities to mobilize social supports, to use effective coping skills, or to maintain their self-esteem.

An examination of the equation helps the client to understand that he or she can take steps both to lessen stress and thereby decrease the above-the-line values or build up the values below the line. Listing his or her current characteristics according to the categories shown on the equation gives the client an opportunity to recognize what strengths he or she can build on and what areas are in need of change. Plans of action can then be developed to work on the issues that have come to light.

The Structured Interview

One effective method of filling in the equation's values is through the use of a structured interview in which the counselor focuses questions on the categories to be covered. This approach reminds the counselor as well as the client to assess all aspects of the individual's well-being rather than to focus narrowly on only one issue or problem. Lewis and Fussell (1982) have developed a set of guidelines that are helpful in this regard, especially for beginning EAP counselors. These guidelines are shown in Exhibit 3.1.

EXHIBIT 3.1. *Interview Guidelines*

These interview guidelines have been designed to help you assess the individual client's unique set of problems, circumstances, and personal resources. This approach is based on the assumption that assessment should relate to the individual's overall level of functioning, taking into account whether significant problems exist in the client's life and what strengths he or she has for coping with stress. Assessment considers physiological, social, and psychological factors.

The interviewing guide is one way of developing an assessment strategy to focus on important areas of concern. The interviewer must, of course, take into account the special needs and presenting problems of the client. Alterations in the format should be made if significant issues require more in-depth investigation of one area. Keep in mind that the success of the assessment process depends on the relationship between counselor and client. Accuracy of self-report depends on the degree of trust that has been established.

After basic demographic information has been collected, you should explore the following content areas: (1) client objectives; (2) physical vulnerabilities; (3) stress; (4) life skills; (5) self-concept; (6) social supports.

Client Objectives
1. What made you decide to come here today? Did you come on your own, or did someone else encourage you to make the appointment?
2. What problems or issues are you most concerned about right now?
3. What do you hope will happen as a result of your being here today?
4. Are you under some kind of pressure from your employer, your family, or someone else to work on a problem that they are concerned about?
5. How do you feel about being here? Have you ever had any kind of professional help before? Tell me about how it went.

Physical Vulnerabilities
1. Tell me about any medical problems you're having right now. Are you taking any kind of medication? For how long?
2. What about in the recent past? Have you experienced any physical problems?
3. Has alcohol use ever been a problem for you?
   a. How old were you when you had your first sip of alcohol? Can you remember what it was like?

    b. Do you consider yourself a regular drinker? For how long?

    c. How much do you generally drink in a week's time?

    d. Do you find yourself drinking more when you're under stress or at any other particular time?

    e. Has anyone else—family, friends, employer—ever suggested that you might have a problem with alcohol?

    f. Have you ever had treatment for an alcohol-related problem?

    g. Do any of your family members have problems with alcohol?

4. Has drug use ever been a problem for you?

    a. What kind of drug do you use most often?

    b. Are there other kinds of drugs that you also use?

    c. Do you ever mix drugs and alcohol?

    d. How long have you been using these drugs?

    e. How much do you generally use in a week's time?

    f. Has anyone else—family, friends, employer—ever suggested that you might have a problem with drugs?

    g. Do any of your family members have problems with drugs?

    h. Have you ever tried to stop taking drugs on your own? What happened?

    i. Have you ever had treatment for a drug-related problem?

5. How do you see your own level of physical fitness? Are there things that you do to take care of your own health? (Diet, exercise, etc.)

6. Are there aspects of your health that you think you should do something about improving?

Stress

1. Have you had any significant changes in your life in the last year, either negative or positive events?

2. How have things been going with your family situation? Have there been any significant arguments or problems?

3. What about the work situation? Have things been going smoothly for you at work?

4. Do you feel that you're under a lot of stress right now?

5. What kinds of things do you do when you feel as though your life is getting stressful, when you're under a lot of pressure?

6. What kinds of things do you find tend to put you under a lot of pressure? Are you in any situations like that now?

7. Are there ongoing problems—not just in the last year—that have been troubling you or your family?

8. Are you having any difficulty as far as finances are concerned, or are things going all right for your family right now?

9. Have there been any changes in your family situation lately?

10. Have you had any changes in your work situation?

Life Skills

1. How far did you go in school? Were you a good student?
2. Do you have any kind of special profession or skills that you use in your work? Are you using those skills in your current job?
3. What kinds of things do you like to do in your spare time?
4. Do you have any special skills or abilities that you're proud of?
5. How do you handle it when you have to make a tough decision?
6. Can you think of some problem that you've had lately—even a minor one? How did you go about solving it?
7. How do you get along with other people? Are you comfortable in social situations?
8. How do you get along with the other people at work?
9. What do you think right now about how you'd like your life to be in five or ten years? Do you have some pretty clear-cut goals and some plans for getting there?
10. Do you feel pretty much able to handle whatever comes along in your life? What kinds of situations make you feel stuck? What kinds of problems give you the most trouble?

Self-Concept

1. How satisfied do you feel with the way your life is going right now?
2. What things would you change in your life if you felt you had the choice?
3. What do you see as your best qualities? Do other people seem to see the same strengths in you?
4. What do you see as your weaknesses, or problems? Have other people pointed them out to you?
5. What would you like to change about yourself?
6. Do you feel generally good about yourself?
7. How satisfied do you feel about how you're doing at work?
8. How satisfied do you feel about how you're doing with your family and friends?
9. What kinds of things would help you to feel better about yourself?
10. How do you think other people feel about you?

Social Supports

1. What is your current home situation? Has it been the same for a long time?
2. How well do you get along with other members of your family?
3. What kinds of problems are troubling your family right now?
4. Do you feel as close to your family as you would like?

5. When you have a problem, does your family help you? What kinds of things do they do to help you with a troublesome situation?
6. What other people play important parts in your life?
7. When you have a problem, where do you usually go for help? (Family, friends, work associates, church, professionals, others?)
8. How about the people at work? Do you find them helpful if you have a problem?
9. Are there times when you feel completely alone and wish you had more support from others?
10. What do you do when you feel as though you need support or help from other people?

■

The discussion arising out of these questions helps to clarify the nature of the employee's strengths and problem areas. This approach can be further operationalized through use of the Lewis-Fussell Case Conceptualization Form.

Case Conceptualization

The Lewis-Fussell Case Conceptualization Form provides an informal method for documenting the multifaceted assessment process. The counselor who uses this form gains a clear concept of the directions that should be recommended to the client as well as a practical, but unofficial, record-keeping tool. This case conceptualization method uses an open-ended questionnaire format in order to allow the counselor to write down his or her perceptions in an organized manner. The form is shown on pp. 62–65 as Exhibit 3.2.

The case conceptualization form requires that the assessor build in recommendations concerning each factor. When the form has been completed, the counselor has both a personal record of the assessment interviews and a set of guidelines to follow in making referrals or continuing the counseling process. Use of the form thus makes it possible for the assessment procedure to lead naturally into treatment planning. This method was utilized in the cases of Jon Smith and Jane Jones, which are described below.

Case Example: Jon Smith

Jon Smith came to the EAP counselor's office and reported that he had been slightly depressed for a while and that, in recent months, the quality of his work had deteriorated. Jon had a stable family life and a loving wife, but his social contacts had always been centered on the group at work. His

EXHIBIT 3.2. *Lewis-Fussell Case Conceptualization Form*

Client:	Dates Seen:
Address:	

Telephone: Work	Home	

Employer Providing Coverage:	Employment:
	Present Job Title _____
	How Long in Present Position? _____
___ Employee	How Long with Company? _____
___ Family Member of Employee	Referred by: _____

Marital Status:	Dependents:	Age:	___ Male ___ Female

Reason for Referral (Presenting Problem):

Physical Vulnerabilities

Physician:

Medical Problems/Medications:

Pattern of Alcohol Use (Self and/or Family):

Pattern of Drug Use (Self and/or Family):

Previous Treatment (for Substance Abuse):

Level of Health/Fitness:

General Impressions (Physical Strengths/Vulnerabilities):

Assessor's Recommendations for Decreasing Physical Vulnerabilities:

Stress

Significant Life Changes (Last 12 Months):

Marital/Family Stressors:

Work-Related Stressors:

Client's Perception of Stress Factors:

General Level of Stress:

Recommendations for Decreasing Stress:

Life Skills

Professional/Educational Level:

Problem Solving/Decision Making Skills:

Interpersonal Skills:

Life Planning Skills:

Aptitudes/Interests/Hobbies:

Ability to Handle Life Situations:

General Impressions of Life Skills:
Recommendations for Increasing Life Skills:

Self-Concept

Level of Life Satisfaction:
Client's Perception of Strengths:
Client's Perception of Weaknesses/Problems:
Level of Self-Esteem:
Level of Work Satisfaction/Perceived Competence:
General Impressions:
Recommendations for Increasing Self-Esteem:

Social Supports

Stability of Present Home Situation:
Relationship to Family:
Family-Related Problems:

Degree of Family Support for Problem Resolution:

Significant Other Relationships/Support:

Work Relationships/Support:

General Level of Available Support:

Recommendations for Increasing/Using Social Support:

General Level of Adjustment

Psycho-Social Problem Areas:

Developmental History of Problems:

Previous Treatment/Response to Treatment:

General Assessment

Nature of Problem	Recommendation/Referral
____ Everyday Living Issue (No Long-Term Treatment Needed) ____ Psychological ____ Substance Abuse _____ ____ Family ____ Medical _____ ____ Legal/Financial ____ Other _____	
Date of Referral:	Date of Follow-up:

■

feelings of self-worth had also been dependent on his work situation; unfortunately, that situation had changed in the last year.

Until last year, Jon had been part of a very close work group of three men. Jon, Harold, and Luis were very effective in their work. Although other people might not have been aware of their accomplishments, they were unconcerned about being overlooked because they supported one another, complimenting themselves for jobs well done and commiserating with one another when difficulties arose.

This agreeable arrangement was interrupted when a major cutback in funding brought a drastic reduction in the work force at the organization. Harold and Luis lost their jobs, and a departmental reorganization left Jon working alone. He was glad that, through outplacement assistance, Harold and Luis had found employment elsewhere, but he felt completely isolated. He had no trouble doing his work, but he felt no joy and no sense of accomplishment. As a result of the reorganization, his friends were no longer there to "stroke" him for his successes.

Jon's solution was to take on more and more tasks at the office in the hope that he could somehow regain some feeling of success or receive some notice from others in the work setting. But taking on more tasks only meant that he was spread too thin. The more he did, the more the quality of his work suffered. Finally, the organization's manager began to notice that he was making errors and submitting work that had to be redone.

In seeking help, Jon described himself as feeling lost and having the sense that his life was "going nowhere." The assessment process was used to help him find ways to replace the positive aspects of his life that had been lost and to give him some sense of a new direction. Exhibit 3.3 shows how Jon's situation was conceptualized.

In Jon Smith's case, the assessment showed that the client was using faulty methods for coping with what was clearly a stressful change in the work environment. He needed to develop more effective ways to manage the situation, including (a) paying attention to his physical health; (b) revising his work schedule to decrease stress and improve his performance of important responsibilities; (c) developing new personal support systems, both at work and in his personal life; and (d) making plans for safeguarding his own mental health.

Jon was able to begin paying more attention to himself and his changing needs. The counselor let him know about a group of men in other departments at his company who used the lunch hour to walk or take easy runs through a nearby park. He joined this group, both to meet new people and to improve his feelings of physical well-being. He and his wife joined a couples group at their church and began taking some weekend time for entertainment. Jon found that he could plan his time in a very purposeful way so that his work no longer got the best of him. Within two months, his work and his moods had both improved and there was no need to make a referral for psychiatric treatment. The experience of working with Jon

EXHIBIT 3.3. *Lewis-Fussell Case Conceptualization Form:* Jon Smith

Client: Jon Smith	Dates Seen:
Address:	

Telephone: Work   Home

Employer Providing Coverage:	Employment:
ABC Corporation	Present Job Title __Computer Programmer__
	How Long in Present Position? __5 years__
__X__ Employee	How Long with Company? __8 years__
____ Family Member of Employee	Referred by: __Self__

Marital Status:	Dependents:	Age:	__X__ Male
Married	2	35	____ Female

Reason for Referral (Presenting Problem):

Depressed; "burned out" at work.

Physical Vulnerabilities

Physician:

Medical Problems/Medications:

No chronic problems. No medication currently being taken. Wanted to know whether he should be taking medication to deal with depression.

Pattern of Alcohol Use (Self and/or Family):

Moderate.

Pattern of Drug Use (Self and/or Family):

None.

Previous Treatment (for Substance Abuse):

None.

Level of Health/Fitness:

Jon is reasonably healthy, but not involved in any regular physical activity. Says his work gives him no extra time.

General Impressions (Physical Strengths/Vulnerabilities):

Jon's health seems to be ok. His depression is moderate and unlikely to be clinical in nature.

Assessor's Recommendations for Decreasing Physical Vulnerabilities:
Involvement in some regular physical activity might help him to enhance his feelings of well-being. Also, he says that he no longer goes out for lunch but "grabs a quick doughnut." He should take time for lunch.

Stress

Significant Life Changes (Last 12 Months):

Change in work situation.

Marital/Family Stressors:

Work-Related Stressors:

Change in work situation. Loss of close co-workers and changes in duties.

Client's Perception of Stress Factors:

Client is concerned about the stress at work. He seems to be taking on unnecessary tasks that increase stress.

General Level of Stress:

Fairly high.

Recommendations for Decreasing Stress:

Suggest that Jon revise his work load and schedule to decrease stress. Cutting down on some extraneous chores would also improve his job performance.

Life Skills

Professional/Educational Level:

Well-educated professional.

Problem Solving/Decision Making Skills:

Normally able to approach problems very logically. In this instance, he needs to look at problems more objectively.

Interpersonal Skills:

Could benefit by building up skills in developing social contacts outside the work setting.

Life Planning Skills:

Normally ok. Having difficulty adjusting to change over which he had no control.

Aptitudes/Interests/Hobbies:

Very few interests outside of work.

Ability to Handle Life Situations:

Normally ok.

General Impressions of Life Skills:
He is having difficulty coping with the immediate work problem. Also, he seems to need some skill development - or perhaps just encouragement - to build up more support systems away from work.

Recommendations for Increasing Life Skills:
Short-term counseling to work on solving immediate problem and to encourage the development of friendships outside of the work setting.

Self-Concept

Level of Life Satisfaction:
Level of life satisfaction seems to depend on the work situation.

Client's Perception of Strengths:
He is feeling somewhat unsure of himself now; was too dependent on the approval of a support system that is no longer present.

Client's Perception of Weaknesses/Problems:
He is very aware of his weaknesses and overlooking his strengths right now.

Level of Self-Esteem:
Poor.

Level of Work Satisfaction/Perceived Competence:
Jon's feelings of work competence, which were very important to him, have been undermined.

General Impressions:

Recommendations for Increasing Self-Esteem:
Help Jon to make purposeful attempts to take care of himself and his own needs.

Social Supports

Stability of Present Home Situation:
Stable.

Relationship to Family:
Jon has a good relationship with wife and family, but hasn't turned to his family for support in his current situation. Keeps work problems to himself.

Family-Related Problems:

Degree of Family Support for Problem Resolution:
Family could be much more supportive if Jon asks for help.

Significant Other Relationships/Support:

Work Relationships/Support:
Has lost his primary source of support in the work setting and needs to develop new relationships.

General Level of Available Support:
Jon needs to use his family's support more and to build up his social relationships outside of the work setting.

Recommendations for Increasing/Using Social Support:
Jon should choose a method for making new friends away from work.

General Level of Adjustment

Psycho-Social Problem Areas:
Needs to make a better adjustment to a change in the work setting. Could use this as an opportunity to broaden his outlook and build new strengths.

Developmental History of Problems:
This seems to be a situational problem that Jon can develop the skill to address.

Previous Treatment/Response to Treatment:
None.

General Assessment

Nature of Problem	Recommendation/Referral
X Everyday Living Issue (No Long-Term Treatment Needed)	Will work with Jon on a short-term basis to help him choose a more effective plan of action for coping with the change in his work setting. If this works, no referral should be necessary.
___ Psychological	
___ Substance Abuse _____	
___ Family	
___ Medical _____	
___ Legal/Financial	
___ Other _____	
Date of Referral:	Date of Follow-up:

also helped the counselor, who now recognized the need to develop supportive counseling groups for people whose jobs had been affected by the recent reorganization at corporate headquarters. Other people—like Jon—were grappling with problems that could be prevented.

Case Example: Jane Jones

Jane Jones was referred by her supervisor because of a recent pattern of lateness and absenteeism. Her work continued to be competent, but her usual habits of punctuality and dependability seemed to be changing. Her supervisor did not feel that Jane's job was in jeopardy, but she did think it was becoming apparent that Jane was experiencing some kind of personal difficulty.

When Jane appeared at the counselor's office, her nervousness was evident. With some encouragement from the counselor, she shared her main concern: her husband, who had been unemployed for over a year, had begun beating her and their two young children. She had put up with sporadic attacks against her in the past, but the abuse of the children was more than she could handle. She had left home several times to stay with her parents, who welcomed her and the children, but had returned because her husband seemed to need her and promised to control his temper. Sometimes she was absent or late because of family crises; sometimes she accompanied her husband in drinking bouts and was unable to get to work on time the next morning. At this point, she needed to reconsider and reorganize almost every aspect of her personal and family life. The assessment process helped her do it, as shown in Exhibit 3.4.

Jane certainly needed to make an immediate change in her home situation. The assessment process helped her to see that she also needed to take steps to build up her own feelings of self-worth and to give herself some opportunities for success. She needed to create an independent life for herself and her children, and that called for taking stock of her own skills and attributes.

The client did move in with her parents, but only on a temporary basis. Their emotional support helped her and the children to make a transition, and soon Jane was able to find an apartment near the office. She also followed through on a referral to the local YWCA Women's Center, where she joined a support group of women who had similar problems and who were able to convince her that she should not shoulder the blame for being victimized. While at the Y, Jane noticed that a crafts class was being offered. By joining the group she rediscovered talents that had been dormant. Once she was removed from the home situation, Jane had no difficulty at all in eliminating alcohol. She did attend some Al-Anon meetings to help her come to grips with her husband's alcoholism.

Jane has not given up hope for her marriage, but she will not consider

EXHIBIT 3.4. *Lewis-Fussell Case Conceptualization Form: Jane Jones*

Client: Jane Jones	Dates Seen:
Address:	
Telephone: Work Home	

Employer Providing Coverage: _____ABC Corporation_____ _____ __X__ Employee _____ Family Member of Employee	Employment: Present Job Title __Secretary__ How Long in Present Position?__4 years__ How Long with Company?__4 years__ Referred by: __Supervisor__

Marital Status: Married	Dependents: 3	Age: 28	_____ Male __X__ Female

Reason for Referral (Presenting Problem):

Recent pattern of lateness and absenteeism.

Physical Vulnerabilities

Physician:

Medical Problems/Medications:

Complaints of "nervous stomach." No special medication taken.

Pattern of Alcohol Use (Self and/or Family):

Husband abuses alcohol. Jane occasionally joins him in drinking bouts in the hope of appeasing him.

Pattern of Drug Use (Self and/or Family):

Husband is actively using. Jane has avoided drug usage other than alcohol.

Previous Treatment (for Substance Abuse):

None.

Level of Health/Fitness:

Family problems and alcohol use are having negative effect on health.

General Impressions (Physical Strengths/Vulnerabilities):

Assessor's Recommendations for Decreasing Physical Vulnerabilities:

Assess whether decrease in alcohol consumption resolves health problems.

Stress

Significant Life Changes (Last 12 Months):

Husband's abusiveness has been exacerbated by his unemployment.

Marital/Family Stressors:

Extremely high level of stress in the family.

Work-Related Stressors:

Jane reports that she feels best when she is at work.

Client's Perception of Stress Factors:

Jane is aware of high level of stress, but uncertain about how to manage the situation.

General Level of Stress:

Very high.

Recommendations for Decreasing Stress:

Explore the possibilities of removing herself from a home situation that is dangerous for her and her children.

Life Skills

Professional/Educational Level:

Skilled in secretarial work. Interested in education. Has not had the chance to do any college-level work but does seem to have the ability.

Problem Solving/Decision Making Skills:

She is trying single-handedly to maintain stability in the family, but life is out of control at this time.

Interpersonal Skills:

Normally good at making friends, but has cut herself off from most of her social contacts.

Life Planning Skills:

Very poor at this time.

Aptitudes/Interests/Hobbies:

Very interested in art, but has not had the chance to pursue this interest in recent years.

Ability to Handle Life Situations:

The current life situation exceeds her coping ability right now.

General Impressions of Life Skills:

Jane is reasonably skilled in handling life situations and prides herself on being a good mother. She can be expected to make a good adjustment if she can remove herself from the immediate situation.

Recommendations for Increasing Life Skills:

Needs to give herself a chance to explore her educational and avocational options and skills. She is not using her skills right now, except for coping at the most basic level.

Self-Concept

Level of Life Satisfaction:

Very poor right now.

Client's Perception of Strengths:

Jane has a tendency to blame herself for the family's difficulties. The harder she tries to maintain family stability, the worse things get. She has lost sight of her strengths.

Client's Perception of Weaknesses/Problems:

Jane is now seeing many of her family problems as reflections of her own problems and weaknesses.

Level of Self-Esteem:

Very low.

Level of Work Satisfaction/Perceived Competence:

Still perceives herself as good at her job, but recognizes that her work may be jeopardized.

General Impressions:

Jane has many strengths and skills that she is not recognizing right now. Her self-respect is in tatters.

Recommendations for Increasing Self-Esteem:

She needs to get into some situations that allow opportunities for success and personal support. Jane also could use some help in recognizing that her current problems are not her fault.

Social Supports

Stability of Present Home Situation:

Very unstable.

Relationship to Family:

Poor relationship with husband. Good relationship with her own parents and with her two young children.

Family-Related Problems:

Abusive husband.

Degree of Family Support for Problem Resolution: Support from her parents can realistically be expected. They seem willing to take her in and care for the children until she can work out the current problem.	

Significant Other Relationships/Support:

Has cut herself off from most of her friends.

Work Relationships/Support:

Good potential support from her supervisor.

General Level of Available Support:

Jane can gain support from parents, friends, and supervisor, but has not made use of this support in the past.

Recommendations for Increasing/Using Social Support:

Jane needs to take steps to develop new sources of social support. She should also accept the support her parents are offering, at least during this crisis situation.

General Level of Adjustment

Psycho-Social Problem Areas:

Marriage problem must be alleviated.

Developmental History of Problems:

Previous Treatment/Response to Treatment:

None.

General Assessment

Nature of Problem	Recommendation/Referral
___ Everyday Living Issue (No Long-Term Treatment Needed) ___ Psychological _X_ Substance Abuse _____ _X_ Family ___ Medical _____ ___ Legal/Financial ___ Other _____	Recommend that Jane examine the possibility of removing herself from the home situation. Referral is being made to YWCA women's center for temporary help, with family counseling suggested after immediate crisis.
Date of Referral:	Date of Follow-up:

■

returning to her husband unless he agrees to participate in counseling and makes some major changes in his own life. In the meantime, she is building a lifestyle based on her own strengths and hopes to attend college on a part-time basis next year.

Focus on Alcoholism

EAP counselors should always attempt to determine the role that alcohol plays in a client's life problems. When alcohol histories are not routinely taken, alcoholics can be subjected to therapeutic interventions that ignore their real problems. An assessment of alcohol-related issues must take into account the multiple factors examined in the general assessment, including physiological vulnerabilities, stress, self-concept, life skills, and support systems. If alcoholism is the problem, however, the drinking behavior itself must be eliminated before other interventions can meet with any degree of success. In almost every instance, some referral, whether to Alcoholics Anonymous, a treatment facility, or an outpatient counselor, is made to deal directly with the alcohol problem.

The most difficult task the counselor faces is to help the alcoholic client come to grips with the fact that he or she needs assistance. Another challenge is to suggest the most appropriate possible treatment setting. When alcoholism is the issue, this decision must take into account not only the client's personal resources and supports but also the likelihood that the detoxification process will be a medical emergency. "Ideally, an assessment process should take into account all aspects of the client's functioning, should pave the way for a treatment alternative involving the least possible disruption for the individual, and should safeguard the client's physical well-being" (Lewis, Fussell, and Dana, 1982).

Most people with alcohol-related problems do not need inpatient hospitalization and should not be subjected to such an interruption of work and family life. Yet some people, largely because of potential health problems or lack of social supports, do need such interruptions. A careful assessment process must first recognize alcohol problems and then address the issue of appropriate treatment.

If the initial interview shows any sign of possible alcohol problems, the counselor should administer an instrument such as the Michigan Alcoholism Screening Test (Selzer, 1971), which uses a simple checklist with a number of questions related to alcohol consumption. The client is asked to check the questions to which he or she would answer *yes*. This instrument, which is widely used, gives the counselor an opportunity to make a general estimate of the degree to which an alcohol problem is present. The Michigan Alcoholism Screening Test (MAST) is duplicated below as Exhibit 3.5.

EXHIBIT 3.5. *Michigan Alcoholism Screening Test*[1]

_____ 1. Do you feel you are a normal drinker? (By normal we mean you drink less than or as much as most other people.)

_____ 2. Have you ever awakened the morning after some drinking the night before and found that you could not remember a part of the evening?

_____ 3. Does your wife, husband, a parent, or other near relative ever worry or complain about your drinking?

_____ 4. Can you stop drinking without a struggle after one or two drinks?

_____ 5. Do you ever feel guilty about your drinking?

_____ 6. Do friends or relatives think you are a normal drinker?

_____ 7. Are you able to stop drinking when you want to?

_____ 8. Have you ever attended a meeting of Alcoholics Anonymous?

_____ 9. Have you ever gotten into physical fights when drinking?

_____ 10. Has drinking ever created problems between you and your wife, husband, a parent, or other near relative?

_____ 11. Has your wife, husband, a parent, or other near relative ever gone to anyone for help about your drinking?

_____ 12. Have you ever lost friends or girl friends because of your drinking?

_____ 13. Have you ever gotten into trouble at work because of your drinking?

_____ 14. Have you ever lost a job because of drinking?

_____ 15. Have you ever neglected your obligations, your family, or your work for two or more days in a row because you were drinking?

_____ 16. Do you drink before noon fairly often?

_____ 17. Have you ever been told you have liver trouble or cirrhosis?

[1]*Note.* From "Michigan Alcoholism Screening Test: The quest for a new diagnostic instrument" by M. L. Selzer, 1971, *American Journal of Psychiatry, 127,* 1653–58. Copyright 1971 by American Psychiatric Association. Reprinted by permission.

_____ 18. After heavy drinking have you ever had delirium tremens (DT's) or severe shaking, or heard voices or seen things that weren't really there?

_____ 19. Have you ever gone to anyone for help about your drinking?

_____ 20. Have you ever been in a hospital because of drinking?

_____ 21. Have you ever been a patient in a psychiatric hospital or on a psychiatric ward of a general hospital where drinking was part of the problem that resulted in hospitalization?

_____ 22. Have you ever been seen at a psychiatric or mental health clinic or gone to any doctor, social worker, or clergyman for help with any emotional problem where drinking was part of the problem?

_____ 23. Have you ever been arrested for drunken driving under the influence of alcoholic beverages?

_____ 24. Have you ever been arrested, even for a few hours, because of other drunken behavior?

Answer key

Question #	Appropriate Answer	Points	Question #	Appropriate Answer	Points
1.	yes	2	17.	no	2
2.	no	2	18.	no	2
3.	no	1	19.	no	5
4.	yes	2	20.	no	5
5.	no	1	21.	no	2
6.	yes	2	22.	no	2
7.	yes	2	23.	no	2
8.	no	5	24.	no	2
9.	no	1			
10.	no	2			
11.	no	2			
12.	no	2			
13.	no	2			
14.	no	2			
15.	no	2			
16.	no	1			

Points are scored if the answer is different from that listed—Total possible score is 53 points.

Score

- 0–4 points non-alcoholic
- 5–6 points suggestive of alcohol problem
- greater than 7 points—alcoholism
- 10 to 20 points—moderate alcoholism
- greater than 20 points—severe alcoholism

■

A more detailed assessment of the client's referral needs can be made through use of the Lewis-Fussell-Dana Treatment Planning Assessment Scale for Alcoholism, which is shown as Exhibit 3.6.

EXHIBIT 3.6. *Lewis-Fussell-Dana Treatment Planning Assessment Scale for Alcoholism*

Physiological Vulnerabilities

Rating System:
0 = Symptom not present
1 = Mild symptomatology
2 = Moderate symptomatology
3 = Severe symptomatology

Withdrawal symptoms

_____ Insomnia

_____ Restless sleep

_____ Nausea

_____ Tremors

_____ Perspiration

_____ Agitation

_____ Anxiety

_____ Eating disturbances

_____ Disorientation to time, place, person

_____ Blackouts

_____ Seizures

_____ Delusions

_____ Hallucinations (auditory)

_____ Hallucinations (visual)

_____ Hallucinations (tactile)

Drinking-related symptoms

_____ Alcohol on breath

_____ Short attention span

_____ Tremors

_____ Restless sleep

_____ Nightmares

_____ Eating disturbances

_____ Disorientation to time, place, person

_____ Blackouts (self-reported)

_____ Hallucinations

_____ Mood swings

_____ Abrupt personality changes

_____ Memory impairment (remote)

_____ Memory impairment (recent)

_____ Slurred speech

_____ Unsteady gait

Coping Skills

_____ Inability to maintain regular employment

_____ Inability to maintain control over life situations

_____ Inability to make and carry out decisions

_____ Ineffective interpersonal relationships

Self-Concept

_____ Perceived lack of control over drinking behavior

_____ Self-doubts about the ability to change

_____ Low level of self-esteem

_____ Self-doubts about personal resources

Social Supports

_____ Unstable family situation

_____ Lack of financial support

_____ Poor relationships with family members

_____ Lack of support from family

_____ Lack of support from significant others

General Alcohol-Related Problems

_____ Points attained on Michigan Alcoholism Screening Test

Assessor's General Impression of Alcohol Abuse

———— Severe problem, 15 points
Moderate problem, 10 points
Mild problem, 5 points

(Take into account amount of alcohol typically consumed within a given period, number of years of alcohol abuse, age of first alcohol use, pattern of drinking and intoxication.)

Referral Recommendation

■

This scale, like the Lewis-Fussell Case Conceptualization Form, takes into account both physical vulnerabilities and psychosocial factors. The assessor also rates the client's physiological symptomatology by completing the section describing withdrawal symptoms or the section describing drinking-related symptoms, depending on whether abstinence is being attempted. The psychosocial assessment helps in determining the client's prognosis by providing a picture of the assets and supports that the individual brings into treatment. Referral depends both on the seriousness of the individual's physical problems and on the likelihood that the client has sufficient personal and social support to help in the treatment process.

A specialized alcoholism treatment program must be contacted if the client receives a score of 15 or higher on any section of the Lewis-Fussell-Dana Scale or a score of 25 or higher on the total score. If the client receives a score of 15 on the physical vulnerability scale, he or she is referred immediately for a medical examination or for diagnosis in an alcoholism facility. The alcoholism specialist can then assess the need for medical detoxification by considering the individual's medical history, current health problems, blood pressure, blood alcohol content levels, and the symptomatology indicated by the Lewis-Fussell-Dana scale.

The treatment planning assessment for alcoholism builds on the basic information gathered through the initial, more general evaluation, but also takes into account the important factor of physiological symptomatology. With this information, the counselor can make a judgment that balances physical, psychological, and social factors. Thus, James Martin, who lived alone and had few friends other than his "drinking buddies," was referred to a four-week, inpatient rehabilitation center where he could take time out to plan for a sober lifestyle. John Walters' alcohol problem was as severe as Martin's, but he had a stable family life and support from his wife and friends. With the help of Alcoholics Anonymous and a good individual counseling program, he was able to make the necessary changes while living at home and continuing his work. Martha Burns also had a stable home situation but started to develop potentially serious symptoms when she attempted to withdraw on her own from a combination of alcohol and prescription drugs. She needed the kind of attention that an inpatient detoxification facility could give, although she did not need to remain hospitalized after the physical crisis was over. In each situation, the counselor, client, and family members needed to evaluate a number of risk factors before they could decide on the most sensible course of action.

REFERRAL

Using a positive, multifaceted assessment method tends to broaden the EAP counselor's view of the range of community resources appropriate for receiving referrals. Each client's action plan is likely to include several life aspects that he or she would like to address. Many of these areas can be addressed by the client alone, others with the help of the employee assistance counselor. The few remaining problem areas can be addressed most effectively with additional assistance from more specialized community resources.

What of those issues that seem to depend on outside help for effective resolution? Although some intransigent problems may require the attention of professional helpers or traditional agencies, a number can be surmounted through less formal methods. When making a referral, the employee assistance counselor can consider all of the organizations and individuals that make up the community's helping network, including self-help groups and members of the client's natural support system as well as established agencies. In fact, many EAP consultants place a high priority on finding the referral options that involve the least disruption in the client's life and the most opportunity for self-help. The following guidelines can help the EAP counselor to find the way through the maze of community resources.

1. *Locate and Use Self-Help Options Available in the Community.*
Self-help organizations provide the opportunity for people with common concerns to band together and provide mutual assistance and support. In self-help groups, members have the chance to give and receive assistance. Instead of depending on the aid they can receive from professionals, individuals seek both emotional support and practical information from people who have dealt successfully with problems similar to their own.

The self-help phenomenon holds great promise as a valuable approach to problem solving because participation allows individuals to build a number of strengths concurrently. A professional helper and a self-help group both can teach someone to solve a problem or cultivate an important coping skill, but the self-help experience has two additional benefits. First, it creates a social support system that reinforces positive new behaviors and can be long-lasting. Second, it builds self-esteem by providing each member with a chance to help as well as be helped. As Skovholt (1974) points out, the act of helping is in itself therapeutic, and "the effective helper feels an increased level of interpersonal competence as a result of making an impact on another's life" (p. 62).

People who deal with alcohol-related problems have long recognized that any treatment can be enhanced by the participation of the client in Alcoholics Anonymous and of his or her family in Al-Anon. The AA approach has also been successfully adapted to the needs of a number of other groups; organizations like Narcotics Anonymous, Overeaters Anonymous, Parents Anonymous, Gamblers Anonymous, and Families Anonymous are flourishing. A variety of other approaches to self-help have also arisen, as various groups have found themselves in need of mutual communication and united action. Regardless of the nature of the group, each helps people to "acquire a new sense of independence and empowerment as a consequence of dealing effectively with their own problems" (Gartner, 1982, p. 64). For this reason, EAP counselors who are concerned with helping employees to build positive mental health and effective self-management skills examine the self-help possibilities in their communities before they consider other options.

2. Develop a Personal Knowledge of Local Resources.
Each employee assistance counselor needs a comprehensive and continually updated file of local resources that offer help. In many communities there are numerous types of services. Usually, some combination of the following service modalities will be available:

Family Service/Mental Health Services:
Community mental health centers (inpatient and outpatient services)
Private mental health clinics (inpatient and outpatient)
Private practitioners (psychiatrists, psychologists, clinical social workers, counselors, other health professionals)
Family service agencies
Specialized agencies (agencies dealing with specific population groups, such as women, children, seniors, etc.)
Self-help groups (Recovery, Inc., Grey Panthers, American Association of Retired Persons, Parents Anonymous, Association for Retarded Citizens, etc.)

Substance Abuse Treatment Facilities:
Detoxification centers (medical or nonmedical)
Rehabilitation centers (medical or nonmedical)
Inpatient hospital treatment programs

Outpatient individual counseling programs
Outpatient group counseling and education programs
Private practitioners specializing in substance abuse
Self-help groups (Alcoholics Anonymous, Al-Anon, Alateen, Alatot,
    Narcotics Anonymous, Families Anonymous, etc.)

Medical Facilities:
Hospitals
Clinics
Private practice physicians
Health care professionals (nursing services, etc.)
Inpatient health care settings (nursing homes, rehabilitation centers, etc.)

Legal and Financial Counseling Services:
Private attorneys (categorized by relevant specializations)
Public assistance agencies
Legal aid programs
Employment services
Advocacy programs (projects providing quasi-legal help for battered
    women, abused children, and other groups with special needs)
Accountants (especially those specializing in financial planning)
Financial planners
Consumer assistance offices

Maintaining records of available resources requires persistent effort, but it
is only part of the job. The counselor must also have personal knowledge
of the services provided and the atmosphere in which they are offered. Some
of this information is developed over time, as referrals are made and information comes back by way of satisfied or dissatisfied clients. But to keep
the number of dissatisfied clients low, the counselor needs to be aggressive
in developing personal knowledge by visiting frequently used facilities and,
at the very least, maintaining telephone and written communication with
more specialized services.

3. *Develop a Method for Evaluating Local Services.*
Based on their personal knowledge of local facilities, counselors can develop criteria that help them decide which referrals would be most appropriate for which clients. Beyond the obvious information about the types
of services offered by a local human service program, counselors also need
to learn about the philosophy, specialization, fee structure, and professional expertise of service deliverers. They need to know:

- What philosophy or theoretical framework underlies the approach to
  treatment of the agency or practitioner?
- How comfortable and accessible are the services provided?
- What special training or experience does the service provider bring to the
  task of helping?

- What is the fee structure for services?
- Does the agency or practitioner have some special strength in terms of success with particular types of issues or populations?
- Does the agency or practitioner use a particular technique that might be especially useful for specific clients?
- What criteria does the agency itself use to decide whether its services are appropriate for a particular client?
- What statistics can the agency make available concerning its success rate with varying client populations?
- To what degree does the agency or practitioner follow up on clients that have been served?
- To what degree are client rights and agency responsibilities clarified?

Counselors find it worth the time it takes to amass this information because so much time is saved when actual referrals take place. If counselors are aware of the philosophical approach and specialty of each service provider, they can choose agencies that meet their clients' personal needs and goals. If couselors make appropriate choices among agencies that pride themselves on accessibility, they can avoid waiting periods and make sure that the referral process runs smoothly. The successful referral will be one that provides a good fit between client and service provider; this compatibility derives from the counselor's having accurate knowledge of both the individual and the agency.

4. Offer Objective Choices to Each Client.

A major function of any employee assistance program is to link employees with appropriate sources of help. This function can be served only if EAP professionals maintain objectivity in their advice to clients. There may be times when an employee's need is so special that only one community resource can be called upon for help. In general, however, the employee assistance counselor should provide the client with at least two, and preferably three, service options. Clients should learn about the differences among their options, especially in terms of fees, philosophical orientations, helping methods, and length and intensity of treatment. Although the EAP counselor can make strong recommendations, the final decision on the preferred course of action must remain in the hands of the client. To maintain the highest ethical standards, the EAP consultant should not have any relationship with a service provider that means he or she gains more from one choice than from another.

5. Provide Ongoing Linkage Between the Client and the Helping Network.

When helpers talk about making referrals, they usually mean that a particular case is transferred from one professional or agency to another, with the new helper now taking responsibility for the client's treatment. In the

EAP context, what is really taking place is linkage. A community agency or practitioner may now be providing services, but the employee assistance counselor maintains his or her interest in and accountability for the employee's well-being. The EAP counselor links the client with sources of help in the community but continues to provide support and follow-up. In many situations, the employee assistance counselor may make multiple referrals and meet the need to expedite the complex process of dealing with a number of helping agencies.

Suppose, for instance, that the employee being served is dealing with an alcohol-related problem. The EAP counselor might need to take a number of steps, going far beyond a simple "referral." In one example, a counselor needed to:

- Meet with family members, supervisor, and union steward to encourage constructive confrontation leading to the employee's recognition of the problem.
- Make multiple referrals for the individual's alcoholism treatment, which included services by a detoxification unit, a rehabilitation center, and an outpatient aftercare program.
- Link the individual with the local Alcoholics Anonymous chapter.
- Link the employee's family with the local Al-Anon and Alateen chapters.
- After the immediate crisis was past, link the family with sources of assistance for family counseling and financial counseling.
- Maintain contact with the employee on a regular basis for one year in order to evaluate progress and prevent relapse.

Thus, the EAP counselor provided ongoing support for the employee and his family, helping them to find their way through the complex network of helping agencies available in their community. If treatment had not gone smoothly, the counselor might have needed to add the tasks of advocating on behalf of the client and making changes in the choice of helping agencies. These tasks, which go far beyond the simple act of referral, all form part of the employee assistance program's reason for being.

SUMMARY

In an employee assistance program, the goal of the assessment process is to devise an action plan for helping the employee to resolve immediate issues and gain control over his or her life. This goal can be met through an assessment process that focuses on the individual's strengths and resources as well as on his or her deficits, includes the active involvement of the client, develops a plan for dealing with each difficulty, and takes into account the positive and negative factors in the individual's work and personal environments. Thus, the client and counselor work together to identify changes that can help the individual to gain more mastery, to increase self-management, and to withstand stress.

The employee assistance counselor can engage the client in a practical, multifaceted assessment process through use of a structured interview and written documents such as the Lewis-Fussell Case Conceptualization Form. If the employee is troubled with an alcohol-related problem, the counselor can also use the Lewis-Fussell-Dana Treatment Planning Assessment Scale for Alcoholism to assess physiological and psychosocial aspects of the problem. The assessment process should make it possible to devise a treatment plan that involves the least possible disruption in the individual's life, while safeguarding his or her physical health. In all instances, the assessment process should focus on a number of related factors, including the individual's physical vulnerabilities, stress, life skills, self-concept, and social supports.

This broadly based assessment process tends to encourage an equally expansive view of available sources of help in the community. This chapter suggests that EAP counselors should locate and use self-help options, develop personal knowledge of local resources, devise a method for evaluating services, offer objective choices to each client, and provide ongoing linkage between the client and a highly complex helping network.

References

Bandura, A. (1982). Self-efficacy mechanism in human agency. *American Psychologist, 37,* 122–147.

Egan, G. (1982). *The skilled helper* (2nd ed.). Monterey, CA: Brooks/Cole.

Gartner, A. (1982). Self-help/Self-care: A cost effective health strategy. *Social Policy, 12*(4), 64.

Lewis, J. A., and Fussell, J. J. (1982). *Assessment and referral handbook.* Unpublished manuscript.

Lewis, J. A., and Fussell, J. J. (in press). Alcoholism treatment planning: Using the health equation. *Alcoholism Treatment Quarterly.*

Lewis, J. A., Fussell, J. J., and Dana, R. Q. (1982). *A three-stage assessment process for alcoholism.* Unpublished manuscript.

Lewis, J. A., and Lewis, M. D. (1983). *Community counseling: A human services approach* (2nd ed.). New York: Wiley.

President's Commission on Mental Health (1978). *Report of the task panel on prevention.* Washington: U. S. Government Printing Office.

Selzer, M. L. (1971). Michigan Alcoholism Screening Test: The quest for a new diagnostic instrument. *American Journal of Psychiatry, 127,* 1653–1658.

Skovholt, T. M. (1974). The client as helper: A means to promote psychological growth. *The Counseling Psychologist, 4,* 58–64.

Swift, C. (1980). The National Council of Community Mental Health Centers task force report. *Community Mental Health Journal, 16*(1), 7–13.

Chapter Four

COUNSELING IN THE EAP CONTEXT

In the context of an employee assistance program, clients with major health problems, whether physical or psychological, are linked with treatment resources outside of the employing organization. Thus, EAP counselors are not expected to provide treatment or long-term therapy. When they counsel employees, their goal is to give temporary support and assistance so that clients can gain or regain self-responsibility. Employee assistance professionals engage in counseling in the true sense of the word: helping individuals gain skills and mobilize resources so that they can manage problem situations and achieve the highest possible degree of mastery over their environments.

The help provided by the employee assistance counselor is short-term, pragmatic, and oriented toward problem solving. Most clients tend to fall into the following general categories:

• People needing help in the management of specific problem situations.
• People working on the development of specific behaviors.
• People seeking support as they deal with temporary crises.
• People hoping to improve their relationships with family members.

PROBLEM-SOLVING APPROACHES

When counseling is used to help a client make a decision or solve an immediate problem, two positive outcomes can be expected. First, a troublesome issue can be resolved. Second, and even more important, the client can learn problem-solving skills to be used in future situations. A number of approaches are used for counseling and most follow a step-by-step process from problem identification to concrete action.

Egan's three-stage approach. Egan (1982) describes his "problem management process" in terms of three stages. During the first stage, the counselor helps the client to explore and clarify the problem situation. In Stage II, the client is encouraged to view the situation from new perspectives and to set goals based on a better understanding of the problem. These goals are met through action programs that are initiated and carried out in the third stage of the process. Successful completion of each stage depends on the interaction between the counselor's skills and the client's behaviors. The following overview[1] clarifies this model.

Stage I: Initial Problem Clarification
   Helper Behavior: Attending, Listening, Probing, and Understanding. In this phase the helper attends to his or her client both physically and psychologically; works at "being with" the client; listens actively to what the client is saying; facilitates the client's self-exploration through judicious probing; responds with respect and empathy to what the client has to say; and establishes rapport (that is, a collaborative working relationship) by attending, responding, and working with the client.
   Client Behavior: Exploring the Problem Situation. Because of the way in which the helper responds, the client is encouraged and helped to explore specifically and concretely the experiences, behaviors, and feelings that relate to the problem situation. In this way, the problem situation begins to be clarified and defined.

Stage II: Setting Goals Based on Dynamic Understanding
   Helper Behavior: Promoting New Perspectives and Facilitating Goal Setting. The helper assists the client in piecing together the data produced in the self-exploration phase; helps the client develop the kind of new perspectives needed for goal setting; and facilitates the goal-setting process.
   Client Behavior: Developing New Perspectives and Setting Goals. The client begins to see the problem situation in new ways; understands the need for action; and chooses goals (that is, behavioral ways of managing problem situations more effectively).

Stage III: Action—Designing and Implementing Action Programs
   Helper Behavior: Facilitating Program Design and Action. The helper collaborates with the client in working out a specific action program; explores with the client a variety of ways of achieving the goals that have been set; encourages the client to act; gives support and direction to action programs; and helps the client evaluate action programs.
   Client Behavior: Acting, Achieving Problem-Managing Goals. The client explores the best ways of achieving goals, searches for supportive resources within self and environment, chooses action programs, implements programs, manages problem situation more effectively, copes with problems in living, and evaluates the helping process with the counselor (Egan, 1982, p. 51).

[1]From *The skilled helper* (2nd ed.) by G. Egan. Monterey, CA: Brooks/Cole, 1982. Copyright 1982, Wadsworth, Inc. Reprinted by permission.

A key to the counselor's effectiveness in using this model is the ability to differentiate among the helping responses appropriate to each stage. During the period of clarification, the counselor responds in ways that show understanding and create a safe environment for exploration. The working relationship and problem definition that have taken place in the initial stage provide the base upon which further work takes place. During the second stage, the counselor probes more deeply and challenges the client to identify themes and discrepancies made apparent through exploration.

> Counselors are no longer merely responding to clients as they did in Stage I; they are now demanding that the clients take a deeper look at themselves. The genuineness, respect, understanding, and rapport of Stage I have created a power base. Helpers now use this power to influence clients to see their problems from a more objective frame of reference. These demands are still based on an accurate understanding of the client and are made with genuine care and respect, but they are demands nevertheless (Egan, 1982, p. 168).

It would be useless to attempt to goad a client into action without having taken the time to develop this clear, mutual understanding. At Stage III, however, helper and client are ready to take action, identifying and deciding among alternative methods for meeting goals that have, by now, been clearly stated. Once the client has decided on a step-by-step plan for managing the immediate problem, he or she begins to implement it, with the counselor providing ongoing support, encouragement, feedback, and affirmation.

One can best understand how this process works by applying it to a specific case. Consider, for example, the problem situation faced by Jon Smith, whose functioning was assessed in Chapter 3. Jon experienced difficulty coping with an organizational change that brought about the dissolution of a very close work group. He tried to make up for this loss of support by doing more at work but found that he was being spread too thin and that the quality of his output was deteriorating. He came to the counselor knowing that he felt depressed and ineffective but unaware of the real dynamics of his situation.

The climate that was set in Stage I allowed Jon to explore his feelings about himself, his working conditions, and his lifestyle. This background information made the counselor aware of Jon's behavior and allowed the counselor to begin gently challenging the client. The work of Stage II made Jon understand that the coping mechanisms he was using were inappropriate for dealing with a job that had suddenly become more stressful. In fact, his behaviors were increasing his stress levels and moving him farther away from sources of support that he might have been able to use.

When it became clear to Jon that he needed to improve his stress management skills and build new personal support systems, he was able to devise and carry out a plan of action. Stage III involved the initiation of purposeful behaviors, including exercising with new acquaintances during his lunch hour, revising his work schedule, and engaging in more social activities with his wife and family. This action plan helped him to resolve the immediate problem and also laid the foundation for him to deal with future stressors more effectively.

Ivey's decision-making model. Ivey's decision-making approach (1980) also involves three stages. In fact, from the point of view of the client, the two models would not seem to differ greatly. Conceptually, however, the process developed by Ivey involves a series of decision-making events.

According to this model, Stage I is characterized by a focus on problem definition. Although the client might come into the interview with an initial idea of the nature of the problem, he or she might not yet be fully aware of the most appropriate way to define the issue. Working together, the client and counselor generate alternate definitions of the problem and make a mutual decision concerning the one definition that is most suitable to form the basis for further work. Thus, the first stage might involve the exploration of a number of hypotheses. The key decision of Stage I occurs when a commitment is made to one problem definition. The client is then ready to move on to Stage II, the work phase.

The focus of Stage II is on an in-depth examination of the issue, with alternate solutions now being generated and examined. The form that this work takes depends on the theoretical framework from which the counselor operates. One counselor might focus on measurable behaviors, another on cognitions, and still another on affect and self-concept. The model provides room for differing approaches, but the completion of the work phase should lead to the development of a plan for improved coping.

Stage III involves a decision to take action. This stage is concerned with "1. generating further alternative solutions for a client's issue; 2. examining the array of potential solutions and reflecting on the advantages and disadvantages of those solutions; and 3. deciding on which solutions are most appropriate and testing the solutions in the home environment" (Ivey, 1980, p. 36). Like Egan, Ivey stresses the importance of maintaining the counseling relationship during the period in which the client tries out new behaviors or transfers his or her new learning to "real-life" settings. Once this testing has been completed, the client can either terminate the counseling process or return to Stage I to begin the examination of a new issue. Figure 4.1 shows Stages I and II in detail.

It is clear that at any given point counselor and client may proceed to the next step, terminate, or return to an earlier stage in the process. The underlying motivation for these behaviors can be traced to the problem definition and alternative solutions that have been selected.

Consider, for instance, the case of Jane Jones, which was discussed in Chapter 3. Jane's initial definition of the problem was based on the faulty

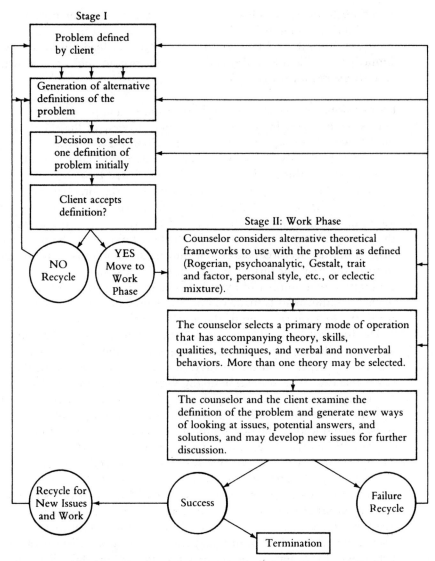

Figure 4.1. *The first two stages of Ivey's decision-making approach.* Note. From *Allen E. Ivey/Lynn Simek-Downing,* Counseling and Psychotherapy: Skills, Theories, and Practice *(p. 34). Copyright © 1980. Reprinted by permission of Prentice-Hall, Inc., Englewood Cliffs, NJ.*

assumption that she was to blame for severe family difficulties and for her subsequent problems at work. In fact, one of the most important aspects of helping this client was accomplished in Stage I, when she learned that her problem could be defined differently. Jane was a victim of her husband's violence; moreover, she was concerned that her children were also beginning to be abused. Her primary problem was redefined in terms of the need to remove herself and her children from a dangerous situation and to build an independent life until her husband was ready to make major changes in his own behavior. With much clearer goals set for herself, Jane was able to find an appropriate place to live, get assistance from a local self-help group, develop new social supports, and begin to use skills that had lain dormant for years.

The proactive counseling approach. The problem-solving approach developed by Lewis and Lewis (1983) pays even more attention to the role of environmental factors both in producing and in resolving problems.

> Most counselors have always assumed that the objects of change should be the attitudes, the feelings, or the behaviors of the counselee. We are becoming more aware every day, however, that the obstacles that keep an individual from meeting his or her goals may be in the environment, rather than in the individual's own behaviors . . . Sometimes individuals have the power to solve their own problems and sometimes they don't (Lewis and Lewis, 1983, p. 98).

The proactive counseling model is based on the idea that the counseling process involves a number of choice points, starting with the basic question of whether the issue or problem can be resolved through change in the individual alone. If it seems likely that change in the individual's behavior or attitudes can resolve the problem, the client and helper can assess alternate methods for encouraging such personal changes. If problem resolution depends on change in the environment, appropriate strategies for confronting others can be devised. Figure 4.2 illustrates this process through the use of a flowchart.

As the chart indicates, the first question asked is, "Is it possible for the issue or problem to be resolved through change in the individual?" If the answer to that question is even a tentative yes, client and counselor try to determine whether interaction between them alone can be expected to bring about the needed adjustments in behavior, feelings, or attitudes. Sometimes, it seems apparent that more input or support is needed; then the client is linked with other people or resources. If the problem is resolved, client and helper can terminate the counseling process or deal with another issue. If not, they can reconsider their first question. Is change in the environment really needed after all?

If, at any choice point, it becomes apparent that solution of the problem at hand depends on changing some factor in the environment, the individual and his or her helper try to determine whether an individual, a group, an organization, or a policy should be addressed. Once strategies have been designed and implemented, the next choice point comes with an assessment of whether the problem has, in fact, been resolved.

These choice points were involved implicitly in the counseling processes used with Jon Smith and Jane Jones. Jon Smith was able to determine quite

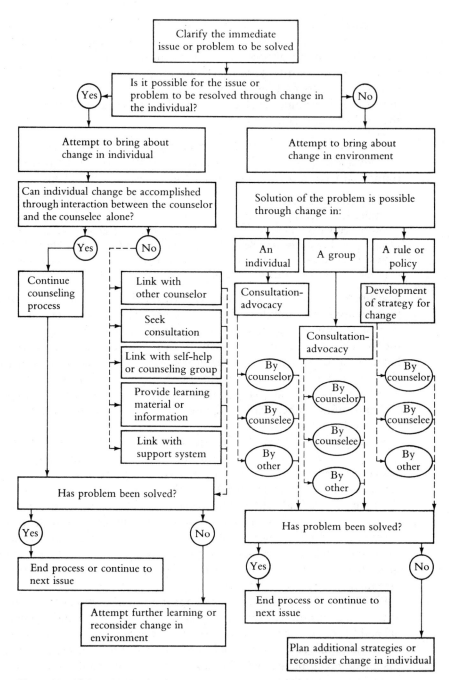

Figure 4.2. *Choice points in the change process.* Note. From Community counseling: A human services approach (2nd ed.) (pp. 99, 100, 102) by J. A. Lewis and M. D. Lewis, New York: Wiley. Copyright 1983 by John Wiley and Sons. Reprinted by permission.

promptly that, although some of his problems could be attributed to organizational factors over which he had no control, the power for resolving the issues lay in his hands. He recognized that he could overcome his difficulties by developing more effective stress-management skills, and there is no doubt that he did improve his life by concentrating on changes in himself. He accomplished these changes by combining counseling with attempts to develop stronger social supports in his work and personal life.

Jane Jones, in contrast, recognized at the first choice point that she could not solve her problems without first making changes in her living environment. Once these changes had been accomplished, she was able to focus her attention on enhancing her own life skills. No amount of stress management training could have prepared her to deal with a situation that was clearly dangerous for her and her children. Once the environmental problems had been addressed, however, she could concentrate on self-management and develop her own resources for growth.

BEHAVIOR CHANGE

Many clients seek assistance from the EAP counselor because they have difficulty making desired behavior changes on their own. Individuals might hope to increase the frequency of desirable behaviors (for example, exercising regularly, speaking up at meetings, studying appropriate professional literature) or decrease the frequency of negative behaviors (for example, smoking, overeating, losing one's temper). In either case, they can make use of learning principles that have long been recognized by behavioral scientists.

Employees can learn the principles of behavorial designing, or "arranging an environment that will produce and maintain specified behaviors in particular situations" (Mahoney and Thoresen, 1974, p. 7), thus enabling themselves to gain control over their lives. The counselor's most useful role is to teach clients the rudiments of behavior change technology and support their efforts at self-management.

> Training in self-management requires strong early support from the helper, with the client gradually relying more and more on his newly developed skills. These include skills in (1) self-monitoring; (2) establishment of specific rules of conduct by contracts with oneself or others; (3) seeking support from the environment for fulfillment; (4) self-evaluation; and (5) generating strong reinforcing consequences for engaging in behaviors which achieve the goals of self-control. The concept of self-control implies that an individual can be taught to rearrange powerful contingencies that influence behavior in such a way that he experiences long-range benefits (Kanfer, 1980, p. 344).

The technology of behavioral management is based on the principles of social learning. People learn to repeat or to avoid repeating particular behaviors because of the consequences the behaviors bring about when they are attempted. If a behavior is reinforced or rewarded, it tends to be duplicated in the future. The response becomes strong and frequent if it is regularly followed by the positive reinforcer. If a behavior is punished or never reinforced at all, it becomes less frequent and may, in time, be extinguished. Sometimes, an individual learns to associate a behavior with a specific stimulus from the environment. This environmental stimulus (the antecedent event) serves as a cue that a given action will be positively reinforced.

Individuals can learn to change their behaviors by purposefully manipulating the cues and reinforcements in their own environments. They can increase the occurrence of positive behaviors by making rewards contingent upon their performance; they can decrease the incidence of negative behaviors by altering environmental cues, removing identified reinforcers, substituting positive behaviors that are incompatible with the undesirable activity, or even using punishment. The effectiveness of this approach depends on the clarity of the client's behavioral goals.

Behavioral goals.   The first step in the process of behavior change is to establish measurable objectives. With the counselor's help, the client translates general goals into specific statements of desired behavior. Behavioral goals differ from the New Year's resolutions with which we are all familiar in several important ways.

1. They identify and describe the behaviors to be performed so that client attainment of the goals can be rewarded.
2. They specify the conditions under which the client will or will not perform the behavior.
3. They indicate the acceptable level of performance, that is, how long, how often, etc., the client is to perform the behavior (Hosford and deVisser, 1974, p. 65).

Clients usually need assistance in translating vague or general goals into measurable terms. "Being more physically fit" becomes "jogging, biking, or swimming for one half-hour four times per week." "Being more assertive at work" becomes "initiating three comments at each staff meeting held this month." If possible, it is best to use positive objectives to form the basis for intervention. Then the client can plan to use some positive reinforcement for successful performance of the behavior at the required rate. If the desired behavior is complex or too difficult to be realistically accomplished at the client's current level of development, subgoals can be identified and used as the basis for behavioral programming. If a client has not exercised in years, he or she might set the objective of walking, rather than jogging, for a half-hour four times per week for two weeks. As this behavior is reinforced, the client might be ready to set a new objective of combined walking and jogging for the second two weeks; jogging for a full half-hour would be a realistic objective for the second month. In this way, the client can gradually shape his or her behavior, coming closer and closer to what might be an ultimate goal of running a marathon. The behavioral plan must begin with a realistic assessment of the individual's current level of performance.

Gathering baseline data.   The behavioral approach requires that individuals obtain base rates for their activities. Clients need to know their current levels of performance before they can begin to work toward their goals. "Gathering baseline data" involves measuring the frequency, quality, or results of the behavior before any intervention takes place. People are often surprised when they obtain concrete evidence about their current behaviors; sometimes their new awareness causes them to become more conservative or more ambitious in setting their objectives. In either case, their objectives are now in line with what they are capable of doing.

Self-observation also helps clients to develop appropriate plans. Observations of the context in which behaviors are performed can give information about the cues that tend to affect actions. Realization that a target behavior is not being performed at all might mean that a client should seek instruction or see someone model the behavior before he or she makes an attempt at self-modification.

Implementing an intervention plan.   Once clients have gathered baseline data and clarified their behavioral objectives, they make plans for intervening to change their own behaviors. Positive reinforcement for successful performance will be part of the plan; clients need to identify what kinds of rewards—tangible or intangible—tend to be reinforcing for them. The individual desiring to speak up at morning staff meetings might reinforce successful performance by treating himself or herself to lunch at a good restaurant after the meeting. The employee trying to engage in a target behavior of reading professional literature might reward himself or herself with an hour of television watching after reading two journal articles. The reinforcement must be contingent upon completion of the performance at the specified rate and must be valued by the individual.

The intervention plan involves a personal contract with the self. The individual schedules specific reinforcements for positive behaviors, gradually increasing the level of performance to be rewarded. If the goal is to decrease a negative behavior, the client attempts to control the environment, eliminating the events and cues that tend to trigger certain activities. An individual trying to maintain sobriety might avoid his or her "drinking buddies" and a dieter would stop keeping high-calorie foods in easily accessible places.

As the plan is implemented, the individual continues to keep careful records, allowing positive changes from the baseline to be readily apparent. At first, the target behavior should be reinforced each time it occurs. Later, intermittent reinforcement—rewarding the behavior only some of the time—should be used. Finally,

> Natural reinforcers eventually replace intervention plans, so that charts and graphs are no longer needed or desirable. The behavioral knowledge involved, however, is now part of the individual's repertoire, giving him or her the more permanent feeling that life is, indeed, controllable (Lewis and Lewis, 1983, p. 32).

Throughout the intervention, the counselor plays an educative and supportive role that Kanfer (1980) suggests can be concentrated in three areas: "(1) . . . helping the individual to establish favorable conditions for carrying out a self-control program and providing initial reinforcement to alter the balance in favor of changing the undesirable behavior (motivation); (2) . . . helping the individual to acquire specific behavior change techniques that ease the process of change (training); and (3) . . . reinforcing the client's efforts and successes in carrying out a self-management program (support and maintenance)" (p. 346).

These kinds of roles are also important as the counselor attempts to intervene with clients in crisis.

CRISIS INTERVENTION

People feel a lack of personal control most intensely when they are in the midst of crisis situations. A crisis is a temporary state during which an individual's usual ways of coping with the world do not seem to be working. When they are in crisis, people tend to feel anxious and upset, not just because of the particular event that precipitated the crisis but because of their apparent helplessness in dealing with it. In fact, no particular event can be identified as always being crisis-provoking. People can find their coping mechanisms suddenly ineffective because of very abrupt life changes or ongoing stressors, purely personal issues, or recognizably difficult situations.

The fact that an individual is going through a crisis does not mean that he or she is suffering from mental illness. A crisis can erupt any time a person is faced with a problem that calls on resources or problem-solving abilities that have not been needed before. Some situations, such as the death of a loved one, divorce, illness, job loss, retirement, or other life changes, are known to place people at risk. Often, however, others perceive an individual's crisis as being unprovoked. The key, as Okun (1982, p. 211) points out, is "people's emotional reactions to a situation, not the situation itself."

By definition, a crisis is temporary. It can be a positive, growth-inducing experience if the individual uses it as an opportunity to learn new, more effective problem-solving skills. It can have negative impact if the situation is not faced and mastered. Because a crisis can be a turning point in an individual's life, timely help is crucial.

In employee assistance settings, counselors are often faced with the need to provide temporary help for normal individuals in crisis. Often, these individuals have already tried without success to use their usual kinds of coping mechanisms. When customary problem-solving techniques have failed, they might have tried a variety of methods to deal with their mounting anxiety. When their lives seem "out of control," they may seek assistance or be referred by others who see that they are troubled.

When the counselor intervenes, his or her goal is to provide temporary intervention, enabling the client to return to effective, independent functioning as soon as possible. Crisis intervention includes the following major components:[2]

1. The focus of crisis intervention is on specific and time-limited treatment goals. Attention is directed toward reduction of tension and adaptive problem solving. The time limits can enhance and maintain client motivation to achieve the specified goals.
2. Crisis intervention involves clarification and accurate assessment of the source of stress and the meaning of the stress to the helpee, and it entails active, directive cognitive restructuring.
3. Crisis intervention helps clients develop adaptive problem solving mechanisms so that they can return to the level at which they were functioning before the crisis.
4. Crisis intervention is reality oriented, clarifying cognitive perceptions, confronting denial and distortions, providing emotional support rather than false reassurance.
5. Whenever possible, crisis intervention uses existing helpee relationship networks to provide support and help determine and implement effective coping strategies.
6. Crisis intervention may serve as a prelude for further treatment (Okun, 1982, p. 216).

Crisis intervention is thus very practical in its application. The helper concentrates on the current situation, encouraging the individual to identify the salient points of the problem as it is being experienced. Because the individual might have difficulty focusing on the problem and identifying alternatives, the counselor uses a relatively directive approach to help the client return to clearer thinking. Emotional support is provided, but client and counselor try to identify more appropriate sources of support in the individual's social network. Throughout the intervention, the counselor models calm and organized problem-solving procedures. A step-by-step process should include the following:

[2]From *Effective helping: Interviewing and counseling techniques* (2nd ed.) by B. F. Okun. Monterey, CA: Brooks/Cole, 1982. Copyright 1982, Wadsworth, Inc. Reprinted by permission.

• *Assess the Nature of the Crisis.*
As step one, the counselor's goal is to learn as much as he or she can about what precipitated the crisis, what coping mechanisms have been attempted, and what patterns the individual usually follows. Of course, the helper must also assess the seriousness of the situation. Is the individual or family in any immediate danger?

• *Help the Client Clarify the Immediate Problem.*
At this point, the individual in crisis might be experiencing difficulty in making a realistic assessment of the major issues. The counselor can help by framing the problem in concrete and realistic terms.

• *Make the Problem Manageable.*
The individual in crisis feels overwhelmed by the demands being faced. He or she can begin to gain control most effectively if the problem is broken down into small, manageable parts. As action is taken to resolve aspects of the problem, the individual can begin to regain a feeling of equilibrium.

• *Identify Additional Sources of Support.*
As the client begins to work on the problems being faced, he or she can identify sources of social support from among family, friends, and associates. In reaching out to others the client gains emotional support and accepts concrete assistance.

• *Identify Personal Strengths.*
The individual might have lost sight of his or her positive attributes. Helping the client to identify resources within himself or herself can enhance the struggle toward self-responsibility.

• *Explore Feelings.*
The client's emotions are deeply engaged in the crisis situation. These feelings can be dealt with most effectively if the individual is helped to identify and express them.

• *Develop a Strategy for Coping with the Situation and Resolving Immediate Problems.*
The counselor works to engage the client in practical problem solving. The strategies employed are similar to those used with clients who are not in a crisis situation. The primary difference is that the client in crisis needs more direction as the stages of exploration, understanding, and action are completed.

• *Plan for the Prevention of Future Crises.*
As the client returns to a more usual level of functioning, he or she can take stock of the situation and identify possible methods for preventing future problems. If new problem-solving skills are accompanied by at-

tempts to maintain personal resources at a higher level, the crisis can prove to be a growth-producing event.

• *Link the Client with Resources for Longer-Term Help.*
When the employee assistance counselor has worked with a client through a crisis, he or she might find the employee amenable to longer-term treatment. Sometimes an individual who could have benefited from more help in the past is ready to accept therapy after experiencing a crisis.

The Chinese characters that represent the word "crisis" mean both danger and opportunity. Crisis is a *danger* because it threatens to overwhelm the individual or his family, and it may result in suicide or a psychotic break. It is also an *opportunity* because during times of crisis individuals are more receptive to therapeutic influence. Prompt and skillful intervention may not only prevent the development of a serious long-term disability but may also allow new coping patterns to emerge that can help the individual function at a higher level of equilibrium than before the crisis (Aguilera and Messick, 1981, p. 1).

The employee assistance counselor who is alert to the presence of a crisis can help to prevent chronic aftereffects and thus safeguard the mental health of an employee and his or her family.

An example of an employee coping with a crisis situation is provided by the case of Harvey Holmes, a factory foreman. Harvey was a valued employee at ABC Corporation, having been known as a steady, dependable worker for over twenty years. He was also noted for the stability of his family life; after their three children had grown up and begun lives of their own, he and his wife looked forward to quiet years together. Without warning, however, his wife suffered a stroke and died.

Harvey's life changed completely when he lost his wife. In the past, he had drunk only at social events and on holidays. Now, he started drinking daily after work. He began to be absent from work, especially on Mondays, developed high blood pressure, and avoided the friends who tried to help him. The plant manager understood the stress of Harvey's situation, but he began to get impatient as the weeks of adjustment stretched into months.

Harvey's referral to the EAP counselor gave him a chance to talk about his grief for the first time. He had tried to cover up his sense of loss, but he needed to talk about it before he could move on with his life.

Client and counselor also worked together to develop a plan of action for regaining his health. Harvey was told to call the counselor if he ever felt lonely and upset. He was able to do this, and this behavior helped him to avoid drinking. He also began to walk in the evenings after the workday was over, and by the time he had worked his way up to three miles a day, his blood pressure had returned to normal. Gradually he began to see women on a social basis, and the counselor encouraged him to return to socializing with his old friends. His work life also regained stability.

Harvey's situation was one in which a particularly stressful event had triggered health problems, including alcohol abuse, that he had controlled in normal times. He had to address his physical vulnerabilities directly, while at the same time learning to develop new social supports to take the place of the one he had lost. By exploring his feelings, clarifying his goals, and attacking the situation piece by piece, Harvey grew to the point where he was even stronger than he had been before the crisis. He now has a degree of self-awareness and physical health that can help him cope with other crisis-provoking situations, such as retirement, that can be expected to arise in the future.

FAMILY COUNSELING

Employees' performances are affected as much by their families' well-being as by their individual concerns. Employee assistance services are usually open to the immediate families of organization members as well as to the workers themselves. Often a concern expressed either by an employee or by a family member is so intricately enmeshed with family relationships that counseling oriented toward the whole family unit is the only appropriate step.

A major function of family counseling is to help members recognize how their feelings and behaviors influence and are influenced by the rest of their family. Although the family may initially consider one member the cause of all the problems, this "identified patient's" behaviors can soon be seen as effects, rather than causes, of troubled relationships.

All family therapists recognize the importance of shifting the focus from the identified patient to the family relationships that create and maintain pathological behavior. The therapist must move the family members from an individualistic and singular-cause way of thinking to thinking about how relationships, not specific behaviors or feelings or thoughts, create problems (Alexander and Parson, 1982, pp. 47–48).

Bringing these relationships to light is the goal of the earliest phases of the family counseling process. In fact, Alexander and Parson suggest that the aim of the first two sessions should be to have each family member leave with the following thoughts and feelings.[3]

1. The therapist "sided" with me as much as with the others.
2. The therapist helped me see how my behavior relates to everyone else's behavior.
3. The therapist made it clear that I am not to blame. Even though I contributed to the problem, I am as much a victim as is everyone else.

[3] From *Functional family therapy* by J. Alexander and B. V. Parson, Monterey, CA: Brooks/Cole, 1982. Copyright 1982, Wadsworth, Inc. Reprinted by permission.

4. The therapist helped me see how everyone else is also a victim and a participant. I now see the rest of my family in a different light.
5. The therapist helped me see that our problem isn't what I thought it was. Whereas I used to think our problem resulted from different needs, goals, and the like, I now see that our problem resulted because we didn't know how to resolve our differences.
6. I feel that if we continue with the program I will be safer, happier, and better able to get what I want (1982, p. 49).

If the counselor is able to establish rapport with family members, he or she can use questions, tentative interpretations, and comments to model an exploratory approach to problem solving that can be learned by clients. As Kramer (1980) points out, "I want the family to begin looking at itself in the same way I do: wondering about the connections between things, speculating as to cause-and-effect relationships, noticing time coincidences in the family system, and looking at themselves with objectivity and compassion" (p. 177).

This diagnostic process points the way toward more active interventions. Sometimes, a family seems to be dysfunctional; nothing short of a major reorganization would enable the system to resolve problems or deal with stress. In such a case, the employee assistance counselor will probably make a referral for family therapy in a more specialized setting. Often, however, family members are ready to learn and change once they have recognized that they make up a functioning system. The EAP counselor can help such a family develop skills and make necessary adaptations.

Coping with change. Many families come to the attention of an EAP counselor because of their difficulties in dealing with changes brought about by new developments in the family's life cycle. According to David (1980), healthy family functioning means that a family unit is able to cope effectively with "cultural-environmental, psychosocial, and socio-economic stresses throughout the diverse phases of the family life cycle" (p. 338). A family, like an individual, is often subjected to crises in living. Such crises may relate to expected transitions, such as the birth of the first child or the departure of the youngest, or to uncontrollable hazards, such as economic changes or sudden illness. Apparently, "stress and health hazards are likely to increase when environmental changes occur at critical developmental periods, such as adolescence, first pregnancy, menopause, and retirement" (David, 1980, p. 339).

Families who are going through transitions that place them at risk of developing problems can be helped to withstand stress through counseling that strengthens their own relationships. Short-term counseling for a family at risk shares some of the characteristics of crisis intervention for individuals: a focus on immediate issues, an emphasis on problem solving, and a strengthening of existing support networks. The counselor's role involves encouraging the family's efforts to act as social supports for one another and actively teaching new problem-solving skills that can be used by children as well as adults in the family unit. In the EAP context, a counselor might consider developing multiple family groups for people expecting to cope with commonly faced pressures, thus preventing many chronic family problems.

Communication skills.   Most families can function more effectively if they have the opportunity to learn better communication patterns. In counseling based on communication theory, "family members learn to get in touch with their feelings, listen to one another, ask for clarification if they do not understand, provide feedback to one another regarding their reactions to what is taking place, and negotiate differences that may arise" (Goldenberg and Goldenberg, 1981, p. 172). Families can learn to live with differing values and goals if all members can clearly express their needs and desires and listen to similar expressions by others. The pioneering work of Virginia Satir has led family counselors in the direction of teaching families to change by opening up their communication processes.

> If parents are poor models of clear and unambiguous communication, Satir believes the therapist must show them how to change, how to get in touch with their own feelings, how to listen to others, how to ask for clarification if they do not understand another person's message, and so on. Through her gentle, matter-of-fact questioning, Satir may help some families for the first time to listen to their children's statements and opinions, and for the children to understand their parents' views and behavior. The process of feedback in an open system flows in both directions. Congruent ways of communicating, expressing genuine feelings to each other, replace . . . blamer/placater/super-reasonable/irrelevant combinations of family communications styles . . . The ultimate result is more functional family behavior (Goldenberg and Goldenberg, 1980, p. 174).

The employee assistance counselor can use family counseling sessions as a setting for modeling and teaching effective communication skills. Some teaching takes place when the counselor points out problem communication patterns as they occur during family interactions. Often, however, exercises in skill building can be purposefully carried out, with the counselor asking family members to attempt and practice such skills as sending clear verbal and nonverbal messages, using active listening techniques, giving concrete feedback, and making assertive statements. Family members can practice congruent communication and negotiation of differences under the counselor's supervision and then be given "homework assignments" to continue skill-building efforts between sessions.

Behavior change.   The time at home between sessions can be used to work on meeting objectives for behavior change. Especially for families with children, the counselor can be most helpful by teaching family members the basic principles of social learning. The family can use counseling sessions to reach agreement on behavioral objectives designed to help both individuals and the family unit as a whole to work more competently. They can then use reinforcement principles to shape appropriate behavior in the home setting.

Ultimately, a behavioral approach to family counseling focuses attention on the family as a "system of interlocking, reciprocal behaviors" (Liberman, 1981, p. 152).

> Changing the contingencies by which the patient gets acknowledgment and concern from other members of his family is the basic principle of learning that underlies the potency of family or couple therapy. Social reinforcement is made contingent on desired, adaptive behavior instead of maladaptive and symptomatic behavior. It is the task of the therapist in collaboration with the family or couple to (1) specify the maladaptive behavior, (2) choose reasonable goals which are alternative, adaptive behaviors, (3) direct and guide the family to change the contingencies of their social reinforcement patterns from maladaptive to adaptive target behaviors (Liberman, 1981, pp. 153–154).

In many families, simply becoming acquainted with learning principles makes parents aware that they have been working against their own goals by paying close attention to negative actions and failing to reward approximations of desirable behaviors. Such families can make good use of tools like contingency contracts: agreements to recognize defined behaviors with reinforcements such as privileges or concrete rewards. If families can devise objectives that allow all family members to achieve gains, they can use "technical aids" (Alexander and Parson, 1982) like contingency contracting, charts, graphs, and time-out and infraction systems as temporary expediences while they learn more potent interaction skills.

THE EAP CONTEXT

The fact that counseling takes place in the context of an employee assistance program affects the nature of the process. First, effective EAP programming depends on the ability of the practitioner to provide time-limited, goal-oriented services. Second, the organizational setting makes recognition of environmental factors an important component of helping.

A counselor in an EAP setting does not have the luxury of following circuitous routes toward vague, general goals.

> A time-limited course of treatment increases the chances of success, while open-ended, long-term therapies usually drag on until the patient realizes that his treatment could go on forever, and drops out. We have found that to the extent that a patient can come up with or agree with a concrete goal (no matter how big and monolithic his problem may seem to him), he is also likely to agree to a time limit (Watzlawick, Weakland, and Fisch, 1974, p. 113).

Clear, limited goals and efficient use of time go hand in hand. Whether counselors find themselves working with problem solving, behavior change, crisis management, or family systems interventions, they need to be working toward specific objectives, both because the EAP model eschews long-term therapy and because corporate cultures insist on clear, measurable benefits of organizational activities. All of the approaches discussed in this chapter share a common emphasis on working toward concrete goals.

The approaches discussed here also share a recognition that each individual client is affected by his or her social environment. Historically, helping professionals have had difficulty recognizing the contextual nature of human development.

> The perspective was myopic, concentrating on intrapsychic functioning to the exclusion of environmental influences. In turn, applications focused on individual self-discovery and insight when, for many, this process failed to alleviate the presenting condition. What seemed called for, therefore, was both a broadening of perspective and a wider array of intervention techniques (Aubrey and Lewis, 1983, p. 2).

The EAP setting is a natural one for broadening the perspective of counselors. Because worksite-based practitioners are familiar with their organizations as social systems, they can take into account both the negative and positive influences of the work environment. They see each client in an organizational context and therefore have valuable awareness of environmental factors.

SUMMARY

In the context of employee assistance programs, counselors provide short-term counseling to help individuals move toward self-management. Most EAP counselors find that they are often called upon to give immediate assistance to (1) people needing help in managing specific problem situations; (2) people hoping to build specific, positive behaviors; (3) people dealing with temporary crises; and (4) people working on relationships within their families.

Problem-solving approaches are used to help clients deal with immediate issues and, concurrently, to teach useful skills in problem management. Among the strategies used by counselors are Egan's three-stage method, Ivey's decision-making model, and a proactive approach that weighs individual and environmental factors.

Counselors also use short-term interventions to bring long-lasting changes by teaching clients the principles of behavior change technology. Many employees seek assistance in developing and maintaining desirable behaviors that can enhance their health or their job effectiveness. Such clients can learn to set behavioral objectives, gather data concerning target behaviors, and implement intervention plans. These skills can help them to maintain more potent control over their lives and to increase their behavioral repertoires.

Employees who are experiencing crises need more active support from their counselors. During a temporary state in which an individual's usual coping mechanisms are not working, the client might require a great deal of direction. A crisis may serve as an opportunity for growth or as a dangerous situation leading to chronic mental health problems. The counselor can enhance the positive aspects of a crisis and limit the risks by providing temporary support and leading the client through a set of carefully organized problem-solving procedures.

Finally, the employee assistance counselor can expect to be confronted by many problems related to family systems. The focus of family counseling is placed on helping family members to recognize the degree to which they influence one another. If clients can learn to view problems in terms of troubled relationships, rather than individual causes, they can be helped to cope with change, learn communication skills, and build desired behaviors.

Whether counselors are working with problem-solving, behavior change, crisis, or family situations, they attempt to provide time-limited, goal-oriented services that take into account the environmental factors affecting each employee.

REFERENCES

Aguilera, D. C., and Messick, J. M. (1981). *Crisis intervention: Theory and methodology*. St. Louis: C. V. Mosby.

Alexander, J., and Parson, B. V. (1982). *Functional family therapy*. Monterey, CA: Brooks/Cole.

Aubrey, R. F., and Lewis, J. A. (1983). Social issues and the counseling profession in the 1980s and 1990s. *Counseling and Human Development, 15*(10), 1–16.

David, H. P. (1980). Healthy family coping: Transnational perspectives. In L. A. Bond and J. C. Rosen (Eds.), *Competence and coping during adulthood* (pp. 332–365). Hanover, NH: University Press of New England.

Egan, G. (1982). *The skilled helper* (2nd ed.). Monterey, CA: Brooks/Cole.

Goldenberg, I., and Goldenberg, H. (1980). *Family therapy: An overview*. Monterey, CA: Brooks/Cole.

Goldenberg, I., and Goldenberg, H. (1981). Family systems and the school counselor. *The School Counselor, 28*, 165–177.

Hosford, R. E., and deVisser, L. A. J. M. (1974). *Behavioral approaches to counseling: An introduction*. Falls Church, VA: American Personnel and Guidance Association.

Ivey, A. E./Simek-Downing, L. (1980). *Counseling and psychotherapy: Skills, theories, and practice.* Englewood Cliffs, NJ: Prentice-Hall.

Kanfer, F. H. (1980). Self-management methods. In F. H. Kanfer and A. P. Goldstein (Eds.), *Helping people change* (pp. 334–389). New York: Pergamon Press.

Kramer, C. H. (1980). *Becoming a family therapist: Developing an integrated approach to working with families.* New York: Human Sciences Press.

Lewis, J. A., and Lewis, M. D. (1983). *Community counseling: A human services approach* (2nd ed.). New York: Wiley.

Liberman, R. Behavioral approaches to family and couple therapy. In G. D. Erickson and T. P. Hogan (Eds.), *Family therapy: An introduction to theory and technique* (2nd ed., pp. 152–164). Monterey, CA: Brooks/Cole.

Mahoney, M. J., and Thoresen, C. E. (1974). *Self-control: Power to the person.* Monterey, CA: Brooks/Cole.

Okun, B. F. (1982). *Effective helping: Interviewing and counseling techniques* (2nd ed.). Monterey, CA: Brooks/Cole.

Watzlawick, P., Weakland, J. H., and Fisch, R. (1974). *Change: Principles of problem formation and problem resolution.* New York: Norton.

Chapter Five

SUPERVISORY TRAINING

One of the most compelling arguments in favor of employee assistance programs is that they lead to the early identification and resolution of a variety of physical and mental health problems. As Foote and Erfurt (1980) point out, any consideration of community mental health delivery systems should take into account the promise and potential of industrial programming. "Industry has a captive population that includes a majority of adults for about half of their waking hours. There is no more effective way to reach these people than at the work site" (p. 152).

The effectiveness of an EAP depends on its success in reaching members of the organization and providing help for those who need it. In a perfect system, all employees needing help would refer themselves long before their problems began to affect the quality of their work. In fact, however, "no matter how excellent a company's health education and prevention program, some employees refuse to recognize the existence of a problem and fail to seek help" (Sonnenstuhl and O'Donnell, 1980, p. 36). Mental health professionals might prefer to wait until individuals feel ready for change before attempting to intervene, but they do not have such a luxury in a business setting *once the problem has spilled over into job performance.* Employers know that they have leverage in encouraging troubled employees to seek help with problems that affect productivity: the threat of job loss if work continues to deteriorate and the promise of job security if performance improves.

> Confrontation with a supervisor at work can provide a chance for the worker to obtain treatment before losing his or her job. The relationship between the employer and employee provides a legitimate reason for confronting and intervention when deteriorating job performance is documented, since the employee is contracted to perform a specific job. If a worker is not performing to capacity, then the employer has a right to take action (Masi, 1979, p. 45).

This concept of the employer's role and responsibility is operationalized through the process of supervisory referral.

The Supervisory Referral

In most companies with EAPs people who have supervisory responsibilities act as "case finders," recognizing performance-related problems and, when appropriate, offering the option of referral for personal assistance. In implementing the employee assistance policy and procedures, the supervisor has four functions: "to observe, to document, to confront, and to refer" (Royce, 1981, p. 204).

Steps in the Referral Process

Each organization's EAP policy emphasizes the need for supervisors to base referrals on job performance and to avoid attempts at diagnosing personal problems. Thus, the first step in the referral process must involve careful documentation of deficiencies in job performance. If this analysis shows that the problem can be attributed to an employee's lack of skill or to some negative aspect of the work environment, the supervisor can take appropriate action to correct the difficulty. But some performance-related problems tend to act as signs that an employee might need help. The following kinds of behaviors can be documented in most settings.

- Unusual attendance patterns (either chronic absenteeism or sudden, unexplained absences).
- A pattern of arriving for work late or leaving early.
- A high accident rate.
- Taking more time with tasks that had previously been accomplished quickly.
- Making errors in work that had previously been done properly.
- Showing increased difficulty in handling routine assignments.
- Alternating between good and poor performance levels for no discernible reason.
- Receiving an unusual number of complaints from clients or customers.
- Having an unusual number of arguments with co-workers.
- Failing to meet deadlines or work up to usual standards.

The key to the recognition of problems involves change, with supervisors attempting to identify not incompetent workers but high performers whose work has clearly lessened in quality.

After documenting changes in performance level, the supervisor's next step involves confronting the employee. The employee is warned that if his or her work does not improve, disciplinary procedures will have to be followed in accordance with the organization's policies. At the same time, the supervisor presents the employee with the option of seeking help through the employee assistance program. If the employee chooses to use the EAP service, the contact remains confidential and does not become part of the personnel record. Whether or not the EAP is used, improvement in job performance is still mandated, as is shown in Figure 5.1.

As the flowchart shows, seeking help does not give the employee an excuse to continue performing below par. What it does give the employee is an opportunity to safeguard his or her position, to choose positive action rather than continued difficulty. Of course, the basic assumption underlying this approach is that work improvement *will* occur if the troubled employee obtains help. This certainty on the part of many EAP consultants is based partially on their experiences with alcoholism treatment.

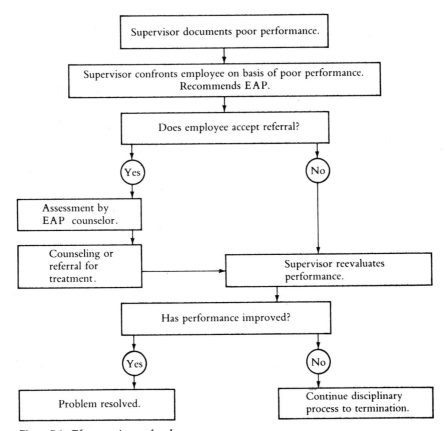

Figure 5.1. The supervisory referral process.

Alcoholism and the Confrontation Process

The confrontation process used by the family and friends of an alcoholic to encourage him or her to seek treatment has much in common with the supervisory ultimatum. Most alcoholism service providers agree that denial plays an important role in the alcoholic's defenses. Often, family members and associates unwittingly encourage this denial by protecting the alcoholic from the negative effects of his or her drinking. Although they wish the drinking would stop, they cover up the problem and allow the problem drinker to avoid the consequences of his or her behavior. Unfortunately, this enables the drinking to continue. "The alcoholic who is sheltered from the reality of his behavior has little reason to stop drinking. He continues to derive satisfaction (no matter how unhealthy) from his drinking and if he does not have to face the consequences, why should he stop?" (Krimmerl, 1975, p. 16).

The most effective intervention in this situation is that which allows a crisis to occur and then offers help when the need for it is recognized.

> The intent of intervention is to (1) intensify the pain of drinking above the pain of not drinking and (2) produce within the alcoholic the awareness that drinking is the source of pain. This means that you stop protecting the alcoholic from the consequences of his own behavior. It means that you begin appropriately confronting him with evidence of his alcohol-related behavior in such a way that he must begin to see the reality of his situation (Miller and Gorski, 1982, pp. 45–46).

If natural consequences do not seem to have the necessary effect on the alcoholic, people who are significant to him or her can force the issue by confronting the person as a group and making it clear that help is needed. Johnson (1973, p. 49) presents several "rules" that can make the confrontation work.

1. Meaningful persons must present the facts or data. . . .
2. The data presented should be specific and descriptive of events which have happened or conditions which exist . . .
3. The tone of the confrontation should not be judgmental. . . .
4. The chief evidence should be tied directly into drinking wherever possible.
5. The evidence of behavior should be presented in some detail . . .
6. The goal of the intervention, through the presentation of this material, is to have him see and accept enough reality so that, however grudgingly, he can accept in turn his need for help.
7. At this point, the available choices acceptable to the interveners may be offered.

Once the alcoholic faces the fact that a problem exists, he or she may be ready to accept a treatment option that is immediately available.

Most alcoholism counselors have seen numerous examples both of families that have continued to enable the alcoholic to drink and of alcoholics

who have been coerced into successful treatment through network confrontation. In recent years, we have become more aware that the enabling
process is just as prevalent in the work setting. Supervisors as well as peers
often allow problem drinking to continue by looking the other way or even
doing extra work to make up for the alcoholic's work deficiencies. They
cover up the problem because they are uncomfortable dealing with it, because they do not understand what is happening, or because they do not
want to cost the individual his or her job.

> Saving a person's job is a noble act. However, when the alcoholic or drug addict
> is hidden, excused, or allowed to continue his or her self-disguised "antics," it
> is not a simple case of whitewashing a friend's mistakes. It is actually allowing
> an illness to gnaw away at the victim's health and happiness . . . The realization
> that detection is the greatest favor a supervisor can offer a subordinate, with the
> understanding that anything short of this is unfair not only to the company but
> to the friend in question, is the foundation of the program (Brisolara, 1979, p.
> 97).

Employee assistance programs have their roots in alcoholism programs.
Most EAP practitioners are well aware that the supervisor who refuses to
cover up problems is, in fact, doing the friend a favor. Because people's
jobs are so important to them, confrontation by a supervisor does start
them toward treatment. Moreover, their prognosis for recovery is better
than that of people who come into treatment through different avenues.

This understanding leads advocates of employee assistance programs to
perceive that one does not necessarily have to choose between loyalty to
the organization and humane treatment of the individual employee. The
network confrontation, which was designed by Johnson as a method of
helping troubled individuals, bears strong similarity to the process used by
supervisors attempting to perform their duties. Each focuses on the description of concrete behaviors, each is designed to help the individual recognize the existence of a problem, and each involves giving the person being
confronted a choice that may not have been present before.

But it is not the EAP specialist who confronts the employee in the work
setting. The burden of making a referral based on job performance falls on
the shoulders of a first-line supervisor, who cannot be expected to succeed
in this effort without special training.

The Union Representative's Role

Special training is also needed for union representatives, who can be expected to play a major role in the referral process. As Royce (1981, p. 204)
notes, "unsatisfactory work performance is the concern of management;
protection of the employee's job and health is the concern of labor." Since
the purpose of an EAP referral is to satisfy both of these concerns simultaneously, an uncommon commitment to cooperation is required.

One important aspect of the union representative's role is to ensure that the employee's rights are protected. A union member should have the right to have his or her steward present during any disciplinary interview. If supervisory confrontations are regularly observed in this manner, the union membership can feel assured that employees are being treated fairly in the referral process, that confrontations are based on objective job performance criteria, and that the voluntary nature of the EAP is being preserved.

Union representatives frequently play an even more active role in the referral process. If management is considering dismissal of an employee, leaders of the appropriate union are normally consulted. Sometimes the result of this consultation is one last chance in the form of an EAP referral. In a recent case, for instance, an employee in an industrial setting continued a pattern of being absent from work on Monday mornings despite repeated warnings and one suspension. Although management felt that they had ample justification for dismissal, the shop steward suggested that a final attempt be made to recommend that the employee seek help. The union representative, direct supervisor, and industrial relations manager jointly confronted the employee, who was convinced to make an appointment with the EAP counselor. All agreed that the employee would be suspended for two weeks and that he would be reinstated at the end of that time if he saw the counselor during the suspension and presented a plan of action upon his return. The employee succeeded in getting his problem under control. Of course, a return to unacceptable levels of absenteeism would still lead to termination, but as long as his job performance remains stable, he retains the job security and seniority he had before his personal problems began. Without labor–management cooperation in support of the EAP concept, his job would not have been saved.

Union representatives can also expect to make some direct referrals without the involvement of the employee's supervisor. Shop stewards are often seen as trusted co-workers who gain the confidence of employees. Sometimes employees share their concerns with union representatives. Often people ask for advice about how to help troubled colleagues and friends. If they know how to use the program effectively, union representatives can be a major source of referrals, frequently encouraging use of the services by employees whose difficulties have not yet manifested themselves in noticeable performance problems.

Because their role is so important to the success of the employee assistance program, union representatives have as much need as supervisors for training in the referral process. In fact, anyone likely to have responsibilities in this area—personnel and other managers, first-line supervisors, union representatives, medical specialists, and others—should attend training workshops whenever a new EAP is launched. Whether these role groups are trained separately or together depends on the needs of the organization and the size of the group to be trained.

PREPARING THE TRAINING WORKSHOP

When the employee assistance program is initiated, the EAP consultant normally leads a workshop designed to train supervisors and key employees in the knowledge and skills they will need to play their parts in the system. Although follow-up training is always available for individuals and groups, the initial training workshop is, for many, their introduction to the EAP concept and its implementation. Their enthusiastic support of the program is crucial to its success, and this training workshop provides the first—and possibly the last—opportunity to get supervisors, managers, and labor involved. If this involvement is to become a reality, the training workshop must be more than just an information-giving session. The leader needs to plan experiences that will encourage active learning and problem solving among participants. A few basic guidelines, based on principles of adult learning, help to point the way.

1. *Design Learning Experiences to Bridge the Gap between Current and Desired Competencies.*
The workshop planner must begin by specifying the behaviors or competencies that participants should be able to demonstrate after training. If the trainer can also assess the participants' current level of performance, he or she can design the experience to help them develop in the right direction without repetition of material with which they are already familiar.

For example, virtually all EAPs require that supervisors demonstrate the ability to confront employees on the basis of impaired job performance. Organizations differ, however, in the amount and nature of the training needed to develop this competency. ABC Company might have a carefully devised performance appraisal system and a clear policy spelling out the steps to be taken in progressive discipline. If these systems have been in place for some time, experienced supervisors might need additional training only to practice their personal confrontation skills and learn about the referral process. In contrast, XYZ Corporation might never have trained supervisors in documenting work-related behaviors. XYZ's supervisors would need more extensive practice in identifying and measuring performance problems. If information about current levels of performance were overlooked, a training design that achieved excellent results in one organization might prove unworkable in another.

2. *Make Sure Participants Can See Benefits for Themselves in the Training Process.*
Adults in the work setting tend to resent having to spend time in meetings or training sessions unless they derive concrete benefits from them, such as the acquisition of new skills and knowledge. EAP training does lead to concrete benefits, since it is meant to help supervisors perform their own jobs more effectively. If supervisors and union representatives can learn to

use the employee assistance program as a backup resource, they can make their own work easier and avoid the buildup of problems.

Although EAP consultants know how beneficial these training sessions are, they should not assume that their usefulness is clear to everyone. Each workshop needs to be designed so that these points are made in introductory activities. The trainer might find it helpful to allow supervisors to identify real problems they have had to face on the job. At least part of the focus of the remaining activities can then be on developing more efficient methods for coping with the real-life situations that have been identified.

3. Provide Opportunities for Immediate Application of New Learning.
Since the focus of training is on the development of practical skills that will be needed in the work setting, participants should have a chance to try out their new learning. If they have been involved only in passive listening, they will not feel ready to implement new concepts when problems arise. A discussion of confrontation methods, for instance, should be followed immediately by a role-playing activity in which supervisors apply the basic concepts to a problem situation. This kind of exercise accomplishes several tasks at once: (a) giving the participant an opportunity to assess his or her skill level, (b) demonstrating the usefulness of the skill for solving real problems, (c) clarifying difficulties in implementation, and (d) enhancing the learning process. Especially when changes in attitudes and skills are needed, the training process should always be based on methods that encourage active, rather than passive, learning.

4. Provide Reinforcement of New Learning.
Reinforcement is part of the learning process, whether the learner is a child or an adult, an employee or a manager. One of the objectives of EAP training is to add to the repertoire of behaviors the supervisor, manager, or union representative can use when faced with problems related to employees. The training session allows supervisors both to attempt previously untried behaviors and to strengthen existing skills in relating to supervisees. Immediate, encouraging feedback for attempts at skill development can provide positive reinforcement in the workshop setting. Continued reinforcement can be expected to occur when the supervisor succeeds in helping troubled employees on the job.

5. Allow for Opportunities to Build on Past Experience.
A group of experienced supervisors and union representatives will have success stories, as well as problems, to share. Like all adult learners, these workshop participants can build on a wealth of life experience, adding new skills to their existing abilities and sharing hard-earned knowledge with others. Some of the required confrontation methods will be new to many, but they will be built on a foundation of existing supervisory skills.

Although the training session should include discussion of problems in the workplace, it can also incorporate comments about positive experiences. Many workshop participants will be able to relate incidents showing that troubled employees can be helped. Workshop attendants may hear statements like "one of my guys got into treatment a year ago and he's been sober and completely on top of things ever since" or "I kept putting off saying anything to one employee about his performance and when I finally gave it to him he straightened himself out and thanked me." Comments like these help to show that the EAP approach can be practical, while providing a way for participants to use one another as resources.

6. Use a Variety of Methods and Activities to Accomplish the Workshop's Goals.

Adults are seldom accustomed to spending long periods of time in passive listening. They expect variety in the trainer's presentation and learn best when several methods are combined. Within the workshop format, the leader can choose from among a number of learning approaches, including short lectures, discussions, simulations, role-plays, skill practices, films, tapes, case conferences, exercises, self-assessment tools, questionnaires, and group problem solving.

But variety is not just an end in itself. The effective trainer uses the methods that best fit his or her training objectives. To build communication skills among participants, the trainer might use demonstrations, experiential exercises, and role-plays. Knowledge about the purpose and functions of employee assistance programs might best be disseminated through lecturettes, question-and-answer sessions, and media. Brainstorming, free discussions, and questionnaires can help in the effort to identify problems in the work setting. In each instance, the type of material to be covered lends itself to particular approaches.

7. Use the Training Session as an Opportunity to Gain Consensus about the Employee Assistance Program.

The training workshop provides the best possible opportunity to ensure that supervisors and union representatives feel a positive sense of involvement with the EAP. Certainly many of them will have been consulted in earlier stages of planning and policy development, but this session should give them another chance to make sure they fully understand the policy and procedures and to give additional suggestions for implementation.

One important training task is to review the company's EAP policy and procedures statements in some detail, allowing time for questions and reactions. Sometimes, the success of a program depends on the degree to which everyone understands the operational details and has his or her expectations met. Supervisors will, at this point, still have questions about the actual day-to-day operation of the program.

- When I want to refer an employee, should I call the EAP office myself or should I let the employee take the initiative?
- If I call to set up the appointment, should I make it during work hours when I know he or she will be available?
- If the employee calls, how will I know whether he or she did make the appointment? Even though the counseling is confidential, how much will I know about whether the employee is following up?
- Will someone get back to me about how someone I've referred is doing?
- Whom should I communicate with—the program director or the counselor?
- If I'm still having problems with an employee after a referral, should I let someone know?
- Should I take it into account if employees are getting counseling and give them more time to improve their performance? I know the disciplinary process supposedly depends just on job performance, but I might be willing to go out on a limb for people who are trying to do something about their problems. Is that okay?
- If I feel uncomfortable about confronting a certain employee, will the EAP consultant help me out?

Many of these questions are likely to be clearly answered in the written statements, but supervisors often need to be certain that they understand more about the details of day-to-day implementation. In addition, supervisors and labor representatives need a chance to give their reactions to operational plans and make suggestions for streamlining procedures. Getting input at this point serves the dual purpose of generating valuable ideas and increasing the participants' sense of inclusion in the employee assistance program.

THE TRAINING WORKSHOP: CONTENT AND PROCESS

Although the particular problems faced by an organization affect the nature of the training process, most EAP workshops deal with the following general content areas: (a) current problems and how they are handled in the organization, (b) methods of identifying and documenting performance problems, (c) approaches to confronting employees with performance problems, and (d) the philosophy and nature of the employee assistance program.

Current Problems

Most trainers find it helpful to deal with current problems and how they are handled at some point early in the supervisory session. Time is allocated for supervisors to discuss performance-related problems they have faced, methods they have used for solving these problems, and—just as important—their feelings about the issues. A carefully designed exercise can show that the organization does face the kinds of issues that are amenable to resolution by an employee assistance program, while helping participants to examine their own attitudes toward employee problems.

One approach that many EAP consultants use is to provide a list of common performance problems and ask supervisors and union representatives to identify the ones they have observed in their own work settings. A possible checklist format is shown in Exhibit 5.1.

EXHIBIT 5.2. *Performance Problem Checklist: Supervisory Responses*

Think about employees you are currently supervising or have recently had to deal with. Examine the list below and place an X next to any problem or characteristic you have noticed in one or more employees.

_____   1. Unusual attendance patterns:

        _____ Chronic absenteeism

        _____ Sudden, unexplained absences

_____   2. Arriving for work late or leaving early.

_____   3. High accident rate.

_____   4. Taking more time with tasks that were previously done quickly.

_____   5. Making errors in work previously done properly.

_____   6. Increased difficulty in handling routine assignments.

_____   7. Alternating between good and poor performance levels.

_____   8. Numerous complaints from clients or customers.

_____   9. Numerous arguments with co-workers, mood swings.

_____   10. Failing to meet deadlines.

_____   11. Failing to work up to usual standards.

_____   12. Other problems. (Write a brief note in the space below.)

■

Obviously, many other problematic behaviors could be listed for the purposes of this exercise. The items used for the checklist shown in Exhibit 5.1 were selected because they represent the kinds of performance problems that seem to lend themselves to EAP interventions. Any supervisor can provide examples of employees who have never developed the skills or motivation to perform effectively, but an employee assistance referral is not appropriate for them. The EAP is designed to safeguard the jobs of competent employees whose work has deteriorated for any one of a variety of personal reasons. Such employees can be recognized because of changes—whether sudden or gradual—from effective to ineffective performance. For this reason, the majority of the items on this checklist mention a disparity between current and customary behaviors and standards.

The checklist can be used as a starting point for a discussion of the kinds of problems faced most frequently in the specific workplace. Supervisors can use this opportunity to share experiences they have had or situations they are currently facing. Many participants will have problems that do not fall under the listed categories, and they should be encouraged to share them. (Of course, participants should be reminded to avoid using the names of employees or information that would identify them to others.)

The general discussion of problem areas can be followed by a consideration of methods used to solve them. Again, a structured exercise can help to focus the participants' thinking. The material shown in Exhibit 5.2 can be used as the next step.

EXHIBIT 5.2. *Performance Problem Checklist: Supervisory Responses*

Go over your performance problem checklist. For each item that you marked "X" and for any problem area that you added, think about how you responded to the problem. Indicate in the left-hand margin what you did about each one by using one of the letters below.

A. I ignored the situation and it got worse.
B. I ignored the situation and it improved.
C. I ignored the situation and there has been no change.
D. I confronted the employee very strongly.
E. I hinted to the employee that something was wrong.
F. I took disciplinary action—suspended or fired the employee.
G. I discussed the problem with my own supervisor.
H. I covered for the employee, making sure the work got done by someone else.
I. I suggested to the employee that he or she get medical attention.
J. I gave the employee an easier job until things got straightened out.

■

Adding supervisory behaviors to the problem checklist helps participants to examine their patterns in responding to troubled employees and to analyze the effectiveness of various approaches. They are likely to find that most of the options they tried either failed to bring about desired changes in performance or caused them to lose the services of a valued employee.

Participants should also be encouraged to talk about their emotional reactions to these issues. Every supervisor and co-worker has felt the anger, frustration, and disappointment of seeing an employee's work continue to deteriorate after he or she has made an apparently sincere promise to change. Too many of these experiences can make a supervisor doubt the efficacy of programs designed to help people with mental or physical health problems. The EAP consultant should allow these doubts to be aired and discuss the difficulties that individuals experience in keeping promises that are unrealistic at best. In fact, this kind of discussion can provide an effective bridge to consideration of the EAP confrontation and referral as an alternative to promises and chronic problems.

Problem Identification and Documentation

The training session makes it clear that the supervisor's responsibility for recognizing and documenting changes in the quality of job performance is at the very core of the employee assistance program. Training supervisors to carry out this vital task requires the use of methods that facilitate the development of both knowledge and skills.

If an organization already has clear disciplinary guidelines and strong performance appraisal mechanisms, the trainer can limit informational aspects to a discussion of ways to integrate the EAP referral into normal processes. In many firms, however, supervisors feel unprepared to give negative performance reviews (Harrison, 1982). They need to be informed about the content and methods of identifying and documenting problems related to employee productivity.

The systematic nature of these tasks should be stressed. Supervisors are on shaky legal ground when they identify troubled employees through their own observations and then begin documenting behavioral deficiencies. If for no other reason than that potential arbitration will lead to questions about the consistency of disciplinary procedures, supervisors should learn to base negative feedback on uniformly applied appraisal methods. This does not mean that the same standards can be applied to all jobs; it does mean that appropriate criteria for performance should be identified for each job classification and then applied evenhandedly. Absenteeism may not be considered an important indicator of performance for certain job classifications, but if it is ever considered a problem behavior, the supervisor needs to keep careful attendance records for every employee under his or her supervision.

Supervisors need to recognize that this attention to performance management is important as a general attitude that can affect daily relationships with employees. Karrass and Glasser (1980), in their discussion of "reality performance management," list the following eight steps to better employee behavior and performance (p. 3):

1. Establishing and keeping a good relationship with each subordinate.
2. Using the ongoing relationship to get the employee to lay on the table what he or she is or isn't doing right.
3. Asking the employee to evaluate his or her behavior in terms of its effect on the job to be done and on fellow workers.
4. Negotiating with the employee to develop a realistic, workable plan to handle the situation in a better way.
5. Getting the employee to agree to follow the plan and providing an equal commitment to help if your help is needed.
6. Asking for and accepting no excuses for why a job cannot be done better.
7. Criticizing in a constructive, not punitive, fashion.
8. Not giving up easily.

Such ongoing attention to the supervisory relationship can prevent many performance-related problems from getting out of hand.

> If you want someone to hammer fifteen nails by 2:00 p.m., don't hope for the best. The effective manager checks the second, the seventh, and the tenth nail at specific times of the day to assure that the fifteenth nail will be driven by 2:00 p.m. The inefficient manager discovers at 2:00 p.m. that the employee didn't even have a hammer (Karrass and Glasser, 1980, p. 68).

Individual supervisors need organizational support in their endeavors. The EAP training session can play a part in the development of an organizational commitment to systematic performance appraisal. A variety of mechanisms can be used to rate employee performance, including traditional rating scales, rankings, and performance tests. More sophisticated mechanisms include critical incident techniques, which use supervisors' logs of important incidents that demonstrate employees' strengths or weaknesses, and behaviorally anchored rating scales, which base performance ratings on measurable behaviors seen to relate to job effectiveness.

If consistent attention is paid to performance levels, a supervisor can easily identify and document problematic behaviors. The employee assistance program referral tends to emphasize *changes* in performance, which can be documented only if comparable rating procedures are used over a reasonably long time span. It may be difficult to confront an employee for making "too many" errors but easier to suggest that a problem exists when it can be shown that an employee has made three times as many errors as he or she made on a comparable job one year ago.

Supervisors who accept the basic concepts of behavioral assessment can develop their skills most easily through practice in the group environment.

Workshop participants can generate cases from their own experience and help one another in their attempts to describe problems in terms of measurable behaviors. This material can provide a bridge to discussion of a closely related topic: the actual confrontation session.

The Confrontation Session

Even supervisors who are aware of employees' performance levels may feel uncomfortable about handling an actual interview.

> The negative performance review . . . is considered one of the least pleasant aspects of a supervisor's job. As such, it tends to be one that is avoided as much as possible . . . Thus, supervisors often put off criticizing subordinates about inferior performance for as long as possible (Alpander, 1980, pp. 216–217).

Unfortunately, problems that are overlooked often become aggravated over time. Situations that could have been resolved through mild confrontations require more severe measures after performance has been allowed to deteriorate without intervention; in short, simple problems become major issues.

Most supervisors are aware that they should deal with problem situations directly, clearly, and promptly. The trainer does not need to spend a great deal of seminar time emphasizing this idea. What supervisors need now are behavioral guidelines and immediate practice in implementing them.

Guidelines.   Supervisors feel more confident about trying out their interview skills if they, themselves, have behavioral guidelines to direct them. The following general principles seem to be adaptable to a variety of supervisory interviews, whether or not an EAP referral is involved.

1. *Specify the Problematic Behaviors in Question.*
At this point in their training, supervisors know that they should come in to the interview with well-prepared documentation concerning the employee's performance. The supervisor should keep the focus of the session on the behaviors in question and avoid letting the discussion drift to other topics. As Royce (1981, p. 204) points out, the ability to present the documented behavior precisely keeps the confrontation from developing into a "fiasco of assertions and denials."

2. *Keep the Focus on Actions Rather than Characteristics.*
The employee should not be treated as an adversary or made to feel that the session is an attack on him or her. One way to do this is to keep the attention on behaviors rather than on the employee's general characteristics. For example, it is appropriate to say, "You left the files unlocked when you went out for lunch and this compromises our confidential records," but inappropriate to say, "You have shown yourself to be an irresponsible person where confidentiality is concerned." The former statement gives the

employee an opportunity to learn what improvements are needed, while the latter simply raises defenses.

The supervisor should also avoid making assumptions about the employee's motivations. "You left the office early on the last two Friday afternoons" is more likely to be effective than "You don't seem to care whether the office is covered or not." Again, one approach gives the employee a direction for improvement while the other simply offers judgments that may not be supported by the facts.

3. *Specify Acceptable Levels of Performance.*

Just as supervisors should specify problems in behavioral terms, they should also be clear about their expectations. The interview can clear up any possible misunderstandings when the supervisor makes statements like, "I see you as being the person who is totally responsible for covering the office in the afternoons, so if you need to leave for any reason—even to go to the bank to deposit the day's receipts—make sure someone else is left in charge." This will leave no doubt in the employee's mind about how many times he or she can leave the office empty on Fridays without feeling the repercussions.

4. *Use a Problem-Solving Approach.*

Alpander (1980) and Maier (1976) differentiate among three approaches to the appraisal session: (a) "Tell and Sell," in which the supervisor persuades the supervisee to improve; (b) "Tell and Listen," which consists of telling the employee the problem and then judging the adequacy of his or her explanation; and (c) "Problem Solving," which emphasizes working out ways to deal with the issues that have been raised. Alpander's point is that positive evaluations always center on problem solving and that this approach is even more important for critical evaluation interviews.

Once the issues have been clarified, the supervisor can focus on the options available to resolve the problem. The employee assistance program may be one option. The employee may be able to suggest others. The choice of which method to use may be optional, but the required change in performance level is not. If the supervisor states that disciplinary measures might be taken, he or she must make clear that discipline will be based on job performance and not on the actions taken toward improvement.

5. *End the Session with a Concrete Plan.*

The employee should be asked to specify exactly what actions he or she plans to take, and according to what time frame, to resolve the problems that have been identified. The supervisor should reiterate his or her plans for action. If a follow-up time is specified, the subsequent appointment can be used both as a deadline for improvement and as an opportunity to acknowledge positive changes in performance.

Practice.   With the above guidelines clearly in mind, workshop participants can try out their skills by role-playing supervisory interviews. The trainer might want to begin by demonstrating a brief interview that can be used as a model. Each supervisor should also have the chance to role-play a session and receive feedback on his or her effort. One way to do this is to divide participants into groups of three, with each member of the trio taking a turn as supervisor, employee, and observer. Participants can choose problems from among issues raised in earlier discussions or, if they prefer, deal with hypothetical cases devised by the trainer. If hypothetical cases are used, they should relate as closely as possible to the needs of the specific work setting and employee group.

Once participants have had an opportunity to try out their skills, the consultant should bring the group back together to discuss their reactions to the exercise. Although some participants might mention problem areas, most will report that their interviews seemed to be on the right track. With this experience behind them, supervisors can be expected to feel more secure when they need to confront members of their own work teams. Follow-up training sessions at later times can be used to deal with unexpected problems and to encourage further use of the EAP referral.

The EAP Concept

Supervisors and union representatives have specific roles to carry out, but they also need to be aware of the total EAP concept. The consultant should spend whatever time is needed to review the organization's employee assistance policy and procedures so that everyone understands how the program is expected to work.

Workshop participants should also learn more about the company's reasons for initiating the EAP. Both supervisors and union representatives find it helpful to obtain general information, not just about their own firm, but about problems faced by organizations throughout the nation. If supervisors know that 10% of any work force can be expected to exhibit physical and mental health problems that interfere with performance, they will understand how important an EAP can be to an organization's efficiency. If they comprehend something of the ways in which personal problems affect job performance, they can increase their insight into the behaviors of all of their supervisees.

Supervisors and union representatives need to be "sold" on the employee assistance concept. Although much of the selling needs to be done by top management and by the employee assistance program consultant, additional aids are available in the form of a vast supply of films and video tapes. Many of the following resources have been designed to explain EAPs and similar concepts or to show supervisory referrals in action.

"Alcoholism: The Bottom Line"
This 29-minute presentation is available in color film or video tape. Lorne Greene narrates the experiences of supervisors dealing with four alcoholics. Both ineffective and effective methods of confronting the problem are demonstrated. (Motivational Media; 6855 Santa Monica Blvd., Dept. E; Los Angeles, CA 90035)

"The Dryden File"
This 28-minute film depicts a white-collar worker—probably himself a manager—whose job performance has deteriorated. Both correct and incorrect methods of dealing with an employee are shown. (Richard S. Milbauer Productions; 21 West 46th Street; New York, NY 10036)

"EAP: A Way to Increased Productivity"
This two-part video tape (45 minutes in length) was designed to be used in supervisory training sessions. The first part covers the fundamentals of EAP and provides intervention guidelines. The second section, which deals with intervention techniques, describes signs of decreased job performance. (Advanced Management Technology; 745 Distel Drive, #10A; Los Altos, CA 94022)

"Intervention and Recovery"
This film deals with the intervention process and is appropriate for family members as well as supervisors. Several approaches to intervention are described. (FMS Productions, Inc.; 1777 North Vine Street, Suite 501; Los Angeles, CA 90028)

"Pandora's Bottle: The Drinking Woman"
Mariette Hartley narrates this 40-minute film about women and alcoholism. Attention is paid to the female alcoholic's support systems, including the ones in the work setting. (Motivational Media; 6855 Santa Monica Blvd., Dept. E; Los Angeles, CA 90035)

"To Meet a Need"
This short film provides an overview of the nature of employee assistance programs and the costs of alcohol-related problems among employees. (Richard S. Milbauer Productions; 21 West 46th Street; New York, NY 10036)

"The Troubled Employee"
This 25-minute presentation, which is available in video cassette or film versions, is designed for supervisory training. As a training film, it provides a five-step formula for correcting problem situations as well as "dos" and "don'ts" for dealing with the troubled worker. (Dartnell; 4660 Ravenswood Avenue; Chicago, IL 60640)

"We Can Help"

This 15½-minute film is oriented toward the white-collar, management, and professional employee. It shows supervisor John Baines as he observes, documents, confronts, and refers two supervisees. (Gary Whiteaker Company, Inc.; 9425 West Main Street, Dept. E; Belleville, IL 62223)

"Women in the Workplace"

In this 20-minute film, Carole Keller discusses the role of the employee assistance program in dealing with troubled women employees. Twelve trouble signs are listed and described. (Gary Whiteaker Company, Inc.; 9425 West Main Street, Dept. E; Belleville, IL 62223)

"Gordon"

This film focuses specifically on employee assistance programming in educational settings. It is available with optional endings: in ending one, Gordon, a teacher, refers himself to the employee assistance counselor; in ending two, he is confronted and referred by a supervisor. (Motivision, Ltd.; 2 Beechwood Road; Hartsdale, NY 10530)

Many of the resources listed above are available in either 16 mm films or videotape cassettes, and most can be either rented or purchased. In the context of an experiential training workshop, these visual aids support the consultant's presentation and show examples with which any supervisor can identify. They can help the trainer meet the training session's ultimate goal: to promote effective use of the employee assistance program by supervisors, union representatives, and other key members of the organization.

SUMMARY

The work setting provides an excellent avenue for reaching individuals with physical or mental health problems. Although self-referrals should be encouraged, some individuals do not seek assistance until their job performance has been affected. In such situations, an employer may intervene, encouraging the employee to obtain assistance in the hope that his or her productivity will be improved.

The supervisory referral process is based on documented work deficiencies, with the supervisor confronting an employee only after he or she has documented such problematic behaviors as absenteeism, high accident rates, or changes in levels of performance. When the supervisor confronts the employee, he or she provides the option of the employee assistance program as a way to interrupt the downward cycle. Even if the employee accepts the suggestion and seeks help from the employee assistance counselor, he or she remains accountable for making specified improvements in work-related behaviors.

The basic assumption underlying this approach is that job performance will improve after help has been obtained. EAP consultants often base this belief on their experiences in dealing with alcohol-related problems. Many alcoholics have been helped because their families and friends stopped shielding them from the effects of their drinking and intervened in the context of crises. An intervention in the work setting can be even more powerful, since the threat of job loss can provide the final impetus to move an individual toward treatment.

If the EAP is to work, both supervisors and union representatives need to be trained in the referral process. The training workshop provides an opportunity both to provide information and to increase the involvement of these key organization members. As in all adult learning situations, the trainer needs to design an experience that seeks to teach specific behaviors that participants see as beneficial to themselves. In the workshop context, learning activities should allow for immediate application of new learning, reinforce skill development, build on life experiences, and encourage positive views of the employee assistance program. The content of the training session should focus on the following topics: (a) current problems and how they are handled in the organization, (b) methods of identifying/documenting performance problems, (c) approaches to confronting employees who are experiencing performance problems, and (d) the philosophy and nature of the employee assistance program. A variety of methods should be used, including discussions, self-assessments, role-plays, skill practices, and use of films and video tapes.

REFERENCES

Alpander, G. G. (1980). Training first-line supervisors to criticize constructively. *Personnel Journal, 59,* 216–221.

Brisolara, A. (1979). *The alcoholic employee.* New York: Human Sciences Press.

Foote, A., and Erfurt, J. C. (1980). Prevention in industrial settings: The employee assistance program. In R. H. Price, R. F. Ketterer, B. C. Bader, and J. Monahan (Eds.), *Prevention in mental health: Research, policy, and practice* (pp. 151–165). Beverly Hills: Sage.

Harrison, E. L. (1982). Training supervisors to discipline effectively. *Training and Development Journal, 36*(11), 111–113.

Johnson, V. (1973). *I'll quit tomorrow.* New York: Harper & Row.

Karrass, C. L., and Glasser, W. (1980). *Both-win management.* New York: Lippincott and Crowell.

Krimmerl, H. E. (1975). The value of a crisis. *Al-Anon faces alcoholism.* New York: Al-Anon Family Group Headquarters, Inc.

Maier, N. R. F. (1976). *The appraisal interview: Three basic approaches.* La Jolla, CA: University Press Associates.

Masi, D. (1979). Combating alcoholism in the workplace. *Health and Social Work, 4*(4), 41–59.

Miller, M., and Gorski, T. T. (1982). *Family recovery: Growing beyond addiction.* Independence, MO: Independence Press.

Royce, J. E. (1981). *Alcohol problems and alcoholism.* New York: Free Press.

Sonnenstuhl, W. J., and O'Donnell, J. E. (1980). EAPs: The why's and how's of planning them. *Personnel Administrator, 25*(11), 35–38.

Chapter Six

THE EAP AND HEALTH PROMOTION

Every day, employee assistance counselors help individuals deal with problems that might, in fact, have been prevented. Although it is useful—even imperative—to intervene when an employee's job performance has been affected by physical or mental health problems, it is even more useful to provide help before the problems have developed. It is cost-effective for an organization to address such issues as absenteeism, high turnover, and poor productivity, but it is even more cost-effective to prevent their occurrence in the first place.

Health promotion activities are a natural extension of the employee assistance concept, with programs oriented toward wellness and stress management acting as the preventive arm of the EAP. Such preventive efforts need a broad focus, since no single, linear relationship between a definitive cause and a specific disorder is likely to be identified. Health problems tend to result from the interplay of a variety of factors, including individual vulnerabilities, stress, and coping capacities. We can identify risk factors that tend to place people in jeopardy as well as positive attributes that tend to act as protectors against disability. We can also develop programs that serve to minimize risks or build strengths, thus preventing a variety of dysfunctions.

> Just as a single disorder may come about as a consequence of a variety of stressful life events, any specific stress event may precipitate a variety of disorders, as a result of differing life histories and patterns of strengths and weaknesses in individuals. For example, an unanticipated death, divorce, or a job loss may increase the risk of alcoholism in one person, coronary artery disease in another, depression and suicide in a third, and a fatal automobile accident in a fourth . . . With this acceptance comes the realization that successful efforts at the prevention of a vast array of disorders (particularly emotional disorders) can take place without a theory of disorder-specific causative mechanisms (President's Commission on Mental Health, 1978, p. 1847).

Even without knowing the unique biological, social, or psychological cause of a particular problem, we can prevent that problem, along with others, by strengthening the health-oriented competencies of employees and by doing what we can to lessen the stressors in the work environment. The efficacy of this broad, positive strategy becomes apparent when we consider some of the issues that EAP counselors most commonly face.

Consider, for example, the problem of excessive alcohol or drug use among employees. For every alcoholic whose obvious problem leads to a supervisory referral, a company is likely to have several employees whose inappropriate use of chemicals leads to more subtle, even indefinable, effects. As Shain (1983) points out, many problems associated with excessive use of alcohol and other drugs do not reach the attention of an EAP counselor either because job performance deficits are too unclear to lead to supervisory confrontation or because a high percentage of the employee population may be involved. "The result of having such people in the workforce, however, is a general depression in productivity and morale and a general elevation in associated absenteeism and accident rates" (Shain, 1983, p. 39).

Shain's contention is that excessive use of chemicals should be prevented, but that this prevention must target a number of factors that affect employees' health and lifestyles. Rather than focusing attention solely on information about alcohol and other drugs, the prevention-oriented consultant should consider the fact that people who are under stress, who have generally poor levels of health, and who are uninformed about the effects of chemicals are at risk of developing problems related to chemical dependency.

> People who live in unhealthy ways are more at risk for becoming excessive drinkers and inappropriate drug users than people whose lifestyles are healthier. This suggests that an appropriate target for preventive activities designed to affect alcohol and drug use is lifestyle itself. Consequently, an intervention based on this hypothesis alone would include education about alcohol and drugs but would do so in the framework of overall lifestyle re-appraisal and reformulation (Shain, 1983, p. 40).

The kinds of health promotion programs Shain espouses for the prevention of drug and alcohol abuse encourage self-regulating activity, build up people's sense of control over their health, and provide supports for the development of new behaviors. The mechanisms for prevention of emotional difficulties are similar. Psychological disorders, like substance abuse problems, come about as a result of the interaction among life stressors, personal characteristics, and situational factors.

> A transit stress reaction interacts with situational and psychological mediators to produce any of three general outcomes. First, a person who experiences stressful life events may undergo psychological growth as a result . . . Another possibility is that the person resumes his life without notable change once the stress-

ful life event and his immediate transient stress reaction are over . . . Finally, an individual may develop psychopathology as a consequence of exposure to stressful life events (Dohrenwend, 1978, p. 5).

We can identify specific life events and environmental stressors that "appear to be capable of triggering patterns of maladaptive behavior in a proportion of the population that experiences those events" (Price, Bader, and Ketterer, 1980, p. 11). But what factors tend to differentiate members of the population who develop psychological/behavioral disorders when overstressed from those who do not?

A number of characteristics seem to act as "buffers," protecting an individual's mental health in the face of strong negative pressures. One factor that has received a great deal of attention from researchers in the field involves the degree of social support available to the individual under stress. Close friends and associates can provide both emotional support and "tangible aid, resources, and information and guidance" (Wilcox, 1981, p. 372) to help a person cope with difficult situations. Just as important is the individual's own sense of being able to exert control over his or her life and environment (Bandura, 1982; Kobasa, 1979). The effects of stress can be moderated by the degree to which people sense that they have potential control over events and that their own actions can make a difference. "When beset with difficulties people who entertain serious doubts about their capabilities slacken their efforts or give up altogether, whereas those who have a strong sense of efficacy exert greater effort to master the challenges" (Bandura, 1982, p. 122). At least part of this sense of efficacy can be seen as a function of the individual's life skills. People who are competent in making decisions, solving problems, interacting with others, planning around their own tolerance for change, and purposefully managing their stress levels can be expected to develop well-founded perceptions of their own abilities to withstand the pressures of daily living.

A general health promotion program can alleviate stress and build life competencies, thus serving a preventive function that does not need to be directed toward specific disabilities. This health promotion program should include components designed to (a) train employees in stress management concepts and skills, (b) encourage the maintenance of health and fitness, (c) develop competencies in daily living, and (d) lessen stressful aspects of the workplace.

STRESS MANAGEMENT

EAP consultants can provide training to help employees understand and manage their reactions to stressful situations, but they need to begin by choosing from among a variety of conceptualizations and definitions.

Ivancevich and Matteson (1980) divide the myriad definitions of *stress* into three categories: stimulus definitions, response definitions, and stimulus-response definitions. Stimulus definitions define *stress* as an environmental situation or event that threatens the individual; if the threat is beyond the person's coping abilities, the response is termed *strain*. In contrast with this definition, which is borrowed from the physical sciences, a response definition sees stress as the individual's physiological or psychological response to an external event, which is termed a *stressor*. Finally, stimulus-response definitions focus on the interaction between the environmental stimulus and the unique individual's response to it. The working definition used by Ivancevich and Matteson takes into account both stimulus and response and seems especially appropriate for a work-based stress intervention model:

> Stress (is) an adaptive response, mediated by individual characteristics and/or psychological processes, that is a consequence of any external action, situation or event that places special physical and/or psychological demands upon a person (1980, pp. 8–9).

This definition recognizes the roles played by both environmental and individual factors and therefore makes it clear that stress management strategies should take into account environmental stressors, individual coping mechanisms, and personal perceptions of threat.

Stress-Related Issues and Problems

Stress-related problems originate in complex processes that begin with demands placed on the individual. An event or situation challenges the person's well-being, forcing him or her to make some kind of adaptation. Short of physical danger, of course, no external event is, in itself, universally stressful. The stress response depends on the individual's interpretation that the situation does, in fact, pose a threat.

Whether someone finds a situation threatening depends on the way the event is interpreted and on the individual's perception of his or her ability to meet the challenge. A number of factors affect the human organism's appraisal of threat, including whether the person feels competent to handle the new demand, whether similar situations have been surmounted in the past, whether the individual feels a sense of control over events, whether the new demand is in conflict with other needs, whether the individual's standards of performance are too high, and whether the person is already coping with an unusually demanding environment. Some people's belief systems make them continually vulnerable to stress, as they "write 'disaster' over every unwanted event at home and at work" (Veninga and Spradley, 1981, p. 20) or insist on perfection in their own performance levels.

Consider, for example, an individual in a work situation who is assigned to perform duties in addition to those normally performed. One employee might see this change as a relief from tedium, while another would find the job expansion stressful. The difference in response can, in part, be attributed to the individual's perceptions—accurate or inaccurate—about his or her ability to perform effectively in the new role. Perceptions of threat can be affected by employees' current states of mind (do they already feel overworked? are they facing pressures at home? do they believe the new tasks are important?) and by their general attitudes and beliefs (do they feel uncomfortable with change and stimulation? do they enjoy work that is so familiar it can be done perfectly? do they tend to worry about any possibility of failure?).

If human beings perceive events as being threatening, they react physiologically, preparing their bodies for the vigorous physical activity needed to cope with physical danger. This "fight or flight" response evokes the same physical changes, regardless of the nature of the stressor.

> It starts in the hypothalamus, a tiny bundle of nerve cells at the center of the brain. Messages race from that command post and spread the alarm throughout the nervous system. Muscles tense. Blood vessels constrict. The tiny capillaries under the skin shut down altogether. The pituitary gland sends out two hormones that move through the bloodstream to stimulate the thyroid and adrenal glands. . . . The adrenals send some thirty additional hormones to nearly every organ in the body. This automatic stress response causes the pulse rate to shoot up; blood pressure soars. The stomach and intestines stop all the busy activity of digestion. Hearing and smell become more acute. Hundreds of other physical changes occur without us even knowing it (Veninga and Spradley, 1981, p. 11).

These responses are appropriate for dealing with physical danger; following fight or flight, the body returns to its original equilibrium. Stress-related problems tend to occur in our complex, modern society because the energy used in the mobilizing process is not adaptive. When stressors are social or psychological rather than physical the stress response builds up tension that is not released, utilizes energy that is not restored, and ultimately leads to exhaustion.

The ongoing effects of stress are many. Individuals who are consistently under stress may find themselves troubled with such physical symptoms as respiratory problems, gastrointestinal symptoms, headaches, backaches, chronic high blood pressure, generally low energy levels, and even cardiovascular disease. Stress also manifests itself in psychological malfunctions such as depression and anxiety. Job performance is certainly affected; ongoing, unrelieved stress in the work setting causes employee burnout, accompanied by low morale, absenteeism, and loss of motivation. "Other changes include increasing discouragement, pessimism, and fatalism about one's work; decline in motivation, effort, and involvement in work; apathy; negativism; frequent irritability and anger with clients and colleagues; preoccupation with one's own comfort and welfare on the job; a tendency to rationalize failure by blaming the clients or 'the system'; and resistance to change, growing rigidity, and loss of creativity" (Cherniss, 1980, p. 6).

Intervention Strategies

Since the development of stress-related problems results from a combination of environmental demands, individual perceptions, and physiological responses, such problems can be lessened through intervention at any of these points. Individual employees can learn to examine the stressors in their lives as well as their own responses and to make purposeful choices about ways to lower their stress levels. Table 6.1 describes possible interventions for dealing with environmental demands or internal processes.

One way that individuals can lessen their stress levels is by learning how to exert more control over their environments. Employees can examine their lifestyles and work situations to identify stressors that are amenable to change. Although some stress will always be present, employees can use problem solving, time management, and interpersonal skills to address problem issues directly. One very important factor is the development of support systems, which can undoubtedly make the environment less threatening and, concurrently, provide sustenance as internal adaptations are attempted.

The next point at which intervention may be made is in the appraisal of environmental demands. Individuals can actually learn to think differently in various situations and thus choose to avoid stress responses. Such "cognitive restructuring" involves altering the effects of problematic events.

Table 6.1. Counseling interventions for points in the stress cycle

Environmental Demands	Internal Processes	
Altering the environment	Altering mental processing	Altering nervous system activation and processing of internal cues
Decision-making and problem-solving counseling	Cognitive modification	Relaxation training
Time perspective counseling	Clarification skills	Meditation
Training in interpersonal skills (assertiveness, leadership, helping)	Values clarification	Sensory awareness training
Self-management procedures	Goal setting	Biofeedback
Support groups	Lifestyle assessment and counseling	
	Problem-solving training	

Note. Adapted from "A model of stress and counseling interventions" by J. C. Barrow and Selina Sue Prosen, 1981, *The Personnel and Guidance Journal, 60,* p. 7. Copyright 1981 by the American Personnel and Guidance Association. Reprinted by permission.

The first phase in restructuring is recognition of certain self-appraisals that play a major role in giving the stressor potency, that is, turning an essentially neutral situation into a highly stressful one: ("Oh no, this is awful.") Second, it is suggested that the individual begin to monitor the self-appraisals to gain awareness of maladaptive ones, such as exaggeration, that tend to maintain the stressful event (Moracco and McFadden, 1982, p. 550).

Being aware of one's tendencies to perceive various stimuli as threats can lead to purposeful efforts to substitute alternate "self-statements" or to utilize other methods for changing mental processes. What Goldfried and Goldfried (1980) call "rational restructuring" can be applied both to stress management and to anxiety states that are unrelated to specific stressors. The process includes four basic steps: (1) helping clients recognize that cognitions mediate emotional arousal, (2) helping clients recognize the irrationality of certain beliefs, (3) helping clients understand that unrealistic cognitions mediate their own maladaptive emotions, and (4) helping clients to change their unrealistic cognitions.

Simply understanding the cause of the problem will do little to alleviate it; clients must consciously and deliberately engage in doing something differently when feeling upset. This emotional reaction must now serve as a "cue" for them to stop and think: "What am I telling myself that may be unrealistic?" They must learn to "break-up" what was before an automatic reaction and replace it with a more realistic appraisal of the situation . . . Clients eventually can totally eliminate the initial upset phase by having made the more realistic appraisal an automatic reaction (Goldfried and Goldfried, 1980, p. 107).

Neither environmental factors nor the individual's cognitive responses are always as controllable as one might wish. Individuals also need to learn to intervene at the point of physiological stress responses. Through such processes as relaxation training, self-hypnosis, biofeedback, or meditation, individuals can learn to substitute relaxation for the fight-or-flight response and thus avoid the long-term, negative effects of stress.

The Stress Management Workshop

A workshop format is appropriate for helping employees develop stress management skills, since at least part of the focus on learning can be placed on opportunities for mutual support and assistance. Sparks and Ingram, for instance, describe the following goals as the bases of their stress management workshops for public school teachers:

(a) to reduce isolation; (b) to identify sources of job-related stress (self-awareness); (c) to identify sources of job satisfaction and job-related strengths that may be drawn on to increase participants' satisfaction with their work; and (d) to formulate a tentative plan and action steps to prevent or alleviate stress (Sparks and Ingram, 1979, p. 198).

Several exercises can be utilized to meet these goals and to introduce methods for intervening in external or internal processes.

Identifying stressors.   Stress management begins with conscious awareness of the stressors in one's life. One exercise that can generate self-awareness and build mutual support is a group assessment of stressors in the work environment. Workshop participants can be divided into small groups and asked to generate a list of work-related factors they find stressful. Once these lists have been created and shared, participants can discuss commonalities in their concerns and potential methods of solving problems in the work setting. The trainer can use this opportunity to emphasize the importance of support systems in coping with stress and to encourage the development of ongoing groups.

Cognitive restructuring.   Self-awareness can be further enhanced by allowing individuals to examine their own patterns of dealing with work conditions. Participants can be asked to list specific recent events that made them anxious. By analyzing each situation and their reactions to it employees can recognize what kinds of events they tend to perceive as threatening. A short lecture and discussion can help participants consider alternate methods of thinking about the work environment and its impact on them.

Stress reduction.   The workshop leader should provide an overview of the physiology of stress. Once participants become aware of the nature of the fight-or-flight response, they can also understand what methods can be used to break into the cycle at the point of arousal. Participants usually enjoy the experience of relaxation training or introductory self-hypnosis exercises.

Identifying successful approaches.   Employees are usually able to share approaches to dealing with stress that they have used successfully. As they discuss the ways they manage stress, they tend to notice that the commonly used tactics run the gamut from environmental problem solving to changes in cognition to relaxation methods. Participants also find it encouraging to discuss job satisfactions and rewards as a counterpoint to the workshop's emphasis on negative aspects of the individual's relationship to work.

Making stress management plans.   Finally, the long-term effects of the workshop can be enhanced by creating individualized stress management plans. Each participant should select several stress-related issues and identify immediate steps that can be taken to deal with them. A follow-up workshop can be used to evaluate employees' success in making the initial lifestyle changes that alleviate stress and prevent the development of health problems.

The Focused Workshop

In addition to providing general stress management training, the EAP consultant can also devise workshops or seminars focused on specific methods for relieving anxiety and enhancing relaxation. Relaxation techniques can be based either on mental imagery or on muscle relaxation; regardless of the approach used, training sessions can teach employees to relax at will and thus interfere with the cycle of stress. Self-hypnosis can go beyond muscle relaxation to place individuals in a special frame of mind for receiving self-suggestions, including suggestions for complete calm and total release of tension. Meditation also produces a calm state of consciousness, whether the method for freeing oneself from senses and thoughts involves visual imagery, controlled breathing, or repetition of a word or sound. Benson (1975) suggests that the "relaxation response" is an alternative to the stress response; thus, employees who are skilled in controlling tension levels can be expected to withstand environmental demands more effectively than those who are not.

WELLNESS PROGRAMS

In recent years, many companies have found it cost-effective to develop programs oriented toward health and fitness. Programs that are focused on wellness, rather than merely on the absence of disease, teach employees to take control of their own health needs and, ideally, prevent the occurrence of problems requiring medical care. Part of the rationale for the creation of these programs is based on the drastic rise in health care costs in the United States.

> Our total spending as a nation for health care mushroomed from 192 billion dollars in 1978 to over 300 billion in 1982. For American business, which bears 23 percent of this burden, these figures are a great concern. Rising health care costs, along with sagging productivity, an ailing economy, and declining employee health, have mobilized many business leaders to change their philosophy regarding employee health. The question is no longer *whether* health management is a corporate responsibility—the issue has become *how* to promote better employee health and reduce health care expenditures (Ardell and Tager, 1982, p. 132).

Another basis for corporate interest in wellness programs involves the nature of contemporary health problems. The vast expenditures for health care have not had the impact they should on the general health of the population, at least in part because changes in the prevalence of various conditions require new approaches. A century ago, infectious diseases were the leading causes of death. During the course of the twentieth century, health patterns have changed. Because of scientific advancements diseases like tuberculosis, measles, poliomyelitis, influenza, and pneumonia are no longer the killers they once were. "Unfortunately, the reduction in these conditions has occurred along with an increase during the same years in such conditions as lung cancer, major cardiovascular disease, drug and alcohol abuse, and motorcycle and alcohol-related automobile accidents" (Matarazzo, 1982, p. 3).

Today, most deaths are caused by the kinds of afflictions that are likely to be affected by changes in personal lifestyle. Cardiovascular disease alone accounts for half of the mortalities among Americans; cancer and accidents are also major causes of death. These problems are preventable and, in fact, do not respond well to traditional medical interventions.

> Clearly, the next health revolution must be aimed at these new killers and cripplers, and it clearly makes sense to emphasize strategies in that revolution for preventing these afflictions rather than to rely on treating them after they have already struck . . . As much as half of all mortality in the United States is due to unhealthy behavior or life-style. Of the rest, 20% is due to environmental factors, 20% to human biological factors, and only 10% to inadequacies in health care. In spite of that, only a minuscule percentage of the 1982 federal budget [was] specifically identified for prevention-related activities. Yet it is clear that improvement in the health of our citizens will not be made predominantly through the treatment of disease, but rather through its prevention (Michael, 1982, pp. 936–937).

And how can health be improved and the costs of medical care lowered? According to Michael, most Americans can improve their health and extend their life spans through "elimination of cigarette smoking, reduction of alcohol misuse, moderate dietary changes to reduce intake of excess calories and excess fats, moderate exercise, periodic screening for major disorders such as high blood pressure and certain cancers, adherence to traffic speed laws, and use of seat belts" (1982, p. 937).

All of these behaviors constitute lifestyle changes that can be affected by education and support. Because employers have a stake in maintaining employee health, their interest in such educational endeavors continues to grow. The workplace is recognized as an appropriate site for the encouragement of healthy lifestyles. Although most organizations cannot offer their employees luxurious physical fitness facilities at the worksite, even small companies can afford to invest in health by affecting attitudes and providing information.

Health promotion programs should offer some activities focused on special issues (smoking cessation clinics, weight loss groups, exercise classes). Just as important, however, is a general orientation toward wellness concepts. People need to be convinced that they have the power to prevent illness through their own initiatives and that they can take responsibility for meeting their own health needs. A sense of personal power does seem to be among the most important factors in helping people to avoid chronic illness. Research by Kobasa (1979) indicates that, among people facing comparable degrees of stress, the factors that distinguished between those who became ill and those who remained healthy included vigorousness in one's attitude toward the world, strong self-commitment, a sense of meaning in life, and an internal locus of control. People who believed in themselves, who believed that they could control events through their own behavior had a "hardiness" that protected them against illness. A central purpose of health promotion programs should be to develop hardiness along with concrete skills.

The employees' attempts to optimize health should begin with some form of assessment to indicate the nature of individual risk factors and lay the groundwork for planning. If facilities are available, initial assessment can include stress tests, measures of aerobic capacity, tests of body composition, and other fitness assessment tools. (Even if companies do not have extensive facilities on-site, they can contract with local agencies that do.) Employees can also make use of computerized health assessments that identify risk factors in their health histories and current lifestyles. Many companies, for instance, use Control Data's PLATO Health Risk Profile, which appraises individuals' health risks through use of a microcomputer. Even the smallest organization can make available paper-and-pencil inventories that help to identify individual risk factors and at the same time serve as teaching tools to raise awareness levels.

Assessment inventories can certainly alert employees to their risks of developing heart disease, since a number of risk factors that make individuals coronary-prone have been identified. Factors associated with heart disease include (Gatchel and Baum, 1983, p. 110):

Age (being older)
Sex (being male)
Serum cholesterol (elevations)
Intake of animal fat
Blood pressure (elevations)
Cigarette smoking
Diabetes
Family history
Obesity
Lack of exercise

Questionnaires can also be used to identify "Type A" behavioral patterns (Friedman and Rosenman, 1974), which seem to increase one's vulnerability to heart disease. The Type A individual is characterized by a sense of time urgency, competitiveness, aggressiveness, hostility, overinvolvement in work, and strong needs to control all situations. The characteristics of the hard-driving Type A individual can be measured through self-reports; attention can then be paid to substituting more effective and less risky mechanisms for coping with stress.

The purpose of using assessment instruments of any type is to point the way toward appropriate behavioral changes. Each employee should set personal, health-related objectives that are realistic in terms of his or her current level of fitness. A workable plan depends on the quality of the goals that have been set. Ardell and Tager (1982, p. 43) suggest the following standards:[1]

1. *Translate goals and behaviors into specific terms.* Instead of "I would like to improve my health," be specific. How about: "I will lose 10 pounds by monitoring my food intake and beginning a jogging program."
2. *Add a measurement component.* What will it take to achieve the goal? How will you know when you are ready? In the example above, you could weigh yourself weekly, calculate daily calorie intake, and log the number of minutes you jog each day. Measurement components are best when checkpoints for progress are built in. Intermediate and short-range sub-goals can be helpful.
3. Identify a *time schedule* for goal achievement. Pick a date for accomplishing your feat: How about this: "I will weigh 180 pounds by my birthday," or "Next January 1, I will be running five miles four times a week."
4. Make sure your goal is *realistic,* but also *challenging.* A goal should present a challenge that, with dedication and perseverance, can probably be realized. The prospects for accomplishing it should be favorable. Avoid goals that are too easy or too challenging (e.g., "I will lose 30 pounds this month" may be a case of attempting too much, too soon).
5. Goals should always be *in writing.* Seeing your goal statements on paper strengthens your commitment to their pursuit. It serves as a reminder of what you have undertaken and helps you think of ways to progress.

Especially when embarking on new exercise routines, employees need to be careful in making their plans. Different types of exercises meet different goals, so individuals need to choose activities that serve their purposes, whether to increase endurance, to build strength, to improve flexibility, or to lose weight. Novices also need to be cautious in setting objectives; slight, steady increases in the amount of physical activity can be more beneficial than sudden spurts of activity that are too ambitious to be maintained.

It is in the maintenance of health improvements that the work-based program can be especially helpful. Individuals are most likely to adhere to their wellness plans if they have as much support in their new endeavors as they did in their former, less healthy lifestyles. Wellness training provides such support, both from trainers and from fellow participants. In a model training course described by Shea (1981), employees come back for reinforcement of their efforts after a thirty-day wellness tryout period.

---

[1] From *Planning for wellness: A guidebook for achieving optimal health* (2nd ed.) (p. 43) by D. B. Ardell and M. J. Tager, 1982, Dubuque, IA: Kendall/Hunt. Copyright 1982 by Kendall/Hunt Publishing Co. Reprinted by permission.

During a long-term follow-up period, reinforcement continues, with articles and reminders mailed frequently from the training department to each participant.

In Control Data's Staywell Program (McCann, 1981), groups of employees with common problems or interests provide mutual support. The Staywell Program is based on lifestyle change courses dealing with such issues as smoking cessation, nutrition, weight loss, relaxation, hypertension, fitness, and stress management. At the end of each of these courses, ongoing employee groups are formed, with the instructor gradually withdrawing from the leadership position. Groups of employees also form task forces to deal with specific, health-related issues in the workplace.

Wellness programs encourage healthful lifestyles by providing basic guidance, by facilitating the development of effective plans, and by reinforcing new behaviors through ongoing supportive mechanisms. These programs promote feelings of self-efficacy and control, which are as important to the maintenance of mental health as they are to physical well-being.

DEVELOPMENT OF LIFE SKILLS

Another major component of health promotion is helping employees develop competencies in daily living. At least part of the rationale for training programs in this area lies in the realm of prevention. "Prevention activities from a competency enhancement view mean that programs could focus on building adaptive strengths with the assumption that a strengthened individual will be able to deal better with a variety of stresses that might eventually lead to disability" (Heller, Price, and Sher, 1980, p. 293). Life skills can be seen as mediating forces that protect people's mental health and well-being by allowing them to use effective coping mechanisms, to solve problems, and to build and retain social support systems.

Educational approaches to the development of life skills are also built on the rationale that many problems resolved through one-to-one counseling sessions could be handled more efficiently through large group interventions. In any organization, an EAP counselor is likely to serve a number of individual employees having similar concerns. While some problems require personalized interventions, many could be addressed just as effectively through seminars or workshops. In fact, group sessions may be more desirable than individual approaches; the ability of employees to help themselves and one another is emphasized and may, in turn, promote feelings of self-efficacy. If a counselor can effectively reach a number of people during the time period normally needed for individual counseling, he or she should be sure to include life skill seminars as a component of the employee assistance program. Such seminars should prepare employees to deal with the problems seen most frequently among individual clients. Most EAP counselors find that employees tend to value training in the skills of parenting, marriage relationships, self-modification, problem solving, assertiveness, and general communication. In some of these areas, existing materials can be used to carry out structured courses.

Parenting

A number of packaged programs are available to counselors who are attempting to enhance the parenting skills of employees and their spouses. It is well worth a counselor's time to offer such programs periodically because many self-referrals tend to revolve around issues relating to family conflict or problems in rearing children.

One particularly well-organized approach is provided by STEP (Systematic Training for Effective Parenting), a nine-session program developed by Dinkmeyer and McKay (1976). STEP, like the more recently developed STEP/Teen (Dinkmeyer and McKay, 1983), is designed to teach parents a set of skills for raising children. The package includes reading materials for each participant as well as audio tapes and leaders' guides for use by the trainer. Exercises and discussions at each meeting address such issues as understanding behavior, the encouragement process, effective discipline, communication patterns, decision-making methods, and family meetings.

STEP and STEP/Teen are based on a coherent theoretical framework that assumes children misbehave because they want to reach a goal or because they have a purpose. Parents can discipline their children most effectively if they understand the goals of their children's behavior and make youngsters responsible for the natural and logical consequences of their own actions. Through this program, parents learn to communicate more effectively, to apply encouragement, and to implement family meetings for the purposes of decision making, mutual encouragement, conflict resolution, cooperation, and social learning.

Another approach to parenting is provided by Parent Effectiveness Training (Gordon, 1971), a course taught by instructors who have been trained in the PET methods. The course content covered in a series of discussion sessions includes (Gordon, 1971, p. 49):

1. Parents are taught to differentiate between those situations in which the child is making it difficult for himself to meet his own needs . . . and those situations in which the child is making it difficult for the parent to meet his own needs.
2. Parents are given skill-training in . . . verbal communication . . .
3. Parents are given skill training in those forms of verbal communication that have been shown to be most effective when one person wants to influence another person to modify behavior . . .

4. Parents are then given skill training in specific methods of preventing conflicts between parent and child . . .

5. Parents are taught the hazards and harmful effects of using . . . win-lose (power struggle) methods of conflict resolution . . .

6. Parents are then given skill training in using a non-power or "no-lose" method of resolving all conflicts between parent and child . . .

EAP counselors can use structured materials like STEP or PET or develop their own approaches. Regardless of the methods used, counselors can help employees deal with parenting issues before intensive family counseling is required.

Marriage Relationships

Every EAP counselor deals on a daily basis with problems related to marriage or other close relationships. For many employees, a skill-building course can prevent problems and enhance family life.

Although counselors can develop their own seminars or workshops, they can also make use of existing course materials. One such approach is Training in Marriage Enrichment (TIME), a ten-session, multimedia, skill-based marriage enrichment program (Dinkmeyer and Carlson, 1984). Each two-hour session of TIME includes exercises, group discussions, and skill-building practices devoted to such issues as understanding oneself, understanding the relationship, communication, choice making, encouragement, conflict resolution, dealing with anger, and "divorce-proofing" the marriage. Each couple also completes homework assignments between meetings, making use of a book, audio cassette, skill cards, and daily focus cards. In addition to the book, *Time for a Better Marriage,* the set of materials includes tapes, exercise materials, marriage assessment inventories, and a leader's manual.

Communication Skills

Communication skills workshops can vary from sessions for people who have difficulty relating with others to training that helps talented communicators become better helpers for their friends and colleagues. Regardless of their current level of expertise, most people find it useful to enhance their abilities to listen effectively and communicate openly.

A person with a deficit in interpersonal communications skills is usually painfully aware of the negative feelings such as alienation, isolation, and social discomfort that often accompany this lack of skill. Communication skills groups provide a series of structured activities that enable people to develop effective interpersonal skills and rewarding styles of relating, as well as to overcome specific personal barriers to effective communication. The actual format of communication skills groups varies widely, from those that emphasize listening and responding skills to those that focus on reducing social anxiety and improving interpersonal transaction abilities (Drum and Knott, 1977, pp. 81–82).

In general, communication skills workshops are highly experiential, giving participants the chance to practice and receive feedback on such activities as sending and receiving nonverbal messages; paraphrasing verbalizations of other group members; using active listening and confrontation techniques; engaging in cooperative, small-group exercises; or resolving interpersonal or intergroup conflicts. A communication skills seminar designed by Apgar, Riley, Eaton, and Diskin (1982) for presentation in the workplace includes four sessions: (1) barriers to effective communication, (2) nonverbal communication and listening, (3) benefits of assertive expressing, and (4) implementing effective communication skills.

As Apgar et al. point out, seminars dealing with communication skills or other life competencies can assist employees to:

> Increase their awareness of community resources outside the company that can be of help to them.
>
> Increase their awareness of people inside the company who can be of assistance.
>
> Increase their awareness of their own resources for coping with work and family issues.
>
> Learn a variety of responses to help them to cope with work and family situations.
>
> Develop a greater sense of personal competence both on the job and at home (1982, p. 1).

STRESSORS IN THE WORK SETTING

Identifying the effects of environmental factors on employees' health is just as important as strengthening individual coping mechanisms and self-responsibility. Preventive programs have, in the past, tended to focus on the individual's personal responsibilities in the maintenance of wellness. In fact, the effectiveness of this singular focus has not been established.

> Consensus is lacking . . . on the specific programs that should constitute a strategy of prevention. Two etiological theories dictate two very different directions: a theory that blames self-destructive habits and a theory that points to social factors (Taylor, 1982, p. 40).

Especially when considering strategies related to stress management, the EAP consultant needs to take into account both personal and environmental factors. Rather than choosing between individual or organizational emphases, the consultant should consider a systemic approach built on awareness of personal/social interactions. "The effectiveness of *combinations* of stress management strategies (i.e., combinations of personal strategies, combinations of organizational strategies, and combinations of personal *and* organizational strategies) needs to be evaluated . . . Since stress phenomena have open system characteristics, strategies for handling job stress need to be systemic in nature" (Newman and Beehr, 1979, pp. 38–39). Wellness, life-skill, and stress management programs need to be joined by efforts to deal with the work setting itself, taking into account such factors as person-environment fit, physical stressors, organizational climate, and the need for supportive work groups.

Person–Environment Fit

Individuals differ greatly in their responses to various environmental stressors. What one employee considers ideal working conditions another will regard as highly stressful. "The stress-evoking and ultimately perhaps disease-producing effect of a situation in working life is therefore heavily dependent on the degree of fit (or misfit) between the capacity and needs of the individual and the demands and opportunities presented by the environment in industry and elsewhere" (Levi, 1981, p. 37).

If work-based stressors are to be reduced, the organizational environment must be adapted to differences in individual needs. Employees can identify and change those aspects of their roles that they find overly stressful. According to Ivancevich and Matteson (1980), common problems leading to stress in individual employees include role conflict, role ambiguity, work overload, responsibility for people, and career development stressors.

Role conflict. Individuals may be faced with competing role pressures, either because of conflicting sets of expectations expressed by different units within the organization or because of conflicts between the requirements of the role and the individual's own goals and values. Stress can be reduced by changing the organizational context within which the job must be performed (eliminating contradictory demands) or changing the job itself (increasing the degree of fit between the individual and the role).

Role ambiguity. Employees often find it stressful if lack of clarity about their role, job objectives, or responsibilities persists more than temporarily. More adequate information can decrease the anxiety of employees who are troubled because they do not know what is expected of them.

Work overload. Job performance and health may be negatively affected by work overload, whether it involves too much work or a demand to perform at a level beyond the individual's current capacity. Chronic overload as a problem depends on the interaction between the individual's abilities and the organization's expectations rather than on objective measures of work requirements.

Responsibility for people. Many employees find it highly stressful to have responsibility for the activities of other people. Appropriate fit between individuals and their jobs takes this factor into account in the selection process.

Career development stressors.   Stress is increased when employees sense a lack of fit between their work and their career goals or values. "This can happen if an employee feels a lack of job security, is concerned about real or imagined obsolescence, feels that promotion progress is inadequate, and/or is generally dissatisfied with the match between career aspirations and the current level of attainment" (Ivancevich and Matteson, 1980, p. 115). This problem needs to be addressed either by helping the individual to develop more realistic expectations or by changing the reality or the perception of available opportunities.

The same role may be perceived as overload for one individual, understimulation for another; ambiguous for one, happily flexible for another. No one organizational strategy can reduce stress for everyone, unless jobs are designed with individual differences in mind. It is possible, however, to make the organizational climate as a whole more conducive to employee health and well-being.

Organizational Climate

It is possible to identify factors in the work setting that tend to exacerbate the difficulties of stress-prone employees. Strategies designed to reduce stressors in the organization can encompass changes in structures and processes that affect everyone. Newman and Beehr, after reviewing the major research in the field, suggested that strategies can attempt to do any of the following:

> Change the organizational structure (e.g., decentralize, integrate, reduce levels of hierarchy or numbers of channels); change the reward system; change the distribution of resources; change the selection, placement, training and development policies and programs; change the socialization processes; change the policies concerning transfers and job rotation; educate management regarding human relations—especially so they can provide employees with social (emotional) support; develop better communication systems; use temporary work groups; use participative decision making; develop health services (mental and physical) to be provided by the organization's personnel or medical department (1979, p. 21).

In general, an organizational climate that provides stability and support while maximizing employees' control over their own work lives can keep stress levels low.

Physical Stressors

The importance of the physical environment as a stressor cannot be overlooked. Inadequate light, extreme temperatures, excessive noise, noxious fumes, or constant vibration can lead to stress and, in turn, to health problems. In addition, physical factors can also lead directly to disease. "An estimated 100,000 workers die each year, according to OSHA, and three or four times that number are disabled, as a result of occupational disease" (Taylor, 1982, p. 35).

Although some physical stressors may be unavoidable, organizational policy makers can move to identify risks, eliminate toxic agents, and make sure that employees are protected. EAP consultants can work in harmony with specialists in safety and medicine to point out environmental stressors as their clients point them out.

Social Support

The idea that social support can have a buffering effect to protect individuals from stress has become widely accepted. In addition to moderating the effects of environmental stressors, social support systems can also have a direct effect on health and well-being because they meet basic human needs.

Because social support appears to have a major impact on stress levels, attempts should be made to build such support into the organizational structure. "If social support is to be effective in reducing stress, preventing health problems, and increasing workers' ability to adapt to the irreducible stresses at work, all people must be able to obtain support from the persons with whom they routinely work—superiors, subordinates, and co-workers or colleagues" (House, 1981, p. 120). Purposeful efforts can be made to build supportiveness into organizational norms by encouraging open communication among employees, structuring work arrangements to eliminate isolation, training key organizational members in the social support concept, and rewarding supportiveness among supervisory personnel. Specific attention should be paid to the need for special support mechanisms among people dealing with highly stressful situations or major transitions.

Employee assistance counselors can have a major impact on organizational efforts to enhance social support systems and decrease environmental stressors. Because they see the victims of stress every day, they tend to be among the first to recognize problem areas. Moreover, they have the kinds of human relations skills that are needed to bring about positive changes in the work environment. EAP professionals have a natural role to play as internal consultants, helping the organization to balance and integrate individual and organizational goals. If they are experienced in organizational development consultation, they can use a number of strategies to change the company's internal culture. Efforts to change the way an organization addresses its problems can take a number of forms, including intervening in group processes, developing conflict resolution strategies, conducting training programs, gathering and sharing diagnostic data about the work environment, and suggesting changes in the organizational structure. All of these activities should be seen as part of the effective EAP consultant's role.

SUMMARY

Health promotion programs can be seen as the preventive arm of the employee assistance program. Because we cannot yet link all mental and physical health problems with specific causal factors, we need to base preventive programs on strategies to strengthen the general health-oriented competencies of employees while lessening the stressors in the work environment. Such programs can decrease employees' risks of developing chronic physical or mental health problems without being linked to specific disabilities. The health promotion program should include four basic components: (1) stress management training, (2) wellness programs, (3) life skills training programs, and (4) efforts to alleviate stressors in the work setting.

Stress management programs should be based on an understanding of the complex relationship among environmental stressors, individual interpretations, and physiological responses. In workshop sessions, employees can learn to identify sources of stress and satisfaction, to analyze their cognitive reactions, and to control the methods they use for responding to stress.

Individual responsibility is also emphasized in wellness programs, which attempt to teach employees to take control of their own health needs. Many of the leading causes of death among Americans can be prevented through elimination of cigarette smoking, reduction of substance abuse, and changes in diet and exercise patterns. These lifestyle changes can be affected by work-based programs that include assessment, behavior change planning, and support.

Training programs to help employees develop competencies in daily living can also build strengths needed to cope with stressful situations. Group efforts are also useful because they can efficiently address many of the same problems that counselors tend to see in one-to-one situations. Among the issues that lend themselves to educational approaches are parenting, marriage relationships, and communication skills.

EAP counselors can also have an impact on their organizations by assisting in the recognition and elimination of unnecessary stressors in the work environment. Efforts to change the work setting should take into account such factors as person–environment fit, organizational climate, physical stressors, and the importance of social support. Employee assistance consultants can utilize their human relations skills to bring about positive changes in the work environment and prevent stress-related problems from occurring.

REFERENCES

Apgar, K., Riley, D. P., Eaton, J. T., and Diskin, S. (1982). *Life education in the workplace: How to design, lead, and market employee seminars.* New York: Family Service Association of America.

Ardell, D. B., and Tager, M. J. (1982). *Planning for wellness: A guidebook for achieving optimal health* (2nd ed.). Dubuque, IA: Kendall/Hunt.

Bandura, A. (1982). Self-efficacy mechanism in human agency. *American Psychologist, 37,* 122–147.

Barrow, J. C., and Prosen, S. S. (1981). A model of stress and counseling interventions. *The Personnel and Guidance Journal, 60,* 5–10.

Benson, H. (1975). *The relaxation response.* New York: Morrow.

Cherniss, C. (1980). *Professional burnout in human service organizations.* New York: Praeger.

Dinkmeyer, D., and Carlson, J. (1984). *Training in marriage enrichment.* Circle Pines, MN: American Guidance Service.

Dinkmeyer, D., and McKay, G. (1976). *STEP: Systematic training for effective parenting.* Circle Pines, MN: American Guidance Service.

Dinkmeyer, D., and McKay, G. (1983). *STEP/Teen.* Circle Pines, MN: American Guidance Service.

Dohrenwend, B. S. (1978). Social stress and community psychology. *American Journal of Community Psychology, 6,* 1–14.

Drum, D. J., and Knott, J. E. (1977). *Structured groups for facilitating development.* New York: Human Sciences Press.

Friedman, M., and Rosenman, R. H. (1974). *Type A behavior and your heart.* New York: Knopf.

Gatchel, R. J., and Baum, A. (1983). *An introduction to health psychology.* Reading, MA: Addison-Wesley.

Goldfried, M. R., and Goldfried, A. P. (1980). Cognitive change methods. In F. H. Kanfer and A. P. Goldstein (Eds.), *Helping people change* (2nd ed.) (pp. 97–130). New York: Pergamon Press.

Gordon, T. (1971). *A new model for humanizing families and schools.* Pasadena: Effectiveness Training Associates.

Heller, K., Price, R. H., and Sher, K. J. (1980). Research and evaluation in primary prevention. In R. H. Price, R. F. Ketterer, B. C. Bader, and J. Monahan (Eds.), *Prevention in mental health: Research, policy, and practice* (pp. 285–313). Beverly Hills: Sage.

House, J. S. (1981) *Work stress and social support.* Reading, MA: Addison-Wesley.

Ivancevich, J. M., and Matteson, M. T. (1980). *Stress and work: A managerial perspective.* Glenview, IL: Scott, Foresman.

Kobasa, S. C. (1979). Stressful life events, personality, and health: An inquiry into hardiness. *Journal of Personality and Social Psychology, 37,* 1–11.

Levi, L. (1981). *Preventing work stress.* Reading, MA: Addison-Wesley.

Matarazzo, J. D. (1982). Behavioral health's challenge to academic, scientific, and professional psychology. *American Psychologist, 37,* 1–14.

McCann, J. P. (1981). Control Data's Staywell program. *Training and Development Journal, 35*(10), 39–43.

Michael, J. M. (1982). The second revolution in health: Health promotion and its environmental base. *American Psychologist, 37,* 936–941.

Moracco, J. C., and McFadden, H. (1982). The counselor's role in reducing teacher stress. *The Personnel and Guidance Journal, 60,* 549–552.

Newman, J. E., and Beehr, T. A. (1979). Personal and organizational strategies for handling job stress: A review of research and opinion. *Personnel Psychology, 32,* 1–43.

President's Commission on Mental Health (1978). *Report of the task panel on prevention.* Washington, D.C.: U.S. Government Printing Office.

Price, R. H., Bader, B. C., and Ketterer, R. F. (1980). Prevention in community mental health: The state of the art. In R. H. Price, R. F. Ketterer, B. C. Bader, and J. Monahan (Eds.), *Prevention in mental health: Research, policy, and practice* (pp. 9–20). Beverly Hills: Sage.

Shain, M. (1983). Prevention of substance abuse through health promotion in the workplace. *EAP Digest, 3*(6), 39–41, 47–51.

Shea, G. F. (1981). Profiting from wellness training. *Training and Development Journal, 35*(10), 32–37.

Sparks, D., and Ingram, M. J. (1979). Stress prevention and management: A workshop approach. *The Personnel and Guidance Journal, 56,* 197–200.

Taylor, R. C. R. (1982). The politics of prevention. *Social Policy, 13*(1), 32–41.

Veninga, R. L., and Spradley, J. P. (1981). *The work/stress connection: How to cope with job burnout.* Boston: Little, Brown.

Wilcox, B. L. (1981). Social support, life stress, and psychological adjustment: A test of the buffering hypothesis. *American Journal of Community Psychology, 9,* 371–386.

Part Three

CAREER DEVELOPMENT PROGRAMS

Chapter Seven

CAREER COUNSELING

Career counseling is becoming an important component in human resource development as managers begin to recognize the need to blend individual and organizational goals. The continued growth of these programs, however, depends on their quality, their conceptual frameworks, and their integration into the corporate setting.

> All too often, career planning is practiced as an isolated employee activity without either realistic career path information or relevant appraisal and counseling inputs. Techniques such as career-planning or life-planning workshops, structured individual planning exercises, and self-improvement materials are widely popular today . . . However, individual career analysis and planning without career path information and other managerial inputs is like sailing without having a chart or knowing the seas. It is fun for a while, but becomes frustrating for individuals who wish to get somewhere (Walker, 1980, p. 323).

Career counselors who want to help employees "get somewhere" need to base their methods on systems that take into account both the nature of adult career choices and the realities of the organizational context.

THE ORGANIZATIONAL CONTEXT

Career counselors serving employees in their work settings practice within an organizational context. Their attempts to assist individuals can be effective only to the degree that the organization supports employees' career planning efforts.

> The systems approach demands that effective career planning be tied to the organization's identified human resources needs, to its training and development program, and to its selection and placement system. Without these factors, it

won't take employees long to see that career planning amounts to little more than a useless and time-consuming exercise (Vosburg, 1980, p. 837).

Employees need to be assured that their career plans are appropriate to the organization's needs and that they will have a chance of realizing their goals. Both career counselors and their clients need to know that the results of their endeavors are valued by the company. Although the counselor is expected to provide conceptually sound services and the employee to take ultimate responsibility for his or her career, the organization as a whole also has major responsibilities related to career planning. The organizational role includes:

- Developing and communicating career paths.
- Communicating information concerning opportunities within the company.
- Encouraging and training managers to support their employees' career planning efforts.
- Providing support through training, enrichment, and tuition reimbursement programs.
- Encouraging employees to utilize career counseling/planning resources.

Career Paths

The career progression of any individual employee is affected by the career paths available within the organization. Possible sequences of work experiences need to be identified in concrete terms and then communicated clearly to affected employees. These career paths should not be defined strictly in terms of a narrow line toward upward mobility; they should also provide guidelines for lateral progressions between functions, units, or locations. Walker (1980, p. 314) suggests that, in defining career paths, organizations should take the following steps:

1. Gather data on actual work activities, their relative importance, and the relative time allocation to each.
2. Determine, through analysis of these activities, the skill, knowledge, and other qualifications required to perform these activities effectively.
3. Identify patterns of similarity among positions, based on their content and skill-knowledge requirements, and grouping of similar positions as job families.
4. Identify logically possible progression lines among these job families, representing career paths.
5. Integrate the overall network of these paths as a single, career system depicting progression possibilities.

Walker recognizes that some organizations continue to use historical paths, which are based on past patterns of promotion among senior employees, or organizational paths, which rely on management's perception of staffing needs. Behavioral paths, which "represent the logical and possible sequences of positions that could be held, based on an analysis of what people actually do in an organization" (Walker, 1980, p. 318), provide the kind of flexibility and mobility most useful in a career planning context. Once such paths have been identified, they can be elaborated upon by means of brief job descriptions to be made available to employees who are in the process of planning their careers.

Information Systems

In order for employees to develop and carry out career plans effectively, they need to be informed of their options within the organization. One easily implemented aspect of the information system is a job posting program, which informs all employees of job openings within the company. Wallrapp (1981) observes that, within one company, a job posting program for nonexempt employees had impact on individual career development, equal opportunity, organizational communications, the discovery of hidden talent, and the rate of turnover. Because all employees had direct information about opportunities, they could identify themselves as people interested in change or promotion, avoid possible favoritism in supervisors' selections, and gain broader knowledge about the company for future planning.

Vosburg (1980) suggests that organizations strengthen the linkage between individual career planning and organizational human resource planning through an annual "human resource review." The purpose of such a review is to sanction individual plans and develop methods for integrating these plans into the selection process for new positions. If an individual's plan has been approved, it must be considered appropriate to the organization's needs and realistic in terms of the individual's performance. Therefore, selection lists for new positions automatically include the names of people listing such positions in their career plans; "the approved plans identify the relevant talent pool for any position which opens up . . . What can be favorably affected is the quality and completeness of a selection list, as well as the search time required to generate such a list" (Vosburg, 1980, p. 831).

Managerial Support

The integration of career planning into the mainstream of organizational activity depends on the willingness of managers to become involved in their employees' development. Among the responsibilities reserved for managers are six listed by Zenger (1981, p. 49).

1. Inform employees of the opportunities that exist within the company for job expansion and for upward mobility expansion.
2. Give feedback to employees to help them know how their performance is

currently perceived, to better understand strengths and weaknesses, and to agree upon development activities.

3. Provide information to the employee about what the organization seeks in individuals to be promoted . . .
4. Teach individuals how to manage their own careers . . .
5. Assist in the development of action plans for each employee's career development.
6. The manager must also give enormous support to make these action plans happen.

Although professional career counselors can enhance the planning process of individual employees, managerial input is sorely needed. It is the manager or immediate supervisor who knows enough about the employee's strengths and immediate chances for mobility to provide realistic information. Moreover, when managers see themselves as being involved in career planning, they can utilize performance appraisals as a means for promoting employee growth as well as for evaluation.

In general, supervisors become involved in their supervisees' career plans by performing a number of distinct roles, each of which can be considered part of the normal managerial process. Leibowitz and Schlossberg (1981, p. 73) have identified and defined nine:[1]

- *Communicator:* One who promotes a two-way exchange between himself/herself and the employee.
- *Counselor:* One who helps the employee to clarify goals and identify steps to take in reaching these goals, whether or not they relate to the present organization.
- *Appraiser:* One who evaluates an employee's performance, gives feedback to the employee, and helps to work out a development plan so that the employee can negotiate the goals and objectives specific to the current job.
- *Coach:* One who gives instruction or skill training to enable an employee to do his/her job more effectively.
- *Mentor:* One who serves as a sponsor to facilitate an employee's career growth.
- *Advisor:* One who gives information about career opportunities both within and outside the organization.
- *Broker:* One who serves as an agent (go-between) for the employee and appropriate resources such as people, institutions for information.
- *Referral Agent:* One who identifies resources to help an employee with specific problems.
- *Advocate:* One who intervenes on behalf of an employee for benefits, promotions, and elimination of obstacles.

---

[1] From "Training managers for their role in a career development system" by Z. B. Leibowitz and N. K. Schlossberg, 1981, *Training and Development Journal, 35*(7), pp. 72–79. Copyright 1981 by ASTD. Reprinted by permission.

Many of these roles require a high degree of interpersonal skills, and career counseling professionals should be prepared to help supervisors develop proficiency in carrying out their functions. Supervisors, like any employees, also need support and encouragement, and they are likely to make major efforts in the career planning area only if they know that such activities are valued in the organization. "When managers are rewarded for coaching employees, having subordinates move into management, and following through on subordinate development plans, then career planning will happen" (Zenger, 1981, p. 52).

Training and Enrichment Programs

Employees' career plans do not always focus solely on moving into new positions. Often, employees receiving career counseling realize that their next step should be in the direction of broadening their work skills or developing new competencies. Part of the organization's commitment to career development entails the provision of resources and opportunities to bring these plans to fruition.

Most large companies have both internal training programs and tuition reimbursement programs that encourage employees to take college-level courses. If the employee links self-development efforts with the career plan, he or she can usually identify a number of less formal experiences that can accomplish the same ends. Among those suggested by Kaye (1983) are on-the-job training; job rotation, which involves moving employees to diverse tasks at set intervals; special projects; mentor relations; and involvement with groups and associations. These kinds of experiences can serve as individual career development strategies, allowing employees to broaden their knowledge of the company, receive useful advice, assess their interests and capacities, and prepare themselves for career progressions.

Involvement in training and enrichment experiences is most useful for employees who have definite career plans; they can select those contacts and activities that are most likely to help them attain their goals. But informal training resources actually require more commitment and support from the organization than do formal training courses or tuition reimbursement programs. Linking training to the career plan requires management to endorse employee development and to provide the kind of atmosphere that encourages highly individualized structures and arrangements.

Career Counseling/Planning Resources

Finally, the organization demonstrates its commitment to employee career development by encouraging employees to take responsibility for their careers and *providing the resources that allow them to do so*. In discussing the "triad of shared responsibility," Leibowitz and Schlossberg (1981) suggest that the individual employee, the supervisor, and the organization all have important roles to play in developing careers.

> To leave employees entirely on their own is to abnegate corporate responsibility in the increasingly complex world of work; on the other hand, the organization should not be totally paternalistic but should allow the employee some initiative. Thus, besides offering training for managers, the organization must see to it that employees are given an opportunity to participate in career planning and self-assessment activities (p. 75).

The professional counselor serving employees in the workplace can act as a linchpin, connecting the organization, the supervisor, and the employee in the career planning effort. The counselor surely needs organizational support; however, he or she also has the responsibility to provide support in return. The counselor can play a major role in the company by (a) consulting with organizational policy makers as they seek to create an environment that encourages planned career development and (b) training supervisors to carry out their part of the process. The counselor can then provide employees with assistance that is enhanced by a firm organizational commitment and, equally important, informed by a theoretical model of career choice.

THEORETICAL APPROACHES TO CAREER COUNSELING

Career counseling materials for use by individuals or groups have become prevalent in recent years. Unfortunately, some practitioners have used these materials atheoretically, selecting a variety of techniques without being aware of their conceptual bases. In fact, each method used should be tested both in terms of its innate qualities and in terms of its appropriateness to the professional's assumptions and goals concerning vocational development and decision making.

At the very minimum, counselors should be aware of the distinction between what Weinrach (1979) terms structural approaches and process approaches. Structural career counseling theories focus on the interaction between the individual and the environment.

> Studying the *link* between them permits the counselor and the client to explore systematically not only the client's characteristics but also the characteristics of the marketplace . . . The link between the client and the environment is established by means of psychometric instruments and matrices that integrate client personality, needs, or interests with job titles or occupational groups (Weinrach, 1979, p. 56).

Process theories, in contrast, focus on the individual's development over a period of time. Such theories deal either with developmental stages through life or with decision making as an individual process. Although some methods may be appropriate for either structural or process-based counseling, many techniques that would work for one would be inappropriate for the other. Counselors can create coherent programs only if they are aware of the scope of relevant theories and cognizant of their similarities and differences. Each of the many approaches to career counseling offers its own explanation, descriptions, and guidelines for effective planning. Among the frameworks that many counselors have found useful in explaining career choices are trait-and-factor counseling, Holland's typology, Schein's career anchor concept, developmental career counseling, Tiedeman and O'Hara's decision-making paradigm, and social learning theory.

Trait-and-Factor Counseling

The historical roots of career counseling can be found in the work of the trait-and-factor theorists. Beginning in the time of Parsons (1909), counselors holding to this structural view have attempted to match individuals with appropriate work by taking into account characteristics of the individual and the environment. Normally, these counselors begin by examining such personal characteristics as job-related abilities, vocational interests, and personality type. They conclude by providing detailed information concerning occupations. The underlying assumption that guides this work is that human beings are rational and, given accurate information about themselves and the world of work, will make reasonable career choices.

As the counseling process begins, practitioners use interviews, self-reports, and a variety of standardized instruments to collect data concerning attitudes, abilities, interests, personality characteristics, education, family background, and other variables. These data are then analyzed and used to create a profile of the client that can serve as the basis for problem solving.

The individual's problems are analyzed, with attention paid to his or her progress and to any possible discrepancies between measured individual characteristics and declared interests or goals. This diagnostic process leads to a prognosis for resolving the individual's problems and the presentation of alternatives for the client to consider.

The trait-and-factor counselor is likely to take an active stand, advising the client about possible actions that he or she should take to resolve problems or become better adjusted. The counselor then assists the client as needed in carrying out an action program or moving on to the examination of new issues. These activities require a clear view not only of the client's traits but of the world of work. Counselors may present occupational information verbally, bring materials in for consideration as part of the interview process, or direct clients to appropriate sources. Their ultimate goal is to provide clients with sufficient knowledge about employment trends and job requirements to lay the basis for an appropriate selection that matches individual and job. The steps in this process are likely to include the following:

1. *Initial Interview.*

   The counselor and client use one or more interviews to establish a relationship and begin to examine the client's perception of the problem. The counselor uses the interview situation to begin gathering subjective data about the client's interests and concerns.

2. *Test Battery.*

   The counselor selects appropriate instruments that can provide more objective data about the client's characteristics. In general, the battery selected includes a combination of aptitude tests and interest inventories.

3. *Test Interpretation.*

   After the instruments have been scored, the counselor and client meet for a session devoted to interpretation of the results. The counselor is likely to take an active role in explaining the tests and discussing the results and their implications for the client.

4. *Summary of Options.*

   The counselor continues to take an active role, summarizing the results of the data-gathering phase and suggesting possible avenues for career exploration.

5. *Occupational Information.*

   With knowledge of his or her personal characteristics now in hand, the client explores in detail occupations or job roles that are within appropriate limits.

6. *Choice.*

   With the counselor's assistance, the client makes a choice concerning his or her immediate and long-range goals. It is assumed that this choice, based on accurate information, will be rational.

   If the diagnosis in Trait-and-Factor career counseling has been accurate, and if the process has been effective, then certain outcomes are expected. . . . Where there was indecision, there is now decision; where there was unrealism, there is now realism. In general, the goal is for the client to arrive, through a rational process of decision making and problem solving, at a career choice which is consonant with his or her educational-vocational capabilities and which can be implemented in the world of work (Crites, 1981, p. 31).

In the context of a work organization, the occupational information provided would tend to concentrate on career options and job descriptions within the company rather than on the kind of broad introduction to the world of work that a student might need. The counseling process would, however, remain concentrated on the use of objective information to provide the basis for cognitive decision making.

The Holland Typology

A sophisticated and widely used structural approach is the typology developed by Holland (1973). Holland's theory involves an examination of personality types as they relate to particular vocational environments. His assumption is that people of varying personality types will be attracted to careers that allow for their desired lifestyles.

Holland's original work categorized people according to the following types:

1. *Realistic* (people who prefer dealing with "things," rather than with people or data, and who enjoy work that involves the manipulation of machinery or other objects).
2. *Investigative* (people who enjoy analyzing data and who value the opportunity to satisfy their curiosity and use scientific methods for the solution of problems).
3. *Artistic* (individuals who are expressive or creative and who tend to avoid situations calling for very methodical manipulation of details).
4. *Social* (individuals who prefer working with other people and who avoid, if possible, working with data or things in isolated settings).
5. *Enterprising* (people who enjoy working toward economic or organizational goals, often by convincing or managing others).
6. *Conventional* (workers who enjoy systematic, even repetitive tasks, especially involving the manipulation of data).

Environments can be categorized by the same typology. A particular vocational environment may be characterized as falling within one of the six types, both because of the actual tasks being performed and because people of that type predominate in that environment. Specific jobs can be identified in terms of their appropriateness for realistic, investigative, artistic, social, enterprising, or conventional individuals.

Holland's model explains phenomena related to career choices and work satisfaction.

> People grow up to resemble one type or another because parents, schools, and neighborhoods serve as environments which reinforce some behaviors more than others and provide different models of suitable behavior . . . This experience contributes to the development of a characteristic cluster of personal traits. Consequently, when the need for choice of employment occurs, a person is predisposed toward some groups of occupations more than others . . . Satisfaction and success result from a congruency of person and environment (Holland and Gottfredson, 1978, p. 148).

Thus, people who are in environments that are congruent with their own types tend to find satisfaction and rewards in their careers. Most people have what Holland terms "orderly careers" because they know what activities bring them satisfaction and gravitate toward work environments that reward their particular talents and attitudes (that is, their types). Lack of involvement or satisfaction results either because of failure to find the right environment or because a lack of definition of personality type has made it difficult to identify an appropriate work setting.

These ideas form the basis both for a description of the realities of career development and for a prescription for effective career decisions. Holland's *Self-Directed Search* (1979b) uses a series of questions to help the individual identify his or her preferred style. The results are presented as three-letter summary codes that identify the first, second, and third strongest preferences. The use of the three-letter combination is based on the resemblances among types. Selection of an appropriate environment is relatively easy for an individual whose choices are consistent and difficult for one whose preferences are undifferentiated.

Some types are similar to one another; for example, enterprising and social types are similar, as are social and artistic types. Some types are seen as very dissimilar; investigating and enterprising types have little in common, and artistic and conventional categories are also distant.

An individual can be evaluated as consistent if his or her most characteristic types are similar. A person labeled by the letters ASE (artistic as the first choice, social and enterprising as the second and third) is consistent, since his or her types are complementary. A person labeled as SRI would be inconsistent, since the social type normally has little in common with the realistic or investigative. The inconsistent person might have difficulty selecting a rewarding work environment, as would an undifferentiated individual whose scores show a spread among several types.

If an individual has a reasonably consistent personality, he or she can identify congruent work environments. An individual would be likely to be unhappy in his or her work if the environment were characterized as a type that is distant from the individual's own (for example, an artistic type in a conventional setting), but fulfilled in a job in the same or similar type. Holland's *Occupations Finder* (1979a) lists occupations under sets of letters, or codes. Thus, an individual whose own code is SEA can identify a large number of potentially appropriate occupations by studying lists under SEA and, if necessary, closely related categories. In an organizational context, this process might help employees to examine the degree of congruence between their types and their current work environments and to make well-reasoned plans for career changes within the company.

Schein's "Career Anchor" Concept

Schein, like Holland, emphasizes the importance of a coherent set of values and attitudes that is formed at an early stage in career development. "These basic combinations of needs and drives act, in effect, as 'career anchors' that not only influence career choices but also affect decisions to move from one company to another, shape what the individuals are looking for in life, and color their views of the future and their general assessments of related goals and objectives" (Schein, 1975, p. 37). Although an individual's career may be partially anchored in a job description or organizational norms, it is also anchored by the needs and motives that he or she is trying to fulfill.

Schein identified several career themes by studying the histories of a group of Sloan School of Management alumni. These themes seemed to serve as anchors by pulling each person back to a set of values and central concerns. Five anchors were identified (Schein, 1975), including the following:

1. *Managerial Competence.*
Some participants in the study seemed to place primary value on their opportunities to demonstrate effectiveness in such managerial components as interpersonal competence, analytical competence, and emotional stability. These individuals desired increasingly more responsible roles within their organizations, primarily as line managers.

2. *Technical/Functional Competence.*
Individuals identified by their technical/functional anchors met their career needs through excellence in their specialized work. Their concern for carrying out specific functions or working in technical areas made them unwilling to move into general managerial positions.

3. *Security.*
Some respondents demonstrated an overriding concern with security, either remaining identified with one organization or placing emphasis on a desire to remain in one geographical location.

4. *Creativity.*
Participants placed in this category were characterized by a need to create something on an individual level; in the context of the business world, these individuals acted as entrepreneurs, developing new businesses, new products, or new services.

5. *Autonomy and Independence.*
Several respondents were concerned with safeguarding their freedom and autonomy, often leaving organizational settings to become consultants or develop careers allowing for independence.

Schein's approach is especially relevant for the organizational environment.

> If career anchors do indeed function as stable syndromes in the personality, it becomes important for employing organizations to identify these syndromes early. It does little good, for example, to offer promotion into management to someone who basically does not want to be a manager but whose basic goal is attainment of technical/functional competence or who is anchored instead to entre-

preneurial, creative, or primarily autonomous activities. The organization stands to gain by creating career opportunities that are congruent with the basic anchor needs of its human talent (Schein, 1975, p. 38).

The counselor in the work setting can help individuals identify their anchors and seek opportunities to meet their needs within the organization. Often, such an analysis can help an employee avoid the mistaken assumption that the only way to progress in a career is through upward moves toward high-level management positions. People with technical/functional or creative anchors might find lateral moves or moves within a separate, professional/technical hierarchy to be more fulfilling.

Developmental Career Counseling

Career development can be seen as a lifetime process, associated not just with a series of jobs but with the entire self-concept. As formulated by Super, developmental career counseling attempts to examine and affect the process of career maturation over time.

> Vocational preferences and competencies, the situations in which people live and work, and hence their self-concepts, change with time and experience . . . , making choice and adjustment a continuous process . . . Development through the life stages can be guided, partly by facilitating the process of maturation of abilities and interests and partly by aiding in reality testing and in the development of the self-concept (Super, 1953, p. 188).

Career development, as seen by Super, is an orderly process in which individuals move through a predictable series of life stages, including growth, exploration, establishment, maintenance, and decline. As this process unfolds, the individual attempts to develop and implement his or her self-concept. No one occupation or one decision is right for an individual. Instead, satisfactory adjustment is based on compromises among personality traits, social factors, and life events. "Work satisfactions and life satisfactions depend upon the extent to which the individual finds adequate outlets for his abilities, interests, personality traits, and values; they depend upon his establishment in a type of work, a work situation, and a way of life in which he can play the kind of role which his growth and exploratory experiences have led him to consider congenial and appropriate" (Super, 1953, p. 188).

Although developmental career counselors use appraisal methods, such methods tend to be broader in scope than those utilized by structural practitioners. The client's active involvement in exploring his or her current adjustment and past development leads to a tentative analysis of the kinds of work roles most likely to enhance satisfaction. The appraisal also serves the purpose of identifying the client's career life stage. If the client is at an early stage of development, the counselor focuses on increasing his or her readiness for entering a decision-making process. If clients are mature in terms of their vocational development, they can move immediately into active decision making and reality testing.

The holistic approach that characterizes the developmental model is useful for the practitioner who is counseling in an organizational setting. Career development programs in business and industry are built on the notion that adults continue to grow and change throughout their careers and that this developmental process can be enhanced by facilitators in the work setting.

Decision-Making Paradigm

Counselors find it useful to study decision-making models such as that described by Tiedeman and O'Hara (1963). According to this model, decision making involves two aspects: anticipation or preoccupation and implementation or adjustment.

In the first stage, anticipation, the individual becomes involved in exploration, crystallization, choice, and clarification. Exploration begins when the person becomes aware that a decision must be reached. A number of goals or alternatives are considered in a somewhat random fashion. "Those goals available to awareness in the study of a problem are affected by: (1) the individual's prior experience; (2) the degree of investment of himself in the continuation or modification of his existing stage and of the situation in which the problem is to be resolved; and (3) the help he may seek or be given in attacking his problem" (Tiedeman and O'Hara, 1963, p. 38). Crystallization brings recognition of the advantages and disadvantages of several alternatives and a degree of stabilization in the individual's thinking. Choice follows crystallization, the individual being ready now to act in accordance with his or her goal selection. As the individual waits for the implementation stage, further clarification of the choice takes place.

The Tiedeman and O'Hara paradigm recognizes that choice is not the end result of the decision-making process. The stage of implementation means that "imagination meets reality." The first step, induction, involves the first meeting of individual goals and social purposes. If the individual is accepted into the new social system, he or she begins to identify with it, leading to the reformation step, when he or she starts to influence the newfound group in turn. In the final step, the individual is integrated into the larger system and, concurrently, the "new part of the self-system becomes a working member of the whole self-system" (p. 44).

The counselor has a supportive role to play as the decision maker moves from stage to stage in this process. When the client is in the stage of anticipation, he or she is likely to need assistance in clarifying goals and recognizing the range of possible alternatives. At the implementation stage, assistance is needed in action planning and identification of ways to implement the choice that has been made.

Gerstein (1982) suggests that the Tiedeman-O'Hara paradigm could form the basis for a comprehensive program to meet the career development needs of adult workers.

> If the model . . . is used as the organizational matrix for career counseling services, it is possible to establish a process of assessment and counseling specifically tailored to the individual adult. In addition to framing the organizational structure of the career counseling services, the model can also be used by the counselor or human resource utilization specialist to determine which strategies are most appropriate for each client. Once it is implemented, the model can be used to structure the counseling service offered by identifying the services and programs that fit in each major stage of Anticipation and Implementation (Gerstein, 1982, pp. 319–320).

Thus, the career development program can include a variety of interventions aimed toward the needs of employees at various stages in the decision-making process.

Social Learning Theory

Social learning theorists explain career decision making in terms of the interaction among genetic qualities, environmental conditions and events, learning experiences, and task approach skills (Krumboltz, Mitchell, and Jones, 1978). As a result of these interactions, people make generalizations about themselves and their characteristics, develop varying degrees of skill in problem solving, and embark on what they have come to see as appropriate career entry actions. "It is the sequential cumulative effects of numerous learning experiences affected by various environmental circumstances and the individual's cognitive and emotional reactions to these learning experiences and circumstances that cause a person to make decisions to enroll in a certain educational program or become employed in a particular occupation" (Krumboltz, Mitchell, and Jones, 1978, p. 113).

These generalizations hold a number of implications for career counselors and clients, which Krumboltz, Mitchell, and Jones summarize as the following:[2]

1. Occupational placement is the result of a complex interaction of genetic components, environmental events and conditions, and learning experiences which result in the development of various task approach skills.

2. Career selection is a mutual process influenced not only by decisions made by each individual involved but also by social forces which affect occupational availability and requirements. People select, and are selected by, occupations.

---

[2]From "A social learning theory of career selection" by J. D. Krumboltz, A. M. Mitchell, and G. B. Jones, 1978. In J. M. Whiteley and A. Resnikoff (Eds.), *Career counseling.* Monterey, CA: Brooks/Cole. Copyright 1978 by Wadsworth Publishing Company. Reprinted by permission.

3. Career selection is a lifelong process. It does not take place at one point in time, but is shaped by events and decisions that occur from infancy through the retirement years.

4. Career selection is caused—not accidental—but the interaction of causal events is so complex that the prediction of occupational selection for any one individual is virtually impossible with any degree of certainty.

5. Career indecision is due to the unsatisfactory nature of an insufficient number of career-relevant learning experiences or to the fact that the person has not yet learned and applied a systematic way of making career decisions. Indecision is a natural result of not yet having had certain learning experiences. An undecided person has no reason to feel guilty or inadequate.

6. Career counseling is not merely a process of matching existing personal characteristics with existing job characteristics, but instead is a process of opening up new learning experiences and motivating a client to initiate career-relevant exploratory activities.

7. The responsibilities of a career counselor, then, are as follows:
   a. to help the client learn a rational sequence of career decision-making skills.
   b. to help the client arrange an appropriate sequence of career-relevant exploratory-learning experiences, and
   c. to teach the client how to evaluate the personal consequences of those learning experiences.

The social learning approach differs from the other models in that its primary emphasis is placed not on matching people with appropriate jobs but on teaching decision-making behaviors. Among the activities that might be used in behavioral career counseling are decision-making simulations, social modeling, behavioral design, and reinforcement of exploratory and choice-making activities.

Any of the major theories can be adapted for use with individuals or groups. What the counselor's theoretical framework does is to give focus and direction to his or her work with individual employees. All career counselors attempt to help their clients with self-assessment, goal setting, decision making, and long-range planning, but the nature of these processes is affected by the model being used as well as by the exigencies of the specific organization. Combining an awareness of organizational needs with a firm theoretical commitment allows the counselor to work toward the development of individual career plans that are both imaginative and realistic.

INDIVIDUAL CAREER PLANNING

Career counselors in work settings normally use a combination of structured workshops and individual interviews to enhance the planning and decision-making skills of employees. Whichever method is used, the intervention is likely to involve three components: (a) self-assessment procedures, (b) goal-setting activities, and (c) strategy formulation.

Self-Assessment

The self-assessment component allows employees to begin the planning process by examining their own assets, characteristics, interests, and current level of development. The methods of self-assessment made available by the counselor are likely to differ on the basis of the conceptual framework guiding the counseling process. Initially, the counselor and client can choose between standardized instruments or less formal mechanisms.

Standardized instruments.   A number of instruments are available to help clients assess their interests, values, or career stages. Although such instruments cannot replace personal counseling and exploration, they can sometimes serve as tools to complement the decision-making process. Among the standardized instruments available are the following:

The *Career Maturity Inventory* (New York: McGraw-Hill) can act as a useful adjunct to developmentally oriented career counseling. The CMI assesses two aspects of career maturity: attitudes and competence. The attitude scale attempts to measure involvement, independence, orientation, decisiveness, and compromise, all of which are considered important in decision making. The competence scale measures self-appraisal, occupational information, goal selection, planning, and problem solving in an attempt to determine the client's level of development in the cognitive areas involved in career choice. Being aware of the employee's attitudes and cognitions as they affect career decision making can help the counselor decide on the most appropriate steps to take in providing assistance.

The employee's interests can be clarified through use of the *Strong-Campbell Interest Inventory* (Palo Alto, CA: Stanford University Press). This inventory asks subjects to identify their reactions to a number of items as "like," "dislike," or "indifferent." Items deal with occupations, academic subjects, activities, amusements, types of people, and personal characteristics. Scores can be interpreted in terms of basic interests and matched with a number of specific occupations.

The *Kuder Preference Records and Interest Surveys* (Chicago: Science Research Associates) also measure interests. The simple, self-scoring instruments ask the subject to choose the least and most liked choices from among groups of three activities. Interests are measured in terms of ten categories: outdoor, mechanical, computational, scientific, persuasive, artistic, literary, musical, social service, and clerical.

The *Self-Directed Search* (Palo Alto, CA: Consulting Psychologists Press) was developed by Holland to assess the types described in his theoretical model. Clients can use a self-administered, self-scoring workbook to determine the summary code that indicates their vocational types. The summary code is then used with an *Occupations Finder* that lists 500 occupations also categorized by code. This assessment helps individuals begin to identify occupations that are congruent with realistic, investigative, artistic, social, enterprising, or conventional types. Holland also developed the *Vocational Preference Inventory* (Palo Alto, CA: Consulting Psychologists Press), which is based on selections from a list of job titles and which also leads to identification of vocational types.

Informal assessments.   Self-awareness can also be developed through informal exercises, open-ended questions, and nonstandardized checklists. These activities help employees prepare for goal setting by identifying the values, interests, and attitudes that are important to them. Often, an individual's real values become apparent when he or she considers the occasions when life and work have seemed especially rewarding.

Bolles (1977) suggests that decision makers use self-administered exercises to help themselves analyze their memories of the past, their feelings about the present, and their visions of the future. Past-oriented exercises include writing diaries, analyzing hobbies, and remembering satisfying achievements—all designed to provide clues about the skills and activities that give one feelings of satisfaction and achievement. Exercises that make use of current feelings include listing things that make one happy or unhappy and searching for common denominators among various forms of self-identification. Visions of the future can take the form of desired accomplishments or the ultimate goals implied by current, valued activities. All of these exercises combine to give the individual a picture of the kinds of activities that should be involved in any career move being considered.

Life work planning exercises such as the ones developed by Kirn and Kirn (1978) also examine the past, present, and future. Among the activities that are most helpful in laying the groundwork for decision making are describing peak work experiences; writing fantasies; completing self-inventories dealing with skills, attributes, and preferences; identifying positive work environments; and creating life work calendars.

In the organizational context, the self-assessment process can be expanded to include attention to performance appraisals in the current job, input from supervisors, and consideration of the realities of the immediate situation. The application of knowledge derived from these three factors in combination can prepare the employee for the all-important task of formulating career goals.

Goal Selection

With information about the self and the organization in hand, the employee can begin to formulate immediate and long-range goals. It is important at this point for employees to recognize that they can select among a wide variety of options, not all of which involve moving "up the career ladder."

Six of these options are:

1. *Vertical*—Moving to the next higher position.
2. *Lateral*—Moving across functions.
3. *Realignment (downward) in the system*—Moving to a lesser position.
4. *Exploratory research*—Actively investigating other options.
5. *Job enrichment*—Creating more challenge in the present job.
6. *Relocation out of the system*—Leaving the organization (Kaye, 1980, p. 368).

Kaye suggests that, because employees need to keep open as many choices as possible, they should be encouraged to select at least one goal for each of the options rather than concentrate solely on the "long shot" of vertical mobility.

When employees begin to write their goal statements, they can use information about the organization's career paths and resources as the basis for revising their objectives. If the counselor can provide input and also direct employees to supplementary sources of information, he or she can help clients develop goals that are both congruent with their own values and realistic in terms of the specific work organization. Ultimately, the employee needs to devise goal statements that are specific, measurable, and attainable.

> If the employee is ever going to be successful in implementing this goal, it must be one such that:
>
> 1. The employee clearly has the relevant skills, knowledge, experience and other requirements to attain the goal (or can reasonably obtain them)
> 2. The goal is relevant to the needs and desires of the individual so that he or she is motivated to attain it
> 3. The goal represents an organizational need, a demand for the commodity that the employee wishes to supply (Kaye, 1980, p. 372).

In assisting the employee to develop meaningful and attainable goals, the counselor uses both his or her own expertise and the support of other members of the organization. As the employee develops a strategy for reaching his or her goals, organizational encouragement becomes even more important.

Strategy Formulation

The steps of self-assessment and goal-setting gain meaning because they lead to plans of action.

> Self-exploration can be no more than an exercise in self-aggrandizement unless it leads to something. The real purpose of self-exploration is to provide a foundation from which individuals can clarify directions for future growth and development and initiate plans to achieve their goals. And the more specific and

thoughtful the action plans, the greater the likelihood that the goals will be reached (Fisher and Walz, 1982, p. 65).

Each employee should emerge from the career counseling process with a concrete set of strategies for goal attainment, whether the immediate steps to be taken involve self-development or attempts to change one's role within the organization.

For every goal that has been formulated, the employee should be able to design a program of action that is likely to lead to successful attainment. The development of this action plan begins with the generation of a number of alternatives, progresses through a careful weighing of the costs and benefits of each option, and ends with a concrete list of goal-directed activities. Each strategy selected needs to be realistic, controllable, and timed in terms of starting and completion dates.

Some employees may focus their action plans on self-improvement, either in terms of personal or job-related skills. Whether an individual wants to improve assertiveness or learn accounting, manage time or manage people, he or she needs to consider the training options that are available and choose carefully among formal and informal learning processes. The counselor's assistance in identifying organizational resources and encouraging reality checks can be an important part of this process.

Efforts to move toward new roles in the work setting require even more complex strategies, since the individual's success will depend, at least in part, on the behaviors of others. An employee's action plan should be based on steps that he or she can take as an individual. Many of these steps must, however, involve developing visibility and seeking support from mentors and other key figures in the organization. Ultimately, the individual's career plan and the company's human resource needs can prove to be congruent.

Summary

Career counseling designed for employees in their work settings should be informed by theoretical models of career choice and enhanced by organizational commitment. Counselors need to base their work both on the realities of the corporate context and on a systematic examination of adult career development.

Although career counseling theories can guide their work, counselors know that their success depends on the nature of the organizational environment. Aspects of the organization's role in career development include developing and communicating career paths; communicating information concerning opportunities within the company; encouraging and training managers to support their employees' career planning efforts; providing support through training, enrichment, and tuition reimbursement programs; and encouraging employees to utilize career counseling/planning resources. The counselor can enhance these efforts by consulting with organizational policy makers and training supervisors to carry out their part in encouraging employee career progression.

The specific methods used in career counseling should be selected in terms of their appropriateness to the professional's assumptions and goals about vocational decision making. A number of theoretical frameworks have been developed to describe and explain career choice. Among them are trait-and-factor counseling, Holland's typology, Schein's career anchor concept, developmental career counseling, decision-making paradigms, and social learning approaches.

Counseling and organizational support ultimately lead to the creation and attainment of individual career plans. Through structured workshops, individual interviews, and information dissemination, counselors assist employees in self-assessment, goal-setting, and strategy formulation. Ideally, these processes lead to career plans that succeed in meeting both individual and organizational needs.

REFERENCES

Bolles, R. N. (1977). *What color is your parachute?* Berkeley, CA: Ten Speed Press.

Crites, J. O. (1981). *Career counseling: Models, methods, and materials.* New York: McGraw-Hill.

Fisher, D. J., and Walz, G. R. (1982). Self-exploration in career development. In G. Walz (Ed.), *Career development in organizations* (pp. 47–66). Ann Arbor, MI: ERIC/CAPS (Educational Resource Information Center/Counseling and Personnel Services).

Gerstein, M. (1982). Vocational counseling for adults in varied settings: A comprehensive view. *The Vocational Guidance Quarterly, 30,* 315–322.

Holland, J. L. (1973). *Making vocational choices: A theory of careers.* Englewood Cliffs, NJ: Prentice-Hall.

Holland, J. L. (1979a) *The occupations finder.* Palo Alto, CA: Consulting Psychologists Press.

Holland, J. L. (1979b) *Self-Directed Search: A guide to educational and vocational planning.* Palo Alto, CA: Consulting Psychologists Press.

Holland, J. L., and Gottfredson, G. D. (1978). Using a typology of persons and environments to explain careers: Some extensions and clarifications. In J. M. Whiteley and A. Resnikoff (Eds.), *Career counseling* (pp. 146–170). Monterey, CA: Brooks/Cole.

Kaye, B. (1980). How you can help employees formulate their career goals. *Personnel Journal, 58,* 368–372, 402.

Kaye, B. (1983). Career development puts training in its place. *Personnel Journal, 62,* 132–137.

Kirn, A. G., and Kirn, M. O. (1978). *Life work planning* (4th ed.). New York: McGraw-Hill.

Krumboltz, J. D., Mitchell, A. M., and Jones, G. B. (1978). A social learning theory of career selection. In J. M. Whiteley and A. Resnikoff (Eds.), *Career counseling* (pp. 100–127). Monterey, CA: Brooks/Cole.

Leibowitz, Z. B., and Schlossberg, N. K. (1981). Training managers for their role in a career development system. *Training and Development Journal, 35*(7), 72–79.

Parsons, F. (1909). *Choosing a vocation.* Boston: Houghton Mifflin.

Schein, E. H. (1975) How "career anchors" hold executives to their career paths. In J. M. Roach (Ed.), *Career planning* (pp. 37–50). New York: AMACOM (American Management Association).

Super, D. E. (1953). A theory of vocational development. *American Psychologist, 8,* 185–190.

Tiedeman, D. V., and O'Hara, R. P. (1963). *Career development: Choice and adjustment.* New York: College Entrance Examination Board.

Vosburg, R. M. (1980). The annual human resource review. *Personnel Journal, 59,* 830–837.

Walker, J. W. (1980). *Human resource planning.* New York: McGraw-Hill.

Wallrapp, G. G. (1981). Job posting for nonexempt employees: A sample program. *Personnel Journal, 60,* 796–798.

Weinrach, S. G. (1979). *Career counseling: Theoretical and practical perspectives.* New York: McGraw-Hill.

Zenger, J. H. (1981). Career planning: Coming in from the cold. *Training and Development Journal, 35*(7), 46–53.

Chapter Eight

TRANSITIONAL COUNSELING

At any given moment, a number of employees in an organization may be undergoing transitions from one type of role or situation to another. In the work setting, such significant transitions include induction into the organization, relocation to new geographical areas, retirement, and even job loss. Counselors can have a major impact on employee well-being by helping individuals make successful adaptations to these new situations and alleviating the stress that often accompanies change.

Of course, one would expect an event like job loss, over which an employee has no control, to be more stressful and problematic than a freely chosen, positive transition, such as starting a new job. We know, however, that any situation that places new demands on a person can be perceived as threatening. The degree to which an event acts as a stressor depends on the individual's interpretation of the demand and his or her ability to cope with it.

Lazarus (1980) points out that a transaction between a situation and an individual can be appraised by that individual as irrelevant, benign-positive, or stressful. Those situations that are appraised as stressful can be divided into those that represent harm or loss, those that represent anticipated threats to well-being, and those that represent challenges.

> The distinction between harm/loss, threat, and challenge may be very important not only in affecting the coping process itself and the effectiveness with which coping skills are utilized in social transactions, but also in their divergent consequences for morale and somatic health . . . A working hypothesis about the causal antecedents of threat and challenge is that the former is more likely when a person assumes that the specific environment is hostile and dangerous and that he or she lacks the resources for mastering it, while challenge arises when the environmental demands are seen as difficult but not impossible to manage, and

that drawing upon existing or acquirable skills offers a genuine prospect for mastery (Lazarus, 1980, pp. 47–48).

Stensrud and Stensrud (1983) suggest that a useful approach for counselors to take is to encourage clients to take "personal control of their lives, accepting stress as a challenge rather than a harm-loss-threat factor, and finding personal meaning within stressful situations" (p. 216). This kind of attitude holds the promise of mastery, even in the face of very difficult transitions.

As counselors consider the means they can use to increase the likelihood of positive adaptations among employees, they need to take into account the kinds of factors that tend to mediate the effects of potentially crisis-inducing life changes. Once counselors become aware of the personal and situational characteristics that work in favor of successful coping, they can develop methods for creating mastery-enhancing conditions. Several factors seem to characterize people who are successful in making adaptations to trying conditions.

1. *Successful Copers Have Strong Social Support Systems.*
The availability of supportive associates seems to provide a buffer against the effects of stressful situations. Such relationships provide both personal validation and practical assistance; people faced with troublesome situations can turn to family members, friends, or associates for information, advice, and concrete resources as well as emotional sustenance.

2. *Successful Copers Tend to Have a Sense of Control over the Environment.*
Whether we term this factor "self-efficacy" or "internal locus of control," we know that people who cope effectively tend to do so because they believe their actions can have an effect on the world. Individuals differ in their general belief systems concerning their ability to exert power and control when needed. In addition, the sense of control in a specific situation can be affected by the appraisal of the stressor and the presence or absence of adequate resources.

3. *Successful Copers Have the Information and Tools Needed for Effective Problem Solving.*
Individuals' coping success depends, at least in part, on their skill in solving immediate problems and developing appropriate new behaviors. This factor involves both general life competence and situation-specific knowledge.

4. *Successful Copers are Confident that They Can Adapt to the New Situation.*
Realistic feelings of confidence come from the fact that adequate personal and financial resources are available and that the individual has coped successfully with similar transitions in the past. One aspect of confidence-

building, then, is recognizing commonalities between the current situation and prior experiences. While the victim of job loss may never have been fired in the past, he or she has been successful in obtaining a position; the planning skills used at that time may still be valid.

Obviously, these factors are all closely related. Support systems provide help in problem solving, interpersonal skills enhance social relationships, and both help to increase the sense that control is possible. The counselor's task is to increase the chance for individual mastery by purposefully building support systems, encouraging self-efficacy, providing information and skill training, and inspiring confidence.

> We know that people faced with difficult life situations need to develop new and practical problem-solving strategies and approaches to everyday living. We also know that such people need close contact with others, new links to human beings who can provide support and encouragement. We can provide for these needs by creating self-help and educational opportunities for people currently facing volatile life changes (Lewis and Lewis, 1983, p. 113).

These general principles can be adapted to the special needs of employees attempting to cope with career transitions. Whether the transition in question involves induction, relocation, retirement, or job loss, affected individuals need as much help in exerting control and self-responsibility as they do in solving specific problems.

Interventions should serve to demonstrate the existence of an organizational support system that is available to each employee. Likert's principle of supportive relationship states that "the leadership and other processes of the organization must be such as to ensure a maximum probability that in all interactions and all relationships with the organization each member will, in the light of his background, values, and expectations, view the experience as supportive and one which builds and maintains his sense of personal worth and importance" (1978, p. 149). This sense of supportiveness is even more important for individuals dealing with job-related stressors. Leibowitz and Schlossberg (1982) state that "one of the most helpful interventions for individuals in transition and crisis is to structure support systems" (p. 14). Their workshops for employees in transition include three types of support: support from other participants experiencing the same type of transition, support from the workshop facilitators, and support from employees who have successfully dealt with similar transitions in the past.

Having the opportunity to give support may be as important for successful adaptation as receiving sustenance in return.

> When helping becomes a *mutual* occupation, each participant becomes aware of his or her value to others. In "self-help" organizations, people with common bonds have the opportunity to make contact with one another, to provide mutual support, to request or provide active assistance, and to deal with common problems in an understanding but realistic group" (Lewis and Lewis, 1983, p. 124).

A strong self-help component should be built into any counseling effort for employees dealing with retirement or outplacement, since they may feel that their personal/social value is at stake. If several employees are facing similar transitions at once, the counselor should attempt to provide assistance through workshops, seminars, or group counseling situations. This approach can increase the support and practical resources available to each client, while enhancing feelings of usefulness and efficacy.

People in transition also need concrete information and assistance in problem solving. Cognitive information about such practical matters as benefits and finances can enhance the planning process, while "emphasis . . . on helping these employees with anticipatory socialization, learning the rules, norms, roles and expectations of their new or aspired-to roles" (Leibowitz and Schlossberg, 1982, p. 14) can increase their feelings of confidence and security. Training in problem solving related to the immediate transition can use both behavioral models and experiential methods to help individuals assess their needs, set realistic goals, and formulate coping strategies.

Of course, the nature of the transition and the characteristics of the employees affected must dictate the counseling methods utilized. In general, however, each type of transition can be made easier through the use of similar principles.

- Demonstrate the organization's commitment to assist in the transition.
- Use whatever sources of support are available, including peers, counselors, and models of successful coping.
- Give affected employees maximum opportunities to help themselves and one another.
- Provide information concerning the characteristics of the new role or situation.
- Assist employees in self-assessment, goal-setting, and strategy formulation.

These guidelines can help to ensure that employees maintain feelings of confidence and control as they attempt to develop new coping mechanisms.

INDUCTION INTO THE ORGANIZATION

When new employees are inducted into an organization, they may feel anxious and uncertain about the roles they will be called on to perform. Lack of information and reluctance to discuss questions or problems with their new supervisors can exacerbate these feelings and make the transition difficult. Orientation programs designed to familiarize new employees with an organization help to ease what for many can be a stressful transition.

The provision of cognitive information is usually a high priority in orientation programs because successful induction depends on the employee's awareness of the characteristics of the organization and of the job. Most programs cover a great many topics. The following list shows topics often covered in employee orientation programs.[1]

Organizational Issues

History of employer	Product line or services provided
Organization of employer	Overview of production process
Names and titles of key executives	Company policies and rules
Employee's title and department	Disciplinary regulations
Layout of physical facilities	Employee handbook
Probationary period	Safety procedures and enforcement

Employee Benefits

Pay scales and paydays	Insurance benefits
Vacations and holidays	Retirement program
Rest breaks	Employer-provided services to employees
Training and education benefits	
Counseling	Rehabilitation programs

Introductions

To supervisor	To co-workers
To trainers	To employee counselor

Job Duties

Job location	Overview of job
Job tasks	Job objectives
Job safety requirements	Relationship to other jobs

The effective orientation program provides new employees with needed information but does not overload them with details. In such programs the responsibilities for carrying out the orientation program are shared by supervisors, trainers, counselors, and fellow employees. To decide how the tasks should be divided, the question that needs to be asked is, "Who can best relay each piece of data to the inductee?" The details of the job itself may best be supplied by the immediate supervisor; information about the organizational environment as a whole can be disseminated through a standardized process developed by the personnel or training department; encouragement may be the special forte of an employee who has recently completed the probationary period. St. John (1980) suggests that information concerning a company overview, key policies and procedures, compensation, fringe benefits, safety and accident prevention, employee and

---

[1] Adapted from *Personnel management and human resources* (p. 174) by W. B. Werther and K. Davis, 1981, New York: McGraw Hill. Copyright 1981 by McGraw-Hill. Adapted by permission.

union relations, physical facilities, and economic factors should be given to all employees by human resource specialists. The supervisor should be responsible for covering such topics as department functions; job duties and responsibilities; departmental policies, procedures, rules, and regulations; a tour of the department; and introduction to departmental employees.

St. John lists "sixteen cautions" to be observed in establishing an induction program.[2]

1. Be sure to tailor your induction topics and procedures to fit your company.
2. Be certain to fix induction responsibilities and to assure they are understood by all concerned.
3. Don't rely strictly on managers and supervisors to plan the induction program—do include a cross-section of employees.
4. Keep an induction file . . .
5. Avoid overwhelming employees with too much information too fast.
6. Anticipate employees' potential problems and needs for information—be proactive as well as reactive.
7. Identify both company and job-level induction needs, and organize these by personnel department and supervisors respectively.
8. Use a check list system for topics to be discussed . . .
9. Insist that each new employee sign . . . check lists . . .
10. Share the most important information both in writing and verbally . . .
11. Use a loose-leaf notebook rather than a bound employee manual to permit constant and easy updating.
12. Be certain to show how the employee's job is related to other jobs and how his or her duties affect the final result.
13. Spell out clearly job expectations, work responsibilities, goals, performance standards and criteria, and acceptable conduct at work, with a liberal amount of time for questions and discussion.
14. When selecting a "buddy" to assist the supervisor's orientation, be sure he or she is an effective, well-informed worker with positive attitudes toward work, the job, the department and the company.
15. Seek ongoing new employee feedback, conduct a formal annual evaluation of the induction program, and revise the program accordingly.
16. Include the spouse at one session to secure family understanding of and commitment to the job and company.

Such well-organized information dissemination programs, while far superior to the haphazard processes that characterize many organizations, tend to focus somewhat narrowly on the cognitive dimension and on organizational objectives. This approach can help to alleviate some anxiety, but a great deal more can be accomplished if direct attention is paid to the induction as a process of transition.

If several employees can be oriented simultaneously, the work should be

[2]From "The complete employee orientation program," by W. D. St. John, copyright May, 1980. Reprinted with the permission of *Personnel Journal*, Costa Mesa, California; all rights reserved.

done in a group setting that allows for informal exchanges along with formal presentations. "Warm-up" and "get acquainted" exercises may be used as the first stage in developing a supportive group of peers and in presenting the organization's message that the orientation is meant to be more than a one-way communication of information from the company to the newcomer. The presence of employees who have successfully completed a probationary period can encourage inductees and inspire them to ask questions that they might hesitate to raise with supervisory personnel. If current employees are willing to discuss some of the challenges and anxieties they faced in their first weeks on the job, newcomers might see that their own apprehension is normal and recognized as such.

Finally, counselors can utilize the orientation workshop to assist employees in their initial career problem-solving efforts. At this point, self-assessment will be focused primarily on any special needs the employee might have for information, training, or support. But the problem-solving atmosphere also sends the message that this organization values human resources and encourages thoughtful career planning. The results of such a supportive process are likely to be as positive for the company as they are for the employee, since induction problems will be minimized and productivity enhanced.

RELOCATION

Geographical relocation brought about by corporate group moves, individual lateral moves, and promotions affects over 300,000 employees of American businesses each year (Moore, 1981). Regardless of the purpose of the move, a relocation can be highly stressful for an employee and his or her family.

> An impending transfer is a major consideration in a family's life, triggering a multitude of questions and concerns. Robert T. (an employee who has accepted relocation) wonders if he will be successful at his new job. He worries about whether his family will be able to duplicate their lifestyle in the new location. His wife is concerned about finding a new job. The children worry about their school. The whole family is concerned about making new friends and holding onto the old ones "back home" (Moore, 1981, p. 62).

The risk of crisis is inherent in the nature of a major relocation. Support systems, including work groups, extended families, and friendship networks, are lost; daily routines are shattered; and the employee must face induction into a new work setting. Added to these stressors is the fact that financial resources may, at least temporarily, be strained. The family worries about selling their home, purchasing a new one, and financing the move itself. Dual-career families are especially hard-hit if the spouse is unable to find a new job immediately.

Large corporations have become increasingly interested in developing supportive relocation policies, at least in part because many employees have resisted transfers. Generally, relocation departments or consultants have concentrated on the financial aspects of geographical moves, with corporations easing transitions by purchasing the current home, paying moving costs, and reimbursing other expenses. More and more companies have also begun to address the need to assist the employee's spouse in finding new employment.

Liberal relocation policies do help the situation by demonstrating a degree of corporate support and showing understanding of the transferee's plight. Even more important, however, is counseling aimed at assisting the employee to make a successful *personal* adaptation. If a counseling approach is used first to help the employee and his or her family decide whether to accept the offer of relocation, their feeling of control over the situation is enhanced. The employee who has been guided through an effective decision-making process knows that all of the pros and cons have been weighed and that the choice to move has been made freely. "The key to a successful mobility policy is to determine the needs and values of the family members and to measure their propensity and ability to adjust to relocation before the relocation occurs" (Sherwood and DeSimone, 1983, p. 209).

These needs become even more crucial if the relocation being planned is international. Fontaine (1983) suggests that employees need help at each stage of an international relocation process, from selection through predeparture, on-site adjustment, and repatriation.

Selection

A process described by Fontaine (1983) and developed by the Western Psychiatric Institute and Clinic in Pittsburgh involves an assessment process designed to predict a family's success in coping with an international assignment. The consultant, after careful exploration of personal, family, and economic factors, estimates the likelihood of a good fit between individual and assignment. This information is shared with the employer, who then decides whether the foreign assignment should be offered.

The screening predicts the likelihood of the family's adapting to the new location by considering personality, health, stress management methods, values, and goals. In fact, such an approach would be even more useful to help individuals decide whether they should accept the new assignment. Self-assesssment combined with information about the foreign locale could enable the employees themselves to make appropriate, controlled choices.

Predeparture

Once the decision has been made to accept relocation, the family can begin to address the stresses and problems that are likely to affect them. At this point, a counselor can "meet with the couple or family and help them to clarify their expectations of each other and of the cross-cultural experience, to anticipate the stress points in their relationships during the assignment and to begin to plan and prepare for them" (Fontaine, 1983, p. 28). Efforts to enhance self-awareness can be combined with attempts to describe the atmosphere that will be encountered. If the family has an opportunity to meet with employees who have had previous experience in the new setting, they can begin their preparations on a solid base of reality.

On-Site Adjustment

"International relocations intensify stress reactions because they may combine the extremes of cross-cultural impact, distance from social support systems, and the greater dependency of family members on each other for emotional support in the foreign environment" (Fontaine, 1983, p. 29). Some of the subsequent stress can be prevented by thorough preparation before the fact; information dissemination and counseling can let a family know what strains they can expect. If possible, families should seek out a peer support group while in the overseas location. Spouses who do not have the opportunity to work while on foreign soil are especially vulnerable to feelings of isolation and can benefit from sharing their feelings with people in similar situations.

Repatriation

Employees frequently find themselves more unprepared for the shock of repatriation after an overseas stint than they were for relocating in the first place. The employee may face career problems if no long-range plans have been made for reintegration into the organization at home. In addition, the family as a whole may find it more difficult than expected to readjust to American life. This transition is all the more stressful because it is unexpected. Someone from the company might have provided information about the foreign culture before the move; certainly, little effort tends to be made to prepare the individual or family for the culture shock involved in returning home.

Howard (1980) suggests that the organization can pave the way for a smooth repatriation. To ease the professional facet of repatriation, the organization should preplan the return from the beginning of the overseas assignment, develop a formal orientation for the returning family, assist in the development of an effective career plan, provide proper job placement, and make the new assignment professionally challenging. Financial policies should include provision of financial planning services and counseling, loans, reentry bonuses, relocation allowances, and equitable overseas compensation packages. Personal support should include encouraging the employee to retain his or her home in the United States and assisting the spouse in finding employment.

Although organizational policies can offer institutional support, the personal support that can be provided by a counselor is just as important. Throughout every phase of a relocation transition, assistance should be available to expedite decision making and increase the family's feelings of confidence, security, and control over their lives.

RETIREMENT PLANNING

> Company-sponsored retirement advice . . . offers a solid ledge for employees who feel they're sinking under the trauma of facing a whole new scary world—retirement. At the same time, retirement planning is seen as an investment which increases employee and retiree good will and as a fringe benefit for older employees. It's another way of expressing corporate concern for employees, at all levels, from executives to hourly wage earners (Dever, 1981, p. 56).

Many corporations are, indeed, recognizing the fact that retirement planning is a fringe benefit that cannot be overlooked. Older workers need to be prepared for the transition to retirement; in fact, because this transition has so many implications for individual well-being, the preparatory process should begin several years before the actual event.

To understand why retirement can be such a "scary world," we need to consider the importance that work can have in an individual's life. A glance at Table 8.1 indicates something of the depth and breadth of work's potential meaning and purpose.

Table 8.1. Different purposes work can serve

Economic	Social	Psychological
Gratification of wants or needs	A place to meet people	Self-esteem
	Potential friendships	Identity
Acquisition of physical assets	Human relationships	A sense of order
	Social status for the worker and his/her family	Dependability/reliability
Security against future contingencies		A feeling of mastery or competence
Liquid assets to be used for investment or deferred gratifications	A feeling of being valued by others for what one can produce	Self-efficacy
		Commitment
Purchase of goods and services	A sense of being needed by others to get the job done or to achieve mutual goals	Personal evaluation
Evidence of success		
Assets to purchase leisure or free time	Responsibility	

Note. From Edwin L. Herr and Stanley H. Cramer, *Career guidance and counseling through the life span: Systematic approaches* (2nd ed.) (p. 34). Copyright © 1984 by Edwin L. Herr and Stanley H. Cramer. Reprinted by permission of Little, Brown & Company.

A job does not necessarily meet all of an individual's economic, social, and psychological needs, but it will certainly have an impact on each category and leave a void when it is over. The economic impact of retirement is almost universal; even if retirement benefits are good, the individual's income will probably decrease. But social and psychological factors can be equally important to the retiree. If the individual's needs for social status, human relationships, and a sense of being valued have been met primarily through his or her work, these social purposes must be met in some other way after retirement. If an employee has used his or her job to maintain self-esteem, identity, and feelings of competence, his or her psychological well-being can be jeopardized by feeling that a valued career is over. Hawthorne and Menzel (1983) write that a "disruption in job security represents a loss as profound for some individuals as the loss of a loved one" (p. 25) and that employees who lose their jobs need support in their efforts to work through a process of grieving. This is no less true for people who retire than for those who find themselves suddenly unemployed. Retirees need to come to grips with a sense of loss, develop new support systems, and plan for an adjustment to a new lifestyle and environment.

Although individual counseling and printed materials play an important part in retirement planning, opportunities for participation in group seminars should also be offered to employees. Group situations serve a number of concurrent purposes by (a) providing an efficient mechanism for information dissemination; (b) offering a supportive setting for the sharing of concerns and resources; (c) allowing for contributions by people who have made a successful transition to retirement; and (d) giving the counselor a chance to train employees in self-assessment, goal-setting, and strategy formulation. The outcome of this process for each employee should be a retirement plan based on accurate information and covering such factors as finances, health, lifestyle, social systems, and psychological well-being.

Finances

Changes in lifestyle dictated by financial constraints constitute one of the most stressful aspects of retirement. Long before the fact potential retirees need information that can help them project their postretirement income. Among the income sources they should take into account are the following (Downs and Roll, 1981, p. 150):

1. Social Security
2. Company or government pension
3. Individual or supplemental pension (that is, IRA, Keogh plans)
4. High-quality stocks (yielding dividends)
5. High-quality bonds
6. High-interest savings accounts, money market funds, or savings certificates
7. Annuities and endowments

8. Proceeds of sale or refinancing of primary residence
9. Income property
10. Second-career income
11. Cash value of life insurance
12. Dividends of life insurance kept in force
13. Veteran's benefits
14. Disability payments

Financial planning specialists should be present at a planning seminar to provide information about the tax implications of alternative income sources and to ensure that employees know how to get all benefits to which they are entitled. A representative of the company should inform prospective retirees about the retirement benefits available through the organization's package.

All of this information is vital, but it is only a beginning step in the financial planning process. Each employee needs to set retirement goals based on his or her own values and determine how much income will be needed to permit the desired lifestyle. Gaps between projected income and expenses can be analyzed by the employee with a view toward increasing his or her income through work or other methods or adjusting lifestyle expectations.

Health

Employees need to plan for the maintenance of their health and fitness after retirement. Just as a corporate wellness program prepares employees to take charge of their own health needs, a retirement health plan should emphasize personal responsibility for health. Self-assessment in this area should focus on the risk factors that are likely to affect the individual's long-term health. Plans can then be made to develop health-enhancing lifestyles and to decrease the effects of those risk factors that are subject to personal control.

Retirees also need to make contingency plans for dealing with medical problems that arise. They need information about Medicare, with emphasis on knowing how to use it properly. Retirees should also know what other medical insurance might be needed and what the possibilities are for continuing coverage under the current group plan. As in the case of other financial matters, employees should obtain general information through the seminar and printed materials and then integrate the data into a highly personalized retirement plan.

Lifestyle

Decisions concerning postretirement lifestyle are very personal. Among the most important facets of the retirement plan is the question of type and location of residence. Yet, decisions in this area cannot be made on the basis of objective data alone. As one guidebook designed for retirees states,

After all your years of considering needs other than your own—your children's, your employers', maybe your parents'—you and your spouse may have forgotten your actual personal preferences . . . During your working years, your lifestyle was often dictated as much by circumstances, finances, luck, and unconscious gravitation as it was by choice. Now you're faced with finding out what you may never have given serious thought to before: what you really like to do with your time (Consumer Guide, 1981, p. 11).

As employees assess their personal preferences, they can come closer to deciding whether they are likely to be happier remaining in their current home or moving, renting an apartment or owning a residence, living in a retirement community or sharing life with people of varying ages, focusing on climate or seeking cultural milieux, searching for new experiences or remaining close to friends and family. Once goals have been set on the basis of clear values, the employee can begin to develop a specific strategy for making the desired move upon retirement.

Social Systems

Employees who have tended in the past to build their social lives around fellow workers are at risk for difficulties in retirement if they fail to plan for locating new sources of social support. Retirement planning needs to take into acount the meaning that work has had for the individual so that the purposes served by the career can continue to be accomplished. An individual who has depended on the work organization for relationships, achievements, and feelings of personal worth must find a way to meet these needs in other settings. If the individual's self-assessment points the way toward important personal goals and values, the retirement plan can identify ways to accomplish the same ends through nonwork social systems or even new careers.

Psychological Well-Being

Retirees should take what for many is an unusual step: making plans for maintaining their mental health. The information provided in the seminar should deal not just with retirement benefits but also with the nature of the retirement transition itself. If employees understand the stressful nature of retirement as an event, they can prepare themselves to manage their reactions. If employees know that through work they have met many of their psychological needs and formed part of their identity, they can plan to involve themselves in alternate activities that are as meaningful.

The development of retirement plans is obviously a complex process that cannot be accomplished in a short time. In corporate settings that provide assistance in this area, employees are usually encouraged to participate long before the target date for retirement. As the seminar series is being initiated, older employees and their spouses must be given a great deal of encouragement to attend. As Raffel (1980, pp. 845–846) points out, employees have many reasons to resist dealing with the issue of retirement, including the following:

1. *Fear of Admitting to Aging.*
"If I attend this seminar, I have to face the fact that I am getting old and can't go on working forever. By attending, everyone will know that I am over 55."

2. *Feelings of Futility in Planning for the Unknown.*
"Why should I attend a retirement-planning seminar when I don't know what my health will be, what inflation will do to any financial plans I might make, whether I will lose my spouse, or even when I plan to retire? With all of life's uncertainties, it seems futile to think about where to live or plan what I'll do with my time after I retire. I'll meet each obstacle when I come to it."

3. *Fear of Being Pressured into Retirement Decisions.*
"What's my employer's gimmick in offering these seminars at work? I suspect they will ask me to set my retirement date now, and I'm not ready, or at least they will try to sell me on retirement. If they know my retirement plans, it could affect my future raises, promotions or just how they feel about me."

The counselor needs to communicate in the most encouraging way possible that retirement planning is meant, not to take away individual choice, but to enhance personal control. Like any major transition, retirement can be a negative crisis for some, a growth-producing reward for others.

The sensible person doesn't really retire. He or she changes activities or occupations. One who retires to do something else, to live life in a positive new way, is still in command. One who has "been retired" is a victim (Downs and Roll, 1981, p. 2).

OUTPLACEMENT

If any event in the workplace makes people feel like victims, it is job loss. Whether one has been singled out or is part of a general reduction in the work force, the experience of losing one's job is a shock. Adapting to such an event is among the most difficult transitions in life because the individual's identity, sense of efficacy, and material resources are all at stake. Outplacement—helping affected employees to seek and find new positions—is meant to enhance the process of adaptation.

"Outplacement counseling has several objectives: to reduce anxiety and tension produced by career disruption; to increase attractive job leads; to assure systematic, constructive job searching; to decrease unemployment time; and to effect a career change which improves or at least does not reduce the worker's return from working" (Healy, 1982, p. 566). If a number of workers are being laid off simultaneously, services can be provided in a group setting, where mutual support and resource sharing can enhance the process of adaptation. Whether outplacement is provided in a group seminar or on a one-to-one basis, its components include support, career search skill training, information, and problem solving—all aspects of effective transition management.

The outplacement system does more than provide individual services. Outplacement is closely related to the company's policies for dealing with terminations. In fact, the newfound popularity of the concept grows out of the negative results of haphazard policies and procedures. Morin and Yorks (1982) say that poor termination policies have economic, psychological, and organizational consequences.

In economic terms, poor severance policies often mean that a company provides severance benefits of up to one year's salary for a manager who, with assistance, might have found a new job within a few months. Poorly conceived termination methods also cause needless waste, as appropriate terminations are postponed. Lack of effective outplacement adds to corporate costs for unemployment compensation, just as careless termination procedures increase the likelihood of lawsuits.

The psychological consequences of termination are certainly devastating for the fired employee, but they can also be traumatic for the manager carrying out the dismissal.

> Even managers who terminate with some directness usually experience some guilt over the process. A lack of clear-cut direction on how to handle terminations intensifies such feelings, leading to false starts and poorly handled confrontations. Months after a manager is terminated, his boss may still be trying to rationalize his actions. In fact, most outplacement consultants readily admit that the need to relieve the corporate conscience is a major reason for the rapid growth in the practice of providing counseling to terminated managers (Morin and Yorks, 1982, p. 18).

The organizational effects of poorly handled terminations can also be long-lived. The morale of productive employees still with the company can be negatively affected, and a hostile parting can reverberate through the business community.

Many of these adverse situations can be prevented if the company approaches dismissals with an attitude of fairness and a willingness to help dismissed employees move on in their careers. Schlossberg and Leibowitz (1980) suggest that "the pain and trauma connected with job loss can be mitigated by institutional supports (such as) a special program comprising job-finding training and job lead identification" (p. 215). An effective outplacement program can operationalize corporate responsibility and have direct, practical impact on the well-being of employees.

Adams (1980) points out that what we call "outplacement" programs should really be termed "out-training" because emphasis is usually focused on helping the affected employee learn effective job search skills.

Most people don't have much experience with job searching. They can't be expected to have perfected the rather specialized skills job searching requires, and so they need training. I call it "out-training" and approach job searching for the out-of-work employee as I would any training program with a measurable behavioral objective (Adams, 1980, p. 719).

Clearly, most trainers and counselors in the field agree that their role is one of facilitation and that the ultimate responsibility for securing placement in the right job belongs to the client. The phases leading to that outcome include dealing with affect, self-assessment, goal-setting, strategy formulation, and action.

Dealing with Affect

A recently terminated employee is highly likely to have strong feelings of shock, anger, and anxiety about the future. The counseling process can enable the client to identify his or her affective state and ventilate negative emotions in a safe environment (Knowdell, 1983). Efforts to deal with the individual's emotional state is time well spent; hostile or negative thoughts and feelings can be usefully shared in the appropriate setting and, ideally, set aside. Exploration of the client's attitudes also provides an opportunity for the counselor to offer support and reassurance, allowing him or her to discuss the normal readjustment processes that the employee should expect.

Self-Assessment

The client needs to examine his or her career options. Although some employees might be able to move into positions that are comparable to the ones they have left, most need to explore the possibilities for change. Clients should examine both the strengths and skills they bring to the job market and the work-related values that they hold. In some instances, clients realize that their former jobs were not what they would freely choose today. Assessment should take into account the kinds of accomplishments that employees have found most meaningful, the work environments that they have enjoyed, and the ideals that underlie their fantasies for the future. The employee should be helped to focus on positive attributes, thereby encouraging a sense of optimism and laying the groundwork for goal development.

Goal-Setting

On the basis of the self-assessment, the client should be able to state clear-cut goals concerning his or her next career step. Just as in any career counseling situation, the client may need help in formulating objectives that are concrete, realistic, and congruent with his or her interests and skills.

What is critically needed is an appropriate and realistic objective. In some cases, the appropriate objective might be in the same job that was held at termination. In other cases, it might mean a slight redirection or even a radical career change. . . . Just because an individual's previous job title was sales manager doesn't necessarily mean that his/her major skills are in the areas of sales and management (Knowdell, 1983, p. 30).

If employees can specify the kinds of positions they would consider appropriate to their skills and current levels of development, they can begin to channel energy into the active job search.

Strategy Formulation and Implementation

The strategy designed to meet a job-securing objective is, in fact, what Morin and Yorks term a "personal marketing game plan."

Just as the success of any business enterprise rests on its ability to market its product or services successfully, so, too, does the success of a person's job search depend on his or her approach to marketing the talents being offered to prospective employers . . . Just as there are proven skills in corporate marketing, there are established methods that are known to be effective in marketing oneself for a job. One of the greatest needs a person has when entering the job market is access to those kinds of skills—learning one way or another how to make a product of their career planning efforts and convert it into an effective personal marketing plan (Morin and Yorks, 1982, p. 167).

As the client develops a resume, expands his or her network of contacts, and seeks interviews at carefully targeted companies, the role of the counselor remains important. From planning through implementation, from assessment to action, the counselor provides the support and information that can make a successful adaptation possible.

Multiple Terminations

In cases of multiple terminations, employees have a right to expect strong corporate efforts to expedite their transitions to new employment. Major employment shifts can result from divestitures, mergers, plant relocations, automation, fiscal problems, or any of a number of other challenges, but the impact on each affected employee is equally serious regardless of the reason. Self-esteem and feelings of self-efficacy suffer even when employees are informed that the termination is not related in any way to their job performance levels. Mutual supportiveness might be eroded by the fact that specialized workers are now competing for limited job openings in similar settings. Beyond that, the morale of employees remaining on the job may be at stake. Companies forced to terminate a number of employees over a short period of time have everything to gain from prompt outplacement, both because of the psychological and social importance of smooth transitions and because expenditures for severance pay and unemployment benefits can be lessened.

An example of outplacement in practice is provided by Pfizer, Inc., which displaced a number of workers through the divestiture of its subsidiary, Pfizer Medical Systems (Silverman and Sass, 1982). The outplacement program developed to meet the needs of 250 terminated employees included several components: a severance package; an outplacement manual; an outplacement seminar; and an outplacement center, which was staffed by a combination of corporate personnel and counselors, psychologists, and trainers provided by an external consulting group.

The outplacement manual and seminar addressed the specific needs of the Pfizer employees, taking into account local job market factors and dealing with such issues as resume writing, identifying potential job situations, interviewing, and following up. The placement center offered work space for terminated employees as well as reference materials and counseling support. Staff were also able to schedule interviews with comparable local companies. Ultimately, the effort was evaluated as being highly successful, since the following results (Silverman and Sass, 1982, p. 76) were achieved:

- All of the obvious short-term personal, career and family needs of the terminated employees were met . . . ;
- The local community viewed the management effort as a very positive one. . . . ;
- The number of lawsuits filed by employees was reduced from two to none;
- More than 90 percent of all employees found new positions within the 90-day target period;
- Most of the new positions paid more than the previous positions;
- Those who desired to remain in the geographic area were generally able to do so;
- Corporate management has made a commitment to continue to offer similar support in similar situations if they occur;
- No long-term continuing psychological problems were triggered by the termination incident;
- The cost of potential unemployment insurance was reduced by approximately 60 percent, and the cost of the effort was only a small fraction of the monies saved in unemployment and legal settlements avoided.

Similarly positive reactions followed an intensive outplacement program at Interfaith Medical Center (Shahzad, 1984). The merger of St. John's Episcopal Hospital and the Jewish Hospital and Medical Center of Brooklyn to form Interfaith meant that 450 employees had to be laid off over a six-month period. Working closely with District 1199 of the National Union of Hospital and Health Care Employees, the organization took a number of steps to assist affected employees. Mailings were made to directors of personnel at area hospitals, reminding them that the Hospital Closure Incentive Program allowed them to be reimbursed by the state for salary expenditures they incurred by hiring laid-off employees. Direct services to individuals were provided by the Federation Employment and Guidance Service and by Interfaith's human resource development staff and included orientation meetings, information on entitlements, workshops, career counseling, and job referrals.

Smaller organizations have also been successful in outplacing employees affected by major changes. For instance, Wible and Tirpak (1984) describe the processes utilized when the American Society for Personnel Administration relocated from Berea, Ohio, to Alexandria, Virginia. Although only 34 nonrelocating employees needed to find employment in the Cleveland area, ASPA provided a full-service outplacement program with the assistance of an outside consultant. The three phases of this program included: (1) orientation, (2) instruction in job search techniques, and (3) individualized outplacement assistance. The organization supplemented these measures by publicizing the effort, publishing a newsletter summarizing the backgrounds of employees being outplaced, encouraging information sharing, providing time off with pay for job interviews, providing resume typing and duplication services, and inviting employers to conduct on-site interviews.

> The ASPA outplacement experience proved that small organizations can provide professional outplacement assistance for their employees by effectively utilizing both internal and external resources. A well-planned program can provide both tangible and intangible results—jobs for dislocated employees and a positive spirit of appreciation by them toward their former employer (Wible and Tirpak, 1984, p. 76).

Whatever the cause, job loss is for most people a potential crisis. It is an event that calls for enormous reserves of strength, that requires new coping mechanisms, that tests support systems and resources. Like any crisis, it can leave the individual either stronger than ever or chronically troubled. If outplacement is successful, the client can emerge with feelings of self-efficacy and control based on his or her ability to meet and surmount a difficult challenge.

The same principle holds true with regard to any of the work-related transitions discussed here. Successful adaptation—whether to induction, to relocation, to retirement, or to termination—can strengthen the individual's ability to cope with the world, build his or her life competence, and provide evidence of self-efficacy. Subsequent events become more likely to be interpreted as challenges rather than as threats.

SUMMARY

In the context of a work organization, employees are often faced with the need to adapt to transitions from one role or situation to another. Any transition, whether it is normally considered negative or positive, can be stressful to the individual. An event that places new demands on the person can be considered either as a challenge or as a threat, depending on the individual's perceptions of the situation and his or her ability to master it.

In general, several factors seem to characterize people who are able to make successful adaptations. Such individuals tend to have strong social support systems, to believe in their own efficacy and control, to have the information and tools needed for problem solving, and to have confidence in their ability to adapt to the new situation. Transitional counseling programs can enhance employees' potential for managing transitions if they (a) demonstrate the organization's commitment to assist in the transitions; (b) use whatever sources of support are available; (c) give affected employees opportunities to help themselves and one another; (d) provide information concerning the characteristics of the new role or situation; and (e) assist employees in self-assessment, goal-setting, and strategy formulation. These steps are appropriate for dealing with such varying transitions as induction into the organization, geographical relocation, retirement, and job loss.

Induction into the organization can be most successful if orientations for new employees are carefully planned. Some of the new employee's anxiety is likely to be alleviated if he or she is informed about the organization. In addition, however, inductees should have the opportunity to participate in a workshop designed to provide mutual support and to encourage the beginning of a career planning process.

Relocation can also be a difficult transition, since support systems and customary routines may be lost. Employees and their families should have assistance in making a personal adaptation, from selection through predeparture, on-site adjustment, and return.

Retirement planning also requires a great deal of concrete information and support. Group seminars can be especially useful, since they can (a) provide an efficient mechanism for information dissemination, (b) allow retirees to share concerns and feelings, (c) include presentations by people who have successfully completed the transition to retirement, and (d) involve training in self-assessment, goal-setting, and strategy formulation. Each employee should be able to develop a personal retirement plan dealing with such issues as finances, health, lifestyle, social systems, and psychological well-being.

Outplacement counseling should also be available to assist people affected by job loss. Termination is a highly stressful event for almost anyone, since the individual's identity, support systems, self-efficacy, and material resources all seem to be at stake. If the outplacement counselor can help the client to deal with affect and carry out a successful job search, the final results may be very positive for the individual. Job loss, like any potentially crisis-provoking event, can lead to enhanced strength or chronic difficulties. Successful adaptation to any of the work-related transitions can improve the individual's coping skills, life competency, and self-efficacy.

REFERENCES

Adams, D. N. (1980). When laying off employees, the word is "out-training." *Personnel Journal, 59,* 719–721.

Consumer Guide Editors (1981). *Your retirement: A complete planning guide.* New York: A&W Publishers, Inc.

Dever, S. (1981). Pre-retirement planning. *Personnel Administrator, 26*(10), 56–59, 88.

Downs, H., and Roll, R. J. (1981). *The best years book.* New York: Delacorte.

Fontaine, C. M. (1983). International relocation: A comprehensive psycho-social approach. *EAP Digest, 3*(3), 27–31.

Hawthorne, W., and Menzel, N. (1983). Grieving job loss. *EAP Digest, 3*(2), 24–27.

Healy, C. C. (1982). *Career development: Counseling through the life stages.* Boston: Allyn & Bacon.

Herr, E. L., and Cramer, S. H. (1984). *Career guidance and counseling through the life span.* Boston: Little, Brown.

Howard, C. G. (1980). The expatriate manager and the role of the MNC. *Personnel Journal, 59,* 838–844.

Knowdell, R. L. (1983). Outplacement counseling in business and industry. In R. L. Knowdell, C. McDaniels, A. Hessler, and G. R. Walz, *Outplacement counseling* (pp. 1–58). Ann Arbor: ERIC/CAPS (Educational Resource Information Center/Counseling and Personnel Services).

Lazarus, R. (1980). The stress and coping paradigm. In L. A. Bond and J. C. Rosen (Eds.), *Competence and coping in adulthood* (pp. 28–74). Hanover, NH: University Press of New England.

Leibowitz, Z. B., and Schlossberg, N. K. (1982). Critical career transitions: A model for designing career services. *Training and Development Journal, 36*(2), 12–19.

Lewis, J. A., and Lewis, M. D. (1983). *Community counseling: A human services approach* (2nd ed.). New York: Wiley.

Likert, R. (1978). The principle of supportive relationships. In J. M. Shafritz and P. H. Whitbeck (Eds.), *Classics of organization theory* (pp. 149–160). Oak Park, IL: Moore.

Moore, J. (1981). Employee relocation: Expanded responsibilities for the personnel department. *Personnel, 58*(3), 62–69.

Morin, W. J., and Yorks, L. (1982). *Outplacement techniques: A positive approach to terminating employees.* New York: AMACOM (American Management Association).

Raffel, J. (1980). Combating employee resistance to retirement planning seminars. *Personnel Journal, 59,* 845–849.

Schlossberg, N. K., and Leibowitz, A. B. (1980). Organizational support systems as buffers to job loss. *Journal of Vocational Behavior, 17,* 204–217.

Shahzad, N. (1984). Outplacement services at Interfaith Medical Center. *Personnel Administrator, 29*(6), 59–63.

Sherwood, M. B., and DeSimone, J. A. (1983). Relocation counseling: Current status and potential. In J. S. J. Manuso (Ed.), *Occupational clinical psychology.* New York: Praeger.

Silverman, E. B., and Sass, S. D. (1982). Applying the outplacement concept. *Training and Development Journal, 36*(2), 70–77.

Stensrud, R., and Stensrud, K. (1983). Coping skills training: A systematic approach to stress management counseling. *The Personnel and Guidance Journal, 62,* 214–218.

St. John, W. D. (1980). The complete employee orientation program. *Personnel Journal, 58,* 373–378.

Wible, J. R., and Tirpak, J. E. (1984). Even small organizations can provide job search assistance for their employees. *Personnel Administrator, 29*(4), 71–76.

Part Four

CONCLUSION

Chapter Nine

Issues in Program Management

Good (1984a) has pointed out that the counselor practicing in a corporate setting actually works in two worlds: the world of management and the world of the helping professions. "Counseling skills . . . are only a piece of the skills pie needed to survive and grow in the corporate, industrial, or labor world" (Good, 1984b, p. 2).

The fact that managerial and program development skills are as important as clinical skills in worksite-based programs is pointed up by the experience of individuals who have seen programs flourish or fail.

> While serving as a consultant . . . I observed that programs seldom fail because of clinical issues. Invariably, it seemed that failure resulted from insufficient administration, lack of political know-how, or a short supply of appreciation due to the absence of good evaluation. Whatever the causes, programs seemed most vulnerable in the non-clinical areas. And, again in my own experience, these problems usually relate to an inadequate design and implementation process (Wrich, 1984, p. 4).

Services to employees need to be reinforced by excellence in program management. The counselor working in a career development or employee assistance program should be as skilled in consultation and program development as he or she is in counseling. Although all counselors should be aware of the interaction between the individual and the environment (Lewis and Lewis, 1983a; Aubrey and Lewis, 1983), those who provide services to employees are expected to be especially astute in recognizing the impact of corporate values on client and program alike. The organizational context needs to be taken into account as the counselor attempts to market, implement, and evaluate services.

THE COUNSELOR AS ORGANIZATIONAL CONSULTANT

Counselors working with employees usually consider themselves to be organizational consultants as well as direct service providers. The degree of involvement in organizational issues varies widely, however, from practitioners who see the organization as a whole as the "client" to those who simply recognize that their own specialized programs affect and are affected by management policies.

Some EAP or career development specialists view organizational development as inherent in their roles.

> Administration, counseling, advocacy, management consulting, and education are basically "treatment functions." They are behavioral responses to helping employees deal with what exists within an organization. In other words, the "client" is the individual employee. The sixth function, organizational development, focuses on the organization as client. The organizational development function involves an assessment of how the organization creates and nourishes problems for employees and how the organization could be "treated" to heal itself (Winkelpleck, 1984, p. 21).

The organizational development effort thus focuses on the characteristics of the workplace as a whole, with the consultant attempting to use a variety of interventions that can integrate organizational and individual needs. The "OD" specialist helps the organization to change the way problems are currently viewed and solved.

> In order to change the way an organization solves its problems, the consultant may use any of a vast number of interventions, with the most common including: (1) *group process interventions,* such as team building, laboratory training, or observation and feedback concerning group dynamics; (2) *intergroup process interventions,* including conflict resolution strategies, intergroup confrontation meetings, and joint problem-solving sessions; (3) *training programs,* designed to enhance organizational skills and using innovative educational strategies such as simulation and gaming; (4) *survey feedback,* or the gathering and sharing of diagnostic data about the organization and its current norms and processes; (5) *action research,* which involves broad participation in the development of change strategies based on structured research and behavioral science technologies; and (6) *changes in the organizational structure* based on group agreement about suggested alterations (Lewis and Lewis, 1983b, p. 186).

More frequently, counselors have impact on their organizations because their role as helpers gives them an awareness of problems that others are likely to overlook. Even counselors without formal OD responsibilities can affect managerial decisions by sharing generalized information that has been gleaned through numerous contacts with individuals.

> The competently conducted company EAP will generate enough data about the work place to make consultation with top management useful. For example,

program evaluation in which managers and client employees both participate will produce insights regarding selection, training, policies, and work procedures. It will produce information on the degree to which internal resources may be usable for conducting employee support groups. It will produce information on factors related to general job satisfaction and performance. Those data are useful to management because they make planning more intelligent and efficient (Kiel, 1982, p. 19).

Career development counselors can do even more to affect company policies through information sharing, since their counseling functions are thoroughly entwined with human resource planning.

Finally, practitioners working in employee assistance or career development programs need to recognize that the nature of the services being offered implies a great deal about the more general policies under which the organization operates.

> An EAP is not just a loose piece of program material that can be wedged into the chinks of the armor that is the public fare of most organizations: it is a whole system of organizational intervention with its own philosophy, theory and practice. When introducing this system to a company, the consultant is proposing not just a way of "rounding up the drunks" but rather a way of running the organization so that current, acute difficulties with problem employees are dealt with and future problems are recognized in their infancy and corrective action applied. For many organizations this is not a minor adjustment; it is a change in management methods (Shain and Groeneveld, 1980, p. 35).

A program that attempts to provide direct services to employees without recognizing the importance of the organizational context is destined to be short-lived. An employee assistance program cannot survive without commitment by the organization to seek and support early intervention and rehabilitation for troubled employees. A career development program cannot succeed without human resource policies that bolster its efforts. Although some managers might assume initially that their organizations can benefit simply from the act of providing professional help for troubled individuals, they soon learn that worksite-based programs depend on a commonality of purpose among management, labor, and service providers. The need for this common ground becomes clear as the idea of an employee counseling program is explored.

MARKETING THE EMPLOYEE COUNSELING PROGRAM

The initial implementation of an employee counseling program depends on the acknowledgement by decision makers that such an effort is likely to meet organizational objectives. Practitioners who hope to encourage the development of new programs can do so only if they address the needs, problems, and values of targeted organizations. Whether programs are internal or external, they must be *marketed* in the sense that (a) services that meet the needs of targeted organizations are developed and (b) organizational policy makers become convinced of the efficacy of these services. Effective marketing practices are especially important to external service providers who hope to develop contractual relationships with a number of organizations.

Professional counselors hoping to "sell" their services to employers often make the mistake of failing to transfer their planning and counseling skills to this new effort.

> With little or no thought to marketing, a "canned" sales pitch . . . citing data on national percentages of alcohol abusers and alcoholics, troubled employees, recovery rates, costs-to-benefit ratios . . . is delivered. Much of this presentation is viewed by the executive as totally unbelievable or, at best, is viewed with considerable skepticism. At this point, the salesperson is often trying to sell a product or service for which the consumer sees no demand and the sales process is terminated without the sale (Siner, 1983, p. 31).

No counselor would ever attempt to solve an individual client's dilemma by presenting a "canned" solution that overlooks the unique needs and desires of the counselee. Marketing, like counseling, is predicated on the notion of solving real problems and meeting felt needs. Kotler, in a discussion of the skills needed to market employee assistance programs, addresses this issue.

> The primary task must not be selling EAPs. Rather, one must concentrate on creating the possibility of a more productive and satisfying life for the organization. The very same question that one asks in counseling, that is, "What is keeping this client from achieving that which he or she says he desires?" is the very question that might be asked in marketing. That is, "What is keeping this company from functioning at an optimum level?" Instead of concentrating on selling an EAP, we have to concentrate on resolving the organization's chronic problem. The difference is that in counseling, the client works to solve his problem. In marketing, the marketer works to solve the client's problems (1984, p. 69).

The consultant makes a "sale" when he or she understands an individual organization's needs well enough to meet them. The process of "marketing" requires a broader understanding of the marketplace as a whole. As Siner (1983) points out, marketing is what "enhances and paves the way to sales success" (p. 31).

Successful marketing depends on careful analysis and planning. In general, the steps to be followed in the development of an appropriate system include:

1. Conducting an audit of the marketing environment.
2. Analyzing the strengths and weaknesses that the consultant's firm or practice brings to the marketplace.

3. Segmenting and targeting the market.
4. Developing a "marketing mix."
5. Developing and implementing a marketing strategy.

The Environmental Audit

The marketer needs to develop a realistic sense of the options that may be available. Before any contacts are made, the potential consultant must know what factors can be expected to affect sales. What is the current market like for employee counseling programs? Is there a need that seems, at this time, to be unmet? What types of organizations could be approached? What is the nature of the competition? What economic, social, and political factors are likely to have a bearing on future decisions? What trends might be important? What is the size of the potential market for the consultant's services? As the marketer seeks answers to such questions, he or she begins to develop a realistic picture of the marketplace and a practical knowledge of the work organizations that might be served.

Analysis of Strengths and Weaknesses

Along with their analysis of the environment, consultants also need to examine themselves. Each consulting firm or practice has strengths that serve as potential selling points and weaknesses that can act as limiting factors. The marketer needs to make realistic comparisons between his or her program of services and those offered by competitors. What special strengths can point the way toward a marketing advantage? How can weak areas be minimized? Is there a marketing strategy or target that follows naturally from the consultant's unique characteristics?

Segmenting the Market

Analyses of the environment and of the consultant's strengths and weaknesses lead naturally to the study and selection of market segments. Potential clients can be divided into sections according to such variables as geographical location, size of organization, function of organization, or characteristics of the employee population. The consultant can then target a specific segment, depending on what he or she has learned through the environmental audit and self-analysis. A small consulting firm might choose to focus on a specific geographical area, knowing that familiarity with the local environment might be a marketing tool that larger firms could not use. A consultant with experience in a certain type of work setting—say, banking or education—could plan to market exclusively to organizations in that market segment. A service provider whose market analysis indicated that local companies with fewer than 1,000 employees had not been reached might concentrate his or her efforts in that direction. Clearly, the marketer needs to target potential client organizations that seem to provide the best possible opportunities for success. If several appropriate market segments are identified, the consultant might need to develop separate marketing plans for each.

The Marketing Mix

Each consultant or consulting firm must find a position in the market based on an understanding of the problems experienced by prospective client organizations and the solutions that can be offered. Whether one is marketing a product or a service, the "marketing mix" is made up of the same four variables: *product, place, price,* and *promotion.*

The *product* (or service) is determined after investigation of the marketplace through research, customer information, and knowledge of trends. New services are just as important to a service organization as new products are to a manufacturing company. Similarly, the improvement of existing services and the elimination of unprofitable or unwanted services— marginal services—are as important as the elimination of such products would be. Such adjustments should be the result of regular analysis. The services being marketed must be those that have been determined to meet the needs of targeted client organizations.

The second component, *place,* involves both the location and the size of the market area. The marketer must decide whether to limit the market to one area, how far the market will stretch, where the service itself will be delivered. In this case, the consultant's decision must be based on a realistic assessment of his or her firm's ability to service a given area.

The third component is the *price* structure. Because of characteristics unique to service industries, there is great need for managerial skill and creativity in the area of pricing, or fee-setting. The marketer needs to determine both what income is needed to cover costs and what fees are being charged for comparable services by competing firms. Moreover, the billing method selected can have a major impact on the nature of the services to be performed.

In employee counseling programs, consultants generally use one of two possible billing methods: billing on a subscription rate based on the total number of employees covered or billing on a case-by-case basis for services rendered. Subscription rate billing involves a charge to the company that covers all relevant services, including training, orientation, and consultation, as well as provision of direct services to employees. For instance, an EAP consultant might charge $25.00 per employee per year to provide a full program for an organization. Thus, a company with 1,000 employees would be billed $25,000 per year. The coverage would extend to all employees and their family members. There would be no additional charges for any component of the employee assistance program, regardless of the number of clients utilizing the services.

In contrast, a case-by-case approach to billing means that the company is billed only for services actually rendered. If an employee seeks assistance, the company is billed either on an hourly basis or on a case basis for services provided. Thus, the company would not budget in advance a set amount for EAP services. The amount spent would depend on the number of employees actually seen.

The case-by-case billing procedure appeals to some employers, since they know that they will not be charged if the service is not used. As one manager has pointed out, "Our organization felt that they did not want to be billed on a per employee basis, which is the billing method that the majority of organizations use . . . Our organization wanted to pay for each person that actually used the program, thus paying only for services used" (Holman and Zasloff, 1983, p. 21).

However, the same manager also stresses a major shortcoming of this approach.

> We are still struggling with an appropriate way of auditing the services that are provided. That is, how does an organization really know that a bill from an EAP coordinator accurately reflects the number of employees who have been self-referrals? Due to the confidentiality of the program, we cannot ask our coordinator for a list of people he has seen (Holman and Zasloff, 1983, p. 22).

With regard to the case-by-case method of billing, a number of major questions have yet to be answered.

1. How can the company audit services without losing sight of confidentiality?
2. If the company is billed on a case-by-case basis, is there a tendency to refer fewer clients?
3. If the company is billed on a case-by-case basis, will the service provider deemphasize such preventive approaches as training and education?
4. If the company is billed on a case-by-case basis, will clients tend to be seen when problems have become serious, as opposed to receiving help for minor issues not yet affecting productivity?

As the consultant develops a price structure and billing method, he or she needs to take into account the ethical, legal, and practical implications of the alternatives being considered.

Equally important is the fourth factor in the marketing mix, *promotion*. How will the services be sold? What program will be developed in order to reach the target audience? Will it be one method or a combination of techniques?

While variable, these four factors are thought of as controllable. The marketer decides what services will be offered, what price or fee will be charged, what market segment or area radius will be covered, and what methods will be used to communicate information about services to the target consumer. The marketer decides on the promotional mix: what combination of advertising, personal selling, publicity, and group presentations will be used.

Developing the Marketing Strategy

Although the basic components for marketing a service and a product are the same, the distinctive characteristics of service create special marketing challenges and opportunities. Marketing strategies must take into account several characteristics that are unique to services as opposed to products (Sains, 1982):

1. *Intangibility.* Since it is impossible for clients (customers) to taste, feel, see, hear, or smell services before they buy them, the marketing emphasis must be on the benefits to be derived from the service as much as on the service itself.

2. *Inseparability.* Services generally cannot be separated from the person of the seller. When a business buys a product, unless the product breaks down or is found to have some other flaw, the buyer takes it to the place of business and has no other contact with the seller until another purchase is made. In the case of services, an ongoing relationship between buyer and seller is assumed.

3. *Concurrency.* Services are sold, performed (or produced), and consumed simultaneously. A service organization does not maintain an inventory.

4. *Perishability and fluctuating demand.* The capacity and capability to produce a service must exist before any transaction can take place. It must be "in-being" or "in-place," and remain that way, whether the service facilities are used or not.

5. *Heterogeneity.* Because of the "human-intensive" nature of so many services, it is difficult to forecast the quality of a service in advance of buying it.

6. *Risk-taking.* The seller of services is a risk-taker because he or she is dependent on the good faith of the buyer, who usually pays for the service after it has been performed. Once it has been performed, a service cannot be reclaimed.

While the above are the primary differences between a product and a service, there are some secondary differences as well. Services cannot be purchased and resold. Service providers have clients, as opposed to customers, and they charge fees, or have rates, rather than prices. Services are performed, and often require the active participation of the buyer. The service can be only as successful as the commitment of the client allows it to be.

Implementing the Marketing Strategy

Marketing employee counseling programs means marketing an idea. Employers must be convinced that the concept makes sense to them. Because an employee counseling program, like any other service, is intangible, buyers must be convinced that they will derive real benefits if they agree to establish programs. Because EAPs and career development programs are also inseparable from the qualities of service providers, employers must also be convinced that the service they will receive will be professional and competent. The marketing approach should therefore stress both the benefits of employee counseling programs and the specific expertise of the professionals who will be providing assistance. These factors make it important for marketers to use personalized approaches oriented toward helping individual employers recognize the unique benefits that their firms can expect to gain from program implementation. The ability to solve the client organization's problems is acquired through listening well enough to know how those problems are perceived by decision makers in the business setting.

PLANNING AND EVALUATING THE PROGRAM

Employee counseling programs are meant to provide effective means of dealing with problems in the workplace. Each program therefore must be designed to meet specific goals that have been identified as important to the well-being of the organization and its members. Planning a program and evaluating its effectiveness go hand in hand. At the planning stage, goals and objectives are set; at the evaluating stage, the success of the program in meeting its stated objectives is measured.

Counseling programs of various types have implied goals that tend to be common across organizations. Writing in general terms, La Van, Mathys, and Drehmer (1983) list some of the indicators that might be used to assess the impact of specific kinds of programs:[1]

---

[1]From "A look at the counseling practices of major U.S. corporations" by H. LaVan, N. Mathys, and D. Drehmer, 1983, *Personnel Administrator, 28*(6), pp. 143–145. Copyright 1983 by American Society for Personnel Administration. Reprinted by permission.

Career Counseling
- The retention of middle and upper levels of managers compared to some base year.
- Preparation of candidates for various positions selected from within versus hired externally.
- Attitude survey results indicating such dimensions as the degree of satisfaction with promotional opportunities, or the degree to which personal interest and/or preferences are used in selection.
- The degree to which the organization's counseling activity compares to known successful systems.

Outplacement Counseling
- The success rate for placing employees in other organizations.
- The length of time it takes to place an employee elsewhere once the displacement decision has been made.

Personal Problem Counseling
- Improved performance attributable to removal of personal problems.
- The extent to which under-utilization of employee skills is alleviated upon placement.

Retirement Counseling
- The extent to which employees feel prepared for their retirement.
- The timeliness of the counseling activity regarding the types of decisions that are faced by the retiring employee.
- The percentage of employees who willingly take advantage of such counseling.

Alcoholism and Drug Counseling
- Increased productivity.
- Reduction in absenteeism attributable to alcoholism or drugs.
- Reduction in accidents both on and off the job.
- Reduction in the number of co-workers encouraged to experiment with drugs.
- Improved employee satisfaction obtained by self reports, peer reports or decline in absenteeism.

It is possible to identify some commonalities among counseling programs. More important, however, each specific program should be evaluated in terms of its unique goals and objectives. Each EAP or career counseling program has been developed to serve some organizational purpose. If the program is to survive, its success and efficiency in accomplishing that purpose must be assessed. Two types of evaluation should be utilized routinely: the process evaluation and the outcome evaluation.

Process Evaluation

The purpose of a *process evaluation* is to determine whether programs are operating in accordance with stated goals and expectations.

Process evaluation provides a means for determining whether members of target populations were reached in the numbers projected and whether specified services were provided in the degree and with the quality expected . . . Exactly what services were provided, by whom, and how many, in what time period, at what cost? When this information is used to compare accomplishments with objectives, guidelines for needed program improvements become clear, comparison of alternate methodologies becomes feasible, and accountability becomes a reality (Lewis and Lewis, 1983b, p. 150).

In employee counseling programs, a major factor in process evaluation involves penetration rate. Of the number of employees who might be expected to need assistance, how many actually receive services during a given time period? Wrich (1980) suggests that, for employee assistance programs,

The most common expectations are in the area of 1½ to 2 percent of the total work force per year, with chemical dependency referrals constituting approximately 1 percent of the total work force per year . . . If we assume that 10 to 12 percent of the work force have personal problems which can adversely affect job performance or individual well-being, then we might consider how long we want to take to reach and assist that number of employees. Our bias in developing programs is to usually have the number of referrals equivalent to the initial population at risk over a period of five to seven years immediately following complete system-wide implementation (p. 142).

Organizations vary widely, however, both in managerial expectations concerning penetration rate and in the number and types of problems prevalent in their employee populations. Although figures like the ones provided by Wrich might prove helpful as a comparison tool, each program must be evaluated in terms of its unique characteristics.

Ray (1983) suggests that evaluations must also examine the fit between the program and the nature of the employing organization.

Does the program reach employees in close approximation to their actual representation on the payroll? If the workforce is 80 percent female but only 10 percent of those entering EAP are female, something is wrong. If 70 percent of the workforce are hourly and yet only 20 percent using the EAP are hourly employees, again, something is wrong. A really good program should be reaching every category of the payroll in close approximation to what is actually represented on that payroll. If 17 percent is minority, and yet only 2 percent of those using the program are minority employees, someone should be asking why (p. 4).

The way in which a program is evaluated depends on its focus. What kinds of problems have the services been designed to meet? Given the resources at the program's disposal, what time frame has been set for reaching troubled employees or individuals seeking career counseling? Is the program oriented toward the employee population as a whole or is it oriented toward one group (for example, an outplacement program available only to executives or managers)?

Given the program's overall goals, the service providers need to develop specific, measurable objectives on a yearly basis. An example of possible EAP objectives is provided by Shelton (1983, p. 16):

- Increase employee penetration (utilization rate) by 1 percent by end of next FY (fiscal year).
- Deliver training programs to 20 percent of employee population by end of next FY.
- Expand number of recommended alcohol treatment resources from two to five within next six months.
- Mail client satisfaction survey form (by _____) to all employees who have utilized program during past 24 months.

If a program is based on such easily measurable objectives, staff members can collect needed data as part of the daily routine. The individual or group with responsibility for overseeing the process evaluation can decide what kinds of information will be needed to determine whether objectives have been met. A method for gathering and handling evaluation data can then be built into routine operations, allowing process evaluation to be a continual activity.

Outcome Evaluation

Outcome evaluations are also built on measurable objectives. These objectives, however, are stated in terms of expected results. The purpose of the outcome evaluation is to find out what effect services have had on the well-being of individual clients and the organization as a whole.

Traditionally, employee counseling programs have publicized their high success rates in dealing with individual employees. Unfortunately, these figures tend to lack credibility because of the dearth of controlled studies.

> Although outcome measures alone allow evaluators to recognize whether change has taken place, such methods do not demonstrate that the human service intervention caused the effect. Experimental designs help to do this by comparing groups of people who have received the service in question with control groups that have not received the same intervention. True experimental designs require random selection of experimental and control groups, carefully controlled interventions, and scrupulously examined outcome measures (Lewis and Lewis, 1983b, p. 162).

It is unrealistic to think that stringent experimental research could become the norm among worksite-based programs. Although there is a strong need for controlled studies carried out by research specialists, the typical counselor neither has nor desires the luxury to withhold services from a control group. Despite this difficulty, reasonably credible evaluations can be conducted by counselors who carefully monitor their clients' progress, who utilize quasi-experimental designs to study organization-wide outcomes, and who use care in reporting monetary savings.

A number of outcome measures can be used in routine monitoring of individual employees' progress before and after counseling interventions. Among the variables that can be measured for the purpose of outcome evaluation are (a) number and length of absences, (b) number of accidents, (c) uses of medical benefits, (d) supervisory ratings, (e) career advancements, (f) disciplinary actions, (g) self-reported job satisfaction, and, of course, (h) placement or job retention. The outcome measures taken depend on the program's objectives and rationale. No matter what criteria are used, the data tend to be most convincing if measurements have been taken at regular intervals or over a reasonably long time span both before and after the provision of services.

Multiple measures should also be taken to evaluate the program's effect on the organization as a whole. Such quasi-experimental methods as time-series designs provide insight into organizational trends. In a time-series design, the evaluator identifies one measure that indicates progress toward an objective and takes the measure a number of times at regular intervals. Factors that are measured for individual clients have organization-wide equivalents. Thus, evaluators should monitor the organization's rate of employee turnover, absenteeism frequency rate, accident rate, health care costs, and other relevant variables.

Care needs to be taken in translating findings into the financial terms that are important in corporate settings. It is possible to make a convincing case about the cost-saving aspects of employee counseling programs by studying actual cost figures and reporting conservatively. For instance, Gaeta, Lynn, and Grey (1982) report on the program evaluation mechanisms utilized by the employee assistance program of a very large corporation. Evaluators were able to document a savings of $448,000 through services to 110 employees. Dollar amounts were determined by the actual pre- and posttreatment costs, over comparable time periods, for on-the-job accidents, incidental absences, disability absences, and visits to the medical unit. Anticipated losses were measured by multiplying the costs of replacing an employee by forty (the number of employees in jeopardy whose jobs were saved).

Similarly, in a much smaller health organization, dollar savings were determined through an examination of the turnover rate. In a hospital with an average 31% turnover rate, 67 individuals were counseled during the first two years of a new program (Featherston and Bednarek, 1981). Of the 67 employees involved, 21 would be expected to terminate. Only 6 did terminate, however, suggesting that 15 turnovers were avoided. The evaluators interpreted these data as $28,500 saved in turnover and replacement costs, based on replacement costs of $2,000 per nursing employee and $1,800 per nonnursing employee. Additionally, $23,400 in unemployment compensation benefits was saved.

These evaluation mechanisms certainly lack the precision of controlled experimental designs. They are important, however, in that they provide the kind of information that decision makers need. Evaluation, in contrast with research, "is more mission oriented, may be less subject to control, is more concerned with providing information for decision-makers, tends to be less rigorous or sophisticated, and is concerned primarily with explanation of events and their relationship to established goals and objectives" (Burck, 1978, p. 179). Perhaps the "pragmatic approach" described by Ray (1983) provides the most realistic possible approach:

- A number of employees have used the program;
- Those employees were helped in some manner;
- The majority are still on the payroll years later;
- My managers and supervisors say it is an effective tool that makes their work easier in managing employees or resolving job-performance problems; and
- My employees say it is the best thing since sliced bread (p. 3).

SUMMARY

Is an employee counseling program the best thing since sliced bread? Most employers and employees who have experienced such programs do interpret them that positively. The only way more individuals will have first-hand experience with such programs, however, is through the service provider's ability to work effectively in the organizational context. Decision makers in the corporate world must become convinced that counseling services can and do solve organizational problems and meet corporate goals. Concurrently, employees must be convinced that their participation in EAPs or career development programs can help them meet their personal needs. The employee counselor walks a boundary line, with one foot in the managerial realm and the other in the clinical domain.

Most counselors who work with employees tend to see themselves as organizational consultants, but how this role is defined varies widely. Some worksite-based counselors have clear organizational development responsibilities, using group process and structural interventions to affect the overall nature of the workplace. Others work as management consultants, using their skills as service providers to recognize employee problems and needs and then sharing this general information with corporate planners. Even those counselors who view themselves solely as service providers need to recognize that the very existence of an employee counseling program has vast implications for the culture and management style of the work organization.

An employee counseling program can succeed only in the context of an organizational commitment to its goals. When the program is first marketed, it must be as a service that can meet the real needs of targeted organizations. "Selling" a program to a specific client organization involves understanding that setting well enough to present plausible solutions to its real problems. "Marketing" requires an understanding of the entire marketplace. Successful marketing depends on the marketer's ability to carry out a number of steps, including (a) conducting an audit of the marketing environment, (b) analyzing the strengths and weaknesses that the consultant's own firm or practice brings to the marketplace, (c) segmenting and targeting the market, (d) developing a marketing mix, and (e) developing and implementing a marketing strategy.

Once implemented, the employee counseling program needs to continue meeting specific goals that are important to the well-being of the organization and its members. The planning and evaluating of the program are closely intertwined, with objectives set at the planning stage and assessed at the evaluation stage. Each program needs to be evaluated both in terms of process (whether the program is operating in accordance with expectations) and outcome (whether the program is having a measurable impact on individual clients and on the organization as a whole). The successful program tends to be one that is carefully planned, efficiently implemented, and well received by the people it has been designed to serve.

REFERENCES

Aubrey, R. F., and Lewis, J. A. (1983). Social issues and the counseling profession in the 1980s and 1990s. *Counseling and Human Development, 15*(10), 1–16.

Burck, H. D. (1978). Evaluating programs: Models and strategies. In L. Goldman (Ed.), *Research methods for counselors: Practical approaches in field settings* (pp. 177–202). New York: Wiley.

Featherston, A. J., and Bednarek, R. J. (1981). A positive demonstration of concern for employees. *Personnel Administrator, 26*(9), 43–47.

Gaeta, E., Lynn, R., and Grey, L. (1982). AT&T looks at program evaluation. *EAP Digest, 2*(4), 22–31.

Good, R. (1984a, October 3). *Criteria for the employee assistance professional.* Paper presented to the national conference of the Association for Labor Management Administrators and Consultants in Alcoholism, Denver.

Good, R. (1984b). *The employee assistance function: Educating the new professional.* San Francisco: San Francisco chapter of the Association for Labor Management Administrators and Consultants in Alcoholism.

Holman, R., and Zasloff, M. (1983). Providing consultation to corporate employee assistance programs—the time is right. *Consultation, 2*(1), 19–27.

Kiel, E. C. (1982). EAPs: What business are they in? *EAP Digest, 2*(4), 15–20.

Kotler, V. A. (1984). An EAP counselor in marketing land. *Thirteenth ALMACA Annual Conference Journal* (pp. 69–76). Arlington, VA: ALMACA (Association for Labor-Management Administrators and Consultants on Alcoholism).

LaVan, H., Mathys, N., and Drehmer, D. (1983). A look at the counseling practices of major U.S. corporations. *Personnel Administrator, 28*(6), 76–81.

Lewis, J. A., and Lewis, M. D. (1983a). *Community counseling: A human services approach.* New York: Wiley.

Lewis, J. A., and Lewis, M. D. (1983b). *Management of human service programs.* Monterey, CA: Brooks/Cole.

Ray, J. S. (1983). Employee assistance program effectiveness: Are we using the same measuring sticks? *The ALMACAN, 13*(12), 3–5.

Sains, J. (1982). Personal communication.

Shain, M., and Groeneveld, J. (1980). *Employee assistance programs: Philosophy, theory, and practice.* Toronto: Lexington Books.

Shelton, C. K. (1983). *Data collection and program evaluation: Guidelines for employee assistance programs.* Springfield, IL: Division of Alcoholism, Illinois Department of Mental Health and Developmental Disabilities.

Siner, W. E. (1983). Marketing employee assistance programs. *EAP Digest, 3*(6), 28–31.

Winkelpleck, J. M. (1984). Directions EAPs move: Evolvement towards organizational methods. *EAP Digest, 4*(5), 18–21.

Wrich, J. T. (1980). *The employee assistance program: Updated for the 1980's.* Minneapolis: Hazelden.

Wrich, J. T. (1984). President's message. *The Source: Employee Assistance Society of North America.*

Part Five

THE SCOPE OF EMPLOYEE COUNSELING PROGRAMS

C AREER/LIFE PLANNING AT LAWRENCE LIVERMORE NATIONAL LABORATORY[1]

Lawrence Livermore National Laboratory, an applied research facility under the administration of the University of California, has been a leader in career/life planning since the mid-1970s. The impetus for beginning what was then a small-scale program was a reduction in funding that forced the termination of a number of employees who had acceptable performance records and specialized expertise. The workshops used to assist affected employees in making new career plans proved so successful that the program was offered to other members of the organization, first on a trial basis, and, beginning in 1977, as a regular offering of the Employee Development Division. A central focus of this program is helping employees to take responsibility for their own career development. But because managerial supportiveness is also important, career planning, supervisory training, and management development programs are closely associated as part of the human resource development effort.

Career/Life Planning Approaches

The approach to career planning at Lawrence Livermore National Laboratory involves the use of a series of workshops, with self-guided manuals and individual counseling available to complement this effort.

Orientation to career/life planning. The workshop model used at LLNL begins with a four-hour orientation session. At this workshop, small group activities are used to introduce participants to the experiential training process

---

[1] Information about the LLNL program was obtained through personal contact with the managers responsible for developing and implementing the workshops. Marlys Hanson, Jack Brewer, and others have also written extensively about the program. This description has been adapted from those materials, which are listed as a bibliography following this appendix.

and to provide an overview of career planning and its importance. Participants also have an opportunity at this point to discuss their expectations of the program.

Personal assessment and planning strategy.   A two-day workshop format is used to assist employees in assessing themselves and beginning the planning process. The participants, who number between 18 and 25, are divided into small groups to explore their individual goals and options. Among the questions they seek to answer are the following:

- Where are you in your career and your life?
- What are your goals, interests, values, choices, skills, and knowledge?
- Where do you want to be in your career next year? In 3 to 5 years? In 10 years?
- What are your options?
- What knowledge and skills do you need to attain your goal?
- How do you plan to gain knowledge and skills?
- Is your plan realistic? What are the obstacles? What obstacles are self-imposed?
- What is your commitment? What are you willing to do this week? This month? This year?
- What support do you have? What resistance? How do you plan to maximize support and minimize resistance?
- What is the worst thing that could happen and are you prepared to deal with that scene?

The assessment workshop also includes use of assessment instruments, such as the Strong-Campbell Interest Inventory and the Work Values Inventory, which are later interpreted in individual interviews with each participant.

Motivated skills assessment.   A major component of the career/life planning process is the identification of motivated skills: skills the individual performs well and enjoys using. Based on Arthur Miller's System for Identifying Motivated Skills, this aspect of the workshop helps participants to recognize their motivational patterns, including the dimensions of ability, subject matter, preferred relationship style, and valued result or reward.

The search for the individual's motivational pattern is carried out through a process developed by the Livermore staff and termed the Livermore Achievement Motivation Process (LAMP). Each participant is interviewed by a counselor on video tape. This structured interview is devoted to identifying the individual's achievements, both in childhood and adulthood. The participant describes six achievements in detail, discussing what was done, and what was most satisfying about the accomplishment.

After a training session devoted to the motivated skill model, participants work in small groups, observing their videotaped interviews and identifying achievement-related patterns. As a result of this activity, employees learn to recognize their motivated skills, preferred working environments, preferred interaction styles, and "bottom line" motivators. A one-hour, individual counseling session is then scheduled for each participant, with the desired outcome of this appointment being the clarification of a specific life or career goal and of an initial strategy for reaching it.

Career strategy workshop. A final, half-day workshop is devoted to sharing plans of action. Each participant is encouraged to present his or her life/career development strategy in detail and to receive feedback from the trainer-counselor and fellow group members. Each participating employee should, at this point, be able to state what he or she intends to do, when, how, and with what desired results.

Counseling. Professional counselors are available to follow up on the workshop by providing individualized assistance in clarifying goals and objectives or supporting action plans at the implementation stage. In addition, resource counselors, selected from among employees, are available to provide information about job classifications, tasks, and training requirements. This support and information is provided in the context of a Career Resource Center, which provides career information of a general nature as well as material focused on career options at Lawrence Livermore Laboratory.

Planning manual. Because some employees prefer to work on career planning at their own pace, LLNL also provides for an individualized approach. The Self-Guided Career Planning Manual follows the same steps as the workshop, but allows highly motivated employees to complete each phase on their own.

Supervisory Training

Supervisors have a major role to play in developing employees, but they need interpersonal skills in order to carry out this role. At Lawrence Livermore National Laboratory, training is provided for supervisors in order to increase their effectiveness in motivating, leading, coaching, developing, and appraising subordinates.

Motivation. As part of a series of supervisory training sessions, first-line managers are introduced to the general concepts that can help them understand employee motivation and behavior. Emphasis is placed on self examination as well as on incorporating motivational theories in managing others.

Leadership. Trainers introduce participants to the situational leadership model, which prescribes adapting leadership styles to the maturity level of employees. Supervisors learn the theoretical concepts associated with effective leadership and through experiential exercises attempt to put theory into practice.

Emphasis is also placed on the process of communication between supervisor and supervisee. Training focuses on the skills of listening effectively, minimizing misunderstandings, and giving helpful feedback.

Identifying motivated abilities. Supervisors are also introduced to the System for Identifying Motivated Abilities. Just as employees can use awareness of their own motivated skills to make career and life plans, supervisors can utilize this concept to encourage subordinates. By learning to recognize and track motivational patterns a supervisor can increase his or her supervisees' potential for development. Thus, a session of supervisory training is devoted to practice in analysis of patterns.

Counseling/coaching. Although managers should not feel that they are expected to be professional counselors, they do need to use effective human relations skills in dealing with employees. The focus of this aspect of supervisory training is on active listening, feedback techniques, joint goal-setting, and advising.

Developing subordinates. The training program also provides a conceptual base to help managers recognize their potential impact for developing employees. Supervisors learn that their expectations for themselves and their supervisees will have a strong effect on employees' behavior and that sharing high expectations in a concrete way can encourage employees to work toward attainable goals. Emphasis is also placed on the idea that employees should be rewarded for their contributions, allowed increased visibility, and consulted about decisions that affect them.

Performance appraisal. Training sessions are also used to encourage participative performance appraisals. Supervisors learn that frequent performance appraisals, using good interpersonal feedback skills, can be effective in enhancing employees' receptiveness. As in the other aspects of supervisory training, videotaped presentations and experiential skill building methods are used to add to the supervisor's repertoire of available behaviors.

Management Development

Managers at middle and upper levels also benefit from services that allow them to increase their sense of responsibility for their development. For this reason, LLNL has also created several mechanisms for encouraging assessment, planning, and training for managers.

The Assessment Center is used to help the individual manager appraise his or her managerial qualities through exercises, assessment materials, and mutual feedback sessions with peers. This process is aimed, not toward selection, but toward the kind of self-assessment that can form the basis for effective career planning.

When the manager has created a developmental plan, he or she can become involved in training sessions that are appropriate for individual goals. Thus, one manager might need to become involved in training to improve his or her effectiveness in managing people, another in activities designed to improve work management, and a third in programs to enhance career management.

Revitalization

A concern for individual differences among employees is also apparent in LLNL's more recent program: revitalization. This effort is based on the recognition that, in any organization, a number of employees can be recognized as "devitalized" by their lack of movement or change over the years, their decreased energy levels, and their negative views of the organization. Such employees can be a drain on an organization, since their earlier successes and long years of service tend to make it unlikely that they will be terminated.

The revitalization program addresses this group of employees by providing more personal attention and support than would be involved in the more general workshop situations. Identified employees are selected on the basis of supervisory nominations and strongly encouraged to participate in a small group meeting on a regular basis. The group situation allows participants to recognize that they are not alone in their problems, to explore relevant issues, to identify motivational patterns, and to develop plans for action. While the affected employees work together, their supervisors also meet to explore issues related to managing devitalized employees.

Each aspect of the human resource development program at Lawrence Livermore National Laboratory seems to operationalize the basic philosophy that employees can assume responsibility for their own development but that the organization as a whole has a major role to play in encouraging and supporting this development. Change is a constant, as programs are piloted, evaluated, and created; most recently, for instance, the career/life planning workshop has been integrated into an employee assistance program that deals with a variety of employee issues. The concern for enhancing the creativity and quality of employees' work carries over into the work of the Employee Development Division itself; there seems to be little danger of "devitalization" among these HRD professionals.

PARTIAL BIBLIOGRAPHY OF PUBLICATIONS BY LLNL PROFESSIONALS

Brewer, J., Hanson, M., Van Horn, R., and Moseley, K. (1975). A new dimension in employee development: A system for career planning and guidance. *Personnel Journal, 54,* 228–231.

Brewer, J. (1983, October). *Revitalization: An organizational program for the individual.* Paper presented at organizational development conference.

Hanson, M. C. (1977). Career development responsibilities of managers. *Personnel Journal, 56,* 443–445, 465.

Hanson, M. C. (1981). Career counseling in organizational groups. In D. H. Montross and C. J. Shinkman (Eds.), *Career development in the nineteenth eighties: Theory and practice.* Springfield, IL: Charles C Thomas.

Hanson, M. C. (1981). Implementing a career development program. *Training and Development Journal, 35.*

Hanson, M. C. (1981). *Training employees and managers for their role in career development.* Paper presented at the National ASTD (American Society for Training and Development) Conference, Anaheim, CA.

Training and Development Services Unit: The First National Bank of Chicago[1]

At First Chicago, the Training and Development Services Unit provides a full range of career development services for nonofficers of the bank. The unit's programs for employees include counseling services, resource services, training programs, and follow-up services for on-the-job skill application. Services to management include custom-designing programs to meet the needs of specific units and consulting in the design of development strategies. As of 1984–85, the unit's training programs were divided into three general areas: (1) customer service and technical skills training, (2) professional development, and (3) supervisory/management development.

Customer Service and Technical Skills Training

One goal of training and development at First Chicago is excellence in execution. Training programs focus on the interpersonal and communication skills needed for effective service to customers because such service is a high priority of the corporation. Technical skills are also important; courses and skill laboratories allow employees to develop and update their skills in writing, word processing, accounting, data processing, typing, speed reading, and other technical areas.

---

[1] Information for this description of First Chicago's training and development program was obtained through personal contact with Barbara Brooks, manager of the Training and Development Services Unit, and Dr. Judy Mayo, organizational development consultant. Written material was also adapted from the unit's 1984–85 brochure, "Training for Excellence."

Professional Development Services

Professional development specialists are available to provide counseling and information to individuals who seek their services. Many employees find that they need personal assistance in assessing their skills and abilities, identifying career interests, setting goals, and designing career management strategies. The specialists are good resources both for providing individualized career counseling and for disseminating information about the Internal Mobility Program, the structure and function of bank departments, career paths, job descriptions, job postings, and relevant college courses.

Also included in professional development services are a number of workshops and seminars designed to help employees identify and act on their goals. Among the programs that have been offered to First Chicago employees are the following:

- *Career Strategies,* which introduces a process for assessing and directing professional growth.
- *Individual Development Seminar,* which provides an in-depth examination of the tools, techniques, and insights necessary for personal job satisfaction.
- *The First Team,* an overview of the internal job market, corporate structure, and career paths available at The First National Bank of Chicago.
- *Bidding: First Chicago's Internal Job Market,* a seminar providing participants with an overview of the Internal Mobility Program as well as techniques for effective resume construction and strategies for interviewing.
- *Introduction to the Business of Banking,* an overview of the principles of banking and how these principles affect First Chicago's goals and strategies.
- *Responsible Assertiveness,* which defines and teaches assertive behaviors and enhances communication skills.
- *Personal Communication Skills,* which focuses on communication in job-related situations.
- *Selling to a Group: Presentation Strategies,* a seminar on planning and conducting persuasive business presentations.
- *Time Management,* which teaches participants specific techniques for gaining more effective use of their time.
- *Orientation Process for Non-Exempt Employees,* which provides guidance for new employees in obtaining information, determining performance expectations, meeting performance expectations, and developing interpersonal relationships.
- *Supervision: A Career Choice,* a workshop allowing potential supervisors to compare their capabilities with the knowledge, skills, and tasks required for supervision.

- *Managing the Transition from Employee to Supervisor,* which helps the new supervisor to design a strategy for a successful transition.
- *Time Management for Supervisors,* a seminar relating time management issues to unit productivity.

Supervisory/Management Development

The Training and Development Services Unit also concentrates on the special needs of supervisors and managers, basing supervisory training on task-related responsibilities. *Staffing workshops* help supervisors to select, orient, train, and develop their employees. *Directing workshops* focus on the skills of delegating, understanding motivation, team building, conflict management, and planning change. *Controlling workshops* include learning experiences devoted to performance standards, performance measurement, performance evaluation, and performance correction. Among the *development workshops* offered are Time Management, Work Simplification, and Managing the Transition from Employee to Supervisor.

Consulting Services

An important attribute of the program offered to employees of The First National Bank of Chicago is the effective interaction between the training and development unit and other components of the organization. Staff members work closely with other units of the bank, attempting to assess training and development needs. They offer their services to managers of other units to assess the needs of their employees and develop programs that will satisfy those needs. This focus on meeting the changing needs of varying groups of employees helps the bank to maintain excellence in performance.

A good example of this approach is provided by the unit's work with First Chicago's U.S. Banking Department in 1984. At that time, major changes in the nature of the department significantly altered the role of the support staff. The training and development unit was given responsibility for assisting the USBD in its restructuring effort. This effort involved working with management and the support staff, beginning with the secretarial staff, to identify, recommend, and implement a new system for providing support activities to management.

Unit manager Barbara Brooks, along with organizational consultant Judy Mayo, developed a strategy based on the idea that people should be involved directly in identifying and recommending solutions to the problems confronting them in the work setting. Thus, the project was designed to allow for involvement of affected staff.

The first phase of the project was designed to acquire broad-based perceptions concerning administrative tasks that must be performed if the U.S. Banking Department is to maintain its efficiency and productivity. Selected groups of secretaries met to generate lists of tasks involved in giving administrative support. A total list was then generated, with duplicate items eliminated.

With this list in mind, the support staff needed to design a new secretarial work flow system. A newly devised team concept involved team leader/secretaries with coordinating responsibilities. The team leaders were brought together for the purpose of analyzing problems and designing an effective system. Training in a seven-step problem-solving method was used to shape this group into a cohesive planning unit. The team leaders learned to discover problem areas; select and define specific problems; plan strategies for analyzing problems; collect and analyze information; generate alternative solutions; evaluate and select solutions; and plan action steps, accountability, and measurement systems. Using this method, the planning group was able to devise a work flow system that was appropriate to the department's new structure and that served to resolve implementation problems that had been identified. Now, the training and development unit could plan and implement training that would meet the real needs of team leaders and secretaries as they attempted to adapt to reorganization. Even more important, the involvement and commitment of affected employees was ensured.

Appendix C

CONTROL DATA CORPORATION'S STAYWELL PROGRAM

Control Data Corporation, a Minneapolis-based computer and financial services company, offers its employees both a comprehensive health promotion program and an employee assistance program.

StayWell, a program designed to build health-oriented lifestyles, was pioneered as a service for Control Data's own employees and now is also marketed to other companies. A unique strength of this program is the fact that it makes use of Control Data's special expertise by integrating computer-based health appraisals and courses into the highly humanized wellness framework.

An individual employee's introduction to the program involves a health assessment that provides him or her with a picture of the health risks that might merit concern. The computer-generated health appraisal focuses on the individual's health history and indicates aspects of the current lifestyle that might have a long-range effect on health.

The employee has an opportunity to participate in an interpretation session, during which the results of the health assessment are discussed and changes in lifestyle are recommended. Education and action teams are then used to help convert recommendations into reality.

Education

A number of courses are offered to provide support for the individual's own health promotion efforts. Among the courses currently available are the following:

- How to Be Fit
- How to Relax
- How to Eat Right
- How to Lose Weight

• How to Quit Smoking
• How to Protect Your Health: Blood Pressure

These StayWell Lifestyle Change Courses are offered through three options: PLATO computer-based courses, self-study courses, or group courses.

PLATO courses.   Lifestyle change courses are included as part of Control Data's PLATO computer-based education system. The courses that are available for group instructional modes are also available to individual employees with access to the Control Data PLATO system.

Self-study courses.   StayWell courses can also be adapted to the needs of individuals who prefer to work at their own rate. Course materials are provided on a flexible basis, so individual employees can complete the work at times and locations convenient for them.

Group courses.   Many employees choose to complete the lifestyle change courses in groups. Professional instructors provide group seminars that allow for mutual support and interaction among employees with common concerns.

Action Teams

Control Data's program developers recognized that, while individualized instruction can help an employee develop an initial awareness of the need for change, group support is needed to maintain commitment. Participation in an action team is an important component of the employee's involvement with StayWell.

Action teams provide a chance for co-workers to join ranks and support and encourage one another as changes are initiated. Action teams also attempt to have an impact on the environment; they can develop plans to bring about health-oriented improvements in community or work environments and develop new ideas to increase the power of individuals over their milieux. In many cases, action teams remain together after their education courses have ended. Joining forces for fitness and exercise activities makes it more likely that each member of the group will remain sufficiently involved to make permanent changes.

Employee Counseling Service

Control Data also enhances employee well-being through Employee Advisory Resource (EAR), their employee counseling service. EAR, which has been in effect since 1974, handles such concerns as chemical dependency, family problems, physical and mental health, and financial worries. Both face-to-face and telephone counseling (the latter on a 24-hour basis) are available through EAR offices located throughout the United States. The services provided to employees are confidential and include crisis interven-

tion, short-term counseling, advice to supervisors on dealing with troubled employees, referral to prescreened services, and follow-up contacts.
The referral system's foundation is a computerized data base that allows
the counselor to access information about approved community resources
in a number of locations.

Appendix D

THE JOHNSON & JOHNSON LIVE FOR LIFE PROGRAM [1]

The Johnson & Johnson LIVE FOR LIFE Program is a comprehensive health promotion effort intended ultimately for all Johnson & Johnson employees worldwide. The LIVE FOR LIFE Program is specifically designed to encourage employees to follow lifestyles which will result in good health. The Program is based upon the assumptions that:

1. Lifestyle activities, such as eating, exercise, smoking, and stress management contribute substantially to an individual's health status.
2. Lifestyle activities which support good health can be successfully promoted at the work setting.

During the initial phase, Johnson & Johnson is committed to a careful evaluation of the LIVE FOR LIFE Program in terms of its impact on employee health and its overall cost-benefit to the Corporation.

The LIVE FOR LIFE Program began in early 1979 with two primary goals:

1. To provide the means for Johnson & Johnson employees to become among the healthiest employees in the world.
2. To determine the degree to which the Program is cost-effective.

Program objectives include improvements in nutrition, weight control, stress management, fitness, smoking cessation, and health knowledge. Moreover, the proper utilization of such medical interventions as high blood pressure control and the Employee Assistance Program is strongly encouraged. It is anticipated that such improvements will lead to positive changes in employee morale, relations with fellow employees, company

[1]From *The Johnson & Johnson* LIVE FOR LIFE *Program: Technical Overview* by C. S. Wilbur. Copyright 1983 by Johnson & Johnson. Reprinted by permission.

perception, job satisfaction and productivity, as well as reductions in absenteeism, accidents, medical claims and total illness care costs.

Responsibility for the LIVE FOR LIFE Program rests with LIVE FOR LIFE staff at the corporate level. As of December, 1982, the LIVE FOR LIFE staff served about 16,000 employees in active programs at 22 separate Johnson & Johnson locations throughout the United States. By the end of 1985, LIVE FOR LIFE will be available to all Johnson & Johnson employees worldwide (approximately 75,000 employees).

LIVE FOR LIFE is primarily a service organization. Its mission is to provide the direction and resources to Johnson & Johnson employees, their families, and the community which will result in healthier lifestyles and help contain illness care costs. LIVE FOR LIFE supplies participating companies with the consulting expertise, training, core Program components, professional services, and promotional materials necessary for Program success. LIVE FOR LIFE staff are also responsible for program development and evaluation.

It is important to recognize that Johnson & Johnson is a highly decentralized group of companies, each of which operates in a very independent fashion. Acceptance of and full commitment to the Program by a company's senior management is essential to ensure the financial and time commitment to support the program.

Following a decision by a company management to accept and support the Program, voluntary employee leaders at that company are selected and trained to manage it. Working closely with LIVE FOR LIFE staff, these employee leaders assume primary responsibility for promoting good health practices at work among their fellow employees. Employee participation in the Program is voluntary and involves no employee financial outlay. Development of exercise facilities, improving the quality of foods offered in the company cafeteria, and establishment of a company smoking policy are examples of work site environmental changes undertaken by LIVE FOR LIFE Program leaders. Throughout the year the employee leaders also schedule and promote a comprehensive array of LIVE FOR LIFE programs and activities for all employees. Such programs include a Health Screen which allows individual employees to examine how healthy their current lifestyles are, a Lifestyle Seminar which introduces employees to the LIVE FOR LIFE concept in depth, and a variety of lifestyle improvement programs (e.g. Action Programs) in smoking cessation, stress management, exercise, nutrition, weight control, and general health knowledge. LIVE FOR LIFE activities are integrated closely with established medical programs in areas such as high blood pressure detection and control and Employee Assistance Programs. . . .

The program has, from its inception, been a multidisciplinary effort involving professional assistance from a variety of scientific, academic, and commercial institutions. While behavioral scientists have played a key role, many medical disciplines have become involved from the start, as have epidemiologists, health educators, and health economists. However, in the final analysis, it is the managers and employees of Johnson & Johnson companies and staff who have carried the major responsibility for implementation, modification and the success that has been achieved.

Appendix E

THE KEMPER PROGRAM: INTERNAL EAP

To know the history of the Kemper employee assistance program is to know the history of EAPs in the United States. Kemper Insurance and Financial Companies have been in the forefront of this movement since the inception of the Personal Assistance Program in 1962.

Throughout the history of Kemper's program, James S. Kemper, Jr., Chairman and Chief Executive Officer, has supported the program and provided important leadership in the field of alcoholism rehabilitation. (Kemper was one of the pioneers in offering insurance coverage for alcoholism treatment, and the companies have also been noted for the dissemination of information concerning alcoholism and drug dependency.)

The personal assistance program began as an informal alcoholism program in 1962. Under the leadership of Kenneth Rouse and Lewis Presnall, the program grew, adopting a formal policy and serving a number of employees through part-time coordinators in a number of locations.

In the 1970s, after John Lavino became director of the program, the emphasis was broadened beyond the alcoholism focus. Locating the personal assistance program in a single office at Kemper's national headquarters and moving it from personnel to the medical department, Lavino also developed a revised policy statement that included drug addiction and emotional disturbance, along with alcoholism, as treatable illnesses. At the same time, counseling was professionalized; employees received services by visiting the counseling center or telephoning collect.

The Kemper program continues to emphasize alcoholism, since that issue is seen as having major impact on the work force. However, the program is broad-brush, dealing with a variety of employee issues. Supervisors are encouraged and trained to make referrals based on job performance problems; in addition, employees and family members are encouraged to refer themselves on a completely confidential basis.

The personal assistance program is an integral part of the organization as a whole. The program director—since 1983, Mary Ellen Kane—conducts annual training sessions for managers and supervisors at the home office and division offices. Program staff members attempt to maintain the visibility of the program through articles in the house organ and the provision of educational programs. In addition, members of the PAP staff work closely with supervisors who may need consultation as they attempt to confront and refer employees.

In 1977, Kemper received the first national award for the most outstanding occupational alcoholism program in the United States from AL-MACA, the Association for Labor-Management Administrators and Consultants on Alcoholism. At least part of the reason the Kemper program has been so successful has been management's commitment to alcoholism rehabilitation and to the employee assistance concept. In addition, Kemper's program has grown with the field, continuing to help alcoholic employees but also focusing on other issues. (Most recently, the company's EAP professionals have confronted important issues related to family difficulties, including alcoholism among spouses or family members of employees and wife battering and child abuse.) Kemper's personal assistance program can be expected to remain in the forefront.

PACE, PROFESSIONAL ASSISTANCE FOR CORPORATIONS & EMPLOYEES: EXTERNAL EAP

Many organizations find that employee assistance services can be provided most effectively through contractual relationships with independent EAP providers. In some instances, the external program is most cost-effective because the company is small or because decentralization makes it difficult for one office to serve a widely scattered employee population. In other instances, employees decide that they prefer the sense of privacy they gain by seeking help from professionals who remain outside of the organizational structure.

The model utilized by PACE makes it possible for an organization to meet all of its employee assistance needs while enjoying the positive attributes of an external approach. The PACE home office is located in Chicago, but the model used makes it possible to serve employees in any location. Counselors can be located in a variety of sites, since they are not necessarily full-time employees of PACE. Each counselor, however, is trained to use the specific approach to counseling and assessment developed by Professional Assistance for Corporations & Employees, Inc. All counselors are either doctoral-level psychologists or master's-level professionals with specialized expertise. Thus, any employee has access to services by a trained, often specialized professional located in an office convenient to the employee's home or worksite. Each employee knows that the services offered are confidential; in the case of a self-referral, even the client's name is withheld unless the individual requests in writing that information be shared.

PACE, like other external EAP providers, recognizes that an employee assistance program should be comprehensive and designed to meet the unique goals of the employing organization. When a program is initiated, PACE consultants work closely with managers, union representatives, and other key employees to develop a policy that meets national standards while responding to the needs of the specific company or institution. PACE then takes responsibility for (a) training supervisors and employee representatives, (b) orienting employees and family members to the program, (c) providing each employee with the telephone number that can be used to set up a counseling appointment, (d) arranging to provide statistical information on a regular basis, and (e) developing a plan for preventive interventions.

The educational/preventive component of the employee assistance program is an important aspect of the PACE model. Each consulting contract includes allowance for a given number of employee workshops or seminars to be selected jointly by the company and the EAP consultant. Programs are based on the special needs of the organization and its employees. Thus, a school district superintendent requested that an in-service training workshop be provided for teachers on the subject of stress management; an organization employing a number of specialized professionals who were "spread too thin" needed a seminar on time management; an alcoholism treatment facility asked for help in preventing staff burnout; a steel mill was forced to ask for increased attention to outplacement; a company going through reorganization needed help in organizational development, with focus on team building and participatory decision making.

The PACE model allows each company to have access to a large pool of professional counselors, consultants, and trainers. In fact, this approach to employee assistance programming is based on the assumption that the EAP should be prepared to deal with any employee issue and that it is difficult—if not impossible—to make sharp distinctions between personal and work-related problems. If the EAP consulting firm can provide access to a number of professionals, the employer should not need to hire separate, specialized firms to deal with outplacement, relocation, or other special issues. Instead, the EAP can be seen as a general, organizing focus for a number of services that have one thing in common: the goal of returning troubled employees to their optimal level of performance and preventing new problems from arising.

Appendix G

Employee Advisory Service: Internal EAP for Washington State Employees[1]

Established in the Department of Personnel in 1972, Washington state's internal employee assistance program serves 60,000 state employees and their families. Because of the vast size of the program, the Employee Advisory Service divides the state into three regions: Olympia, Seattle, and Spokane.

The current policy statement, developed in 1982, was signed by all nine elected state officials as well as by the presidents of most state colleges and universities. This policy statement recognizes alcoholism and drug dependency as treatable illnesses; ensures the confidentiality and professionalism of help provided by the Employee Advisory Service; places the obligation for effective job performance on the employee; and recognizes the supervisor's role in identifying, documenting, and correcting employee performance problems.

Any employee or family member with a personal problem can receive assistance by calling one of the three EAS offices. The professionals who form the EAS staff help to clarify problems and develop treatment plans. Referrals are supported by an employee health insurance program that pays most of the costs of inpatient or intensive outpatient treatment of alcoholism, drug addiction, or severe mental or nervous problems at approved facilities, as well as some of the costs of outpatient help.

Of course, services are also provided for employees referred by their supervisors due to job performance problems. The EAS focus on the corrective action process is backed up by well-organized supervisory training

---

[1] Information was obtained through personal interviews with EAS manager Everett "Bud" Atkins and members of the professional staff. Written material was also adapted from the Employee Advisory Service resume and brochure.

procedures. Training is provided to any supervisory group at the request of the particular state agency and is accompanied by the EAS Supervisor's Guide, a document providing an overview of the program rationale, the team intervention process, supervisory responsibilities, employee responsibilities, the corrective action procedure, signs of job performance deterioration, documentation, confrontation, confidentiality, and referral methods. Supervisory training emphasizes the importance of a process that precipitates a crisis sufficiently intense to motivate the employee to seek help and then provides the necessary professional assistance to identify and solve personal problems. With this kind of teamwork between supervisor and EAS specialist, the employee can be helped before formal disciplinary actions are needed.

In general, the program's array of services includes the following:

1. Training and consultative services for management and supervision in all state agencies, boards, commissions, and institutions of higher education.
2. Screening, assessment, and problem resolving recommendations.
3. Motivational counseling and referral services for troubled employees or members of their families.
4. Follow-up services for employees involved in recovery from disabling personal problems, including supportive counseling as required during the first few months for both the employee and his or her supervisor and continuous monitoring of the problem resolution process.
5. General education and information provided through programs and printed materials delivered to employees, employee organizations, and management groups.

The ongoing existence of the Employee Advisory Service demonstrates a firm commitment to employees by governmental leaders in the state. This commitment can be explained at least partially in financial terms. The EAS staff estimates that the cost per year of untreated, impaired workers in a 60,000-employee work force would be over $27 million. In one recent year, the EAS provided assistance to 2,870 employees, trained 1,794 supervisors, and made 101 presentations to 17 state agencies and institutions—all with a professional staff totalling seven.

Author Index

Subject Index